WITHDRAWN

JOHN STRACHEY

JOHN STRACHEY

EUROPE: THE RADICAL CHALLENGE

CUBA

THE SPANISH CIVIL WAR

SUEZ

923
St 805t

JOHN STRACHEY

Hugh Thomas

HARPER & ROW, PUBLISHERS
New York, Evanston, San Francisco, London

JOHN STRACHEY. Copyright © 1973 by Hugh Thomas. All rights reserved. Printed in the United States of America. No part of this book may be used or reproduced in any manner whatsoever without written permission except in the case of brief quotations embodied in critical articles and reviews. For information address Harper & Row, Publishers, Inc., 10 East 53rd Street, New York, N.Y. 10022.

FIRST U.S. EDITION

CONTENTS

203834

ILLUSTRATIONS

PREFACE

This biography was written on the invitation of, and with the support of, Mrs John Strachey, who kindly made available to me all papers kept by her late husband. Mrs Strachey has also, as the text makes clear, gone to great lengths to help me in writing the book. So have many friends and relations of John Strachey and I am most grateful to them for their help, encouragement and, often, hospitality. In particular, I am grateful to John Strachey's sister, Amabel Williams-Ellis, for her generous help. Both Mrs Strachey and Lady Williams-Ellis kindly read the book in typescript and made many valuable suggestions; so too did Strachey's children, Charles Strachey and Elizabeth al Quadi.

Among those with whom I had useful conversations or correspondence and whom I should, therefore, like to thank are: Mr Ronald Aird; Lady Allen of Hurtwood; Mr W. E. D. Allen; the late Earl Attlee; Mr David Astor; Alderman Sir Joseph Balmer; Madame Julien Benda; Mr F. A. Bishop; Mr George Bishop; Lord Balogh; Lord Blackett; Lord Boothby; Mr Joseph Brewer; Sir Herbert Broadley; Lord Brockway; Mr Roland Brown; Air Vice Marshal S. O. Bufton; Mr James Callaghan; Sir Michael Cary; Lord David Cecil; Lord Champion; Mr Claud Cockburn; Mr Norman Collins; Mr and Mrs Euan Cooper-Willis; Mr Rupert Crawshay Williams; Mr Anthony Crosland; Mr Richard Crossman; Mr Tam Dalyell; Mr Maurice Dobb;

Mr Paul Draper; Mr R. Palme Dutt; Mr Timothy Eckersley; Mrs Daphne Fielding; Sir Dingle Foot; Mr Michael Foot; Dr Robert Forgan; Lady Gaitskell; Professor J. K. Galbraith; Lord George-Brown; Mr William Gerhardie; Lord Gladwyn; Air Marshal Sir Victor Goddard; Mr Jack Gold; the late Sir Victor Gollancz; Miss Livia Gollancz; Mr Patrick Gordon-Walker; Mrs Julia Gowing; Mr John Gross; Mr R. J. Hammond; Mr Stuart Hampshire; Sir Henry Hardman; Viscountess Head; Mr Denis Healey; Mr Christopher Hollis; Mr Michael Holroyd; Mr Richard Hughes; the Earl of Huntingdon; Mr Ronald Hyde; Mr Douglas Jay; Mr Roy Jenkins; Sir Elwyn Jones; Mr Joe Kelly; Mr R. D. Keynes; Mr Donald Klopfer; Mr Arthur Koestler; Lady Jennie Lee; Rev. John Lewis; Mr Paul Levy; Mr Karl Leyser; Mr Kenneth Lindsay; Lady Llewellyn-Davies; the Earl of Longford; Mr J. P. W. Mallalieu; Sir Francis and Lady Meynell; Mr Malcolm Macdonald; Mr Ivor Montagu; the late Frank Moody; Mr Arthur Morley; Sir Oswald Mosley; Mrs Fred Murphy; Mr Nigel Nicolson; Professor Robert Ochs; Mr Reginald Paget; Lord Ponsonby; Sir Eric Roll; Mr John Rosa; Sir John Rothenstein; Mr Charles Seaton; Mr Peter Shore; Mr James Simmons; Mr Julius Silverman; Marshal of the Royal Air Force Sir John Slessor; Mr Robert Skidelsky; Sir Alec Spearman; Mr Michael Stewart; Lord Stow Hill; Mrs Alix Strachey; Lord Strachie; Mr George Strauss; Mrs Nancy Sweezy; Lady Summerskill; the late Tibor Szamuely; Miss Ann Talbot; Sir William Teeling; Mr George Thomson; Mr Philip Toynbee; Sir George Turner; Mr George Urban; Mr Guy Warrack; Mr Anthony Wedgwood Benn; Mr David Wedgwood Benn; Sir Clough Williams-Ellis; Sir Geoffrey Wilson; Mr Woodrow Wyatt; Mr Allan Young; Sir Kenneth Younger; Mr William Geraghty; Mr Harold Macmillan; Mr Charles Williams; and Mr Nicholas Mosley (Lord Ravensdale).

Part 1

MAN ASLEEP

Lies he happy – who sleeps now?
  Knows he oblivion, timeless, serene?
His face made still is beautiful,
  Chiselled by hands unseen.
Or does the unresting stir of life
  Move under curtained eyes,
Must he ever feel and feel
  Till sleeplessly he dies?

John Strachey, Oxford Poetry, 1922

Chapter 1 / OXFORD

'With you, the young men, the future rests . . . let it be a future of union, strength and progress. . . . I place first the honour and security of the Throne [loud cheers]; I place next the defence of private enterprise and of individual opinion against the socialisation of the state [cheers]. . . .'

With these words, Austen Chamberlain, leader of the Conservative party, member of parliament for his father's old seat of West Birmingham, resumed his chair, to applause, at the end of a simple but stirring speech, at the Oxford Carlton Club, on 3 March 1922, in the course of 'one of the most successful political dinners that have been held in Oxford since the war', as it was put by the editor of the leading Oxford Conservative journal, Evelyn John St Loe Strachey, who was present. Here were gathered a brilliant generation of young men, more mature because of the recent war, in which some of them had served, or, at least, knew only too much about; more gay because of the recent coming of peace; debaters at the Canning or Chatham Clubs, diners at the Carlton, or the more fashionable Gridiron, self-confident, eager, even then, for responsibility: 'Eternal summer gilds them yet; but all, except their sun, is set.'

Let us observe those at dinner more closely. The Magdalen Conservative, Strachey, was the son of St Loe Strachey, then editor of the *Spectator*. He was well over six feet tall, and weighed thirteen stone. He had a deliberate manner: 'a very remarkable mind, but a Christian', he might even at that moment be drawling of a mutual friend to his neighbour.[1] Strachey's looks, too, were surprising, being dark, saturnine, with heavy lips, extremely friendly dark brown eyes, a great aquiline nose, and unusually Jewish in appearance for a high Tory. In the pages of the *Oxford Fortnightly Review*, which he edited at the time, with a subsidy from the Conservative party headquarters, his many editorial articles on politics were heavy with the responsible editorial 'we' that he had picked up from his father; and he regarded himself as a 'Whig' more than a Tory.

The purpose of politics, Strachey had written the previous November, was 'the organization of the mutual relations' of citizens with 'the minimum of friction so that civilization can really get to work on mankind'. Only the Conservative party, despite its 'prejudice' and 'stupidity', could 'deal with each problem as it arises, on its own merits, without reference to some blind rigid rule'.[2] The same paper had also published at least one poem by Strachey, while other journals had published others, typical of the verse written by intelligent undergraduates of the early years of the century; for example, this sonnet:

> Come not to me to satisfy desire,
> Come not to me with courage in your hand,
> Faith on your lips, and your great heart on fire:
> For I am poor and should not understand.
> You give great gifts in queenly fashion still.
> Of life, ask nothing, and so greatly live.
> But I have not your fortitude or will;
> Am weak and have but quiet things to give,
> Quiet gentle things, intangible; the sense
> Of sudden rapture, subtle things half felt
> By frail quick hearts too weak for the immense
> Uncharted sea your glorious ship alone

---

[1] A remark, on another occasion, by Strachey of Lord David Cecil, a fellow undergraduate, literary editor of the *Oxford Fortnightly Review*, and an Eton friend of Strachey's. *See* John Rothenstein, *Summer's Lease*, p. 72.

[2] *Oxford Fortnightly Review*, 3 November 1921 and 7 January 1922.

And proud may sail upon. Oh, we have dwelt
In loveless love and each to each unknown.[1]

Strachey was, however, recognized as being unconventional.
Had he not gone in to bat for the Magdalen College Cricket XI,
wearing a French peasant straw hat, hung with pink ribbons;
'just look at what that bastard Strachey's got on his head,' snarled
some Cousin Jasper among the spectators, doubtless to Strachey's
own delight if he had heard the remark.[2] (Perhaps, indeed, it was
an embodiment of the real Cousin Jasper, since that disagreeable
character's creator, Evelyn Waugh, had been at Hertford College
since January 1921.) Strachey's older sister, Amabel, who had
married, a few years earlier, the Welsh architect, Clough
Williams-Ellis, had not long previously called on her brother in
his rooms, and found him breakfasting at noon on chocolate cake
and crème-de-menthe. In his first year, Strachey, then living in
New Buildings, Magdalen, had indeed seemed more interested in
the theatre than in politics; four one-act plays written by him
were performed by the Magdalen College Dramatic Society in
April 1921, and he had produced and acted in other plays as well.
It is unfortunately impossible to recapture exactly the mood of
the first night of *The Winning Stroke*, a 'moral melodrama' by two
Magdalen undergraduates, at Lady Raleigh's house, on 21 January
1921 – with Strachey as 'Giambattista Raggioti', Robert Boothby
as 'Viscount Lympne', and the brilliant historian, Guy Sich, afterwards a priest, headmaster, and later unfrocked, as a card sharper.[3]
The plays too seem lost; all that remains indeed seems to be the
recollection of one player that Strachey's Aunt Philippa had been
very shocked by the comment in *Hands Up!*, a burlesque played
at the Margaret Morris Theatre, that a dagger coming out of a
body gave out a noise resembling suction. Strachey's one-act plays
also included a *Grand Guignol* melodrama, *Power*, which one
spectator noted as 'most intense', and *Sarcophagus Tyrant of
Momentua*, a Fragment, produced by Strachey in 1921. Could the

[1] *Ibid.*, 9 June 1921. Other poems by Strachey are published as the epigraph to
Books I and II; *see* below, p. 199.

[2] Rothenstein, *op. cit.*, p. 73.

[3] Others in the cast included Mrs Julian Huxley, Guy Warrack, the conductor,
and Gladwyn Jebb (as 'Crew').

MAGDALEN COLLEGE DRAMATIC SOCIETY.

FOUR PLAYS BY JOHN STRACHEY.

I MARRIAGE MAKETH MAN.

—An Unedifying Comedy.

Lady Anne	...	...	JULIA STRACHEY
Lady Betty	...	...	IRENE CHANDLEY
George Farringdon	...	...	F. A. LYON
Bobbie Weston	...	...	P. WARREN

Produced by E. J. Strachey.

II POWER.—A Melodrama. *Grand Guignol*, *navi'intensa*

Juana	...	...	SYLVIA THOMPSON
Fernando	...	...	E. J. STRACHEY
Pepe	...	...	F. A. LYON

Produced by H. R. Lenanton.

III HANDS UP!—A Burlesque.

Man	...	...	H. R. LENANTON *excellent*
Joan	...	...	JULIA STRACHEY
Harker	...	...	P. WARREN
Tailor	...	...	F. A. LYON
Girl	...	...	SYLVIA THOMPSON

Produced by E. J. Strachey.

IV SARCOPHAGUS TYRANT OF MOMENTUA.

—A Fragment by (attributed to Shakespeare).

Nesta	...	...	SYLVIA THOMPSON
Cunidad	...	...	E. J. STRACHEY
King	...	...	H. R. LENANTON
Queen	...	...	IRENE CHANDLEY
Messenger	...	...	F. A. LYON

Produced by E. J. Strachey.

THE MAN OF DESTINY.

—A Trifle.

BY

GEORGE BERNARD SHAW.

Napoleon	...	...	E. J. STRACHEY *excellent*
Giuseppe	...	...	F. A. LYON *good*
The Lady	...	...	JULIA STRACHEY *good & full*
The Lieutenant	...	...	H. R. LENANTON *excellent*

but a little unstudied.

the best.

The Inn at Tavazzano: 12th May, 1796.

Produced by F. A. Lyon.

Characters in order of their appearance.

Costumes and wigs for "Man of Destiny" by W. Clarkson.

The members of the Society wish to thank the following for very valuable help in various ways:

Mrs. WILLIAMS ELLIS.

Mr. CHRISTOPHER CLARKSON.

Mr. G. F. LENANTON.

Mr. J. DARLOWE.

future really rest, as Austen Chamberlain had put it, in hands such as these? True, Strachey soon abandoned the aesthetic attitude characterising his early days at Oxford: 'we have got to give up this 90-ish way in which we have been living, especially you', he had written to an intimate friend, John Rothenstein. Perhaps this letter was written after Strachey had heard an address by E. D. Morel, the writer and founder of the Union of Democratic Control, whose speech was reputed to have much influenced Strachey's political life.[1] But Strachey remained, while at Oxford, and for some years after, an aesthete.

Oxford at that time affected effeminacy and hence exquisiteness was forgivable, even in a would-be politician; and, even if Strachey joined with enthusiasm in the current fashions – did he really carry a handbag in the street, as John Rothenstein recalls? – he was apparently heterosexual. Thus, at one party, at which much luxury seemed, by the standards of Oxford, to have been assembled, a speaker remarked that 'everything save naked houris had been brought to feast the eye'; and then, sternly, he added, with the characteristic affectation of youth, 'but mercifully who of us, save for two people present, would know what to do with houris, naked or otherwise?' The eyes of the gathering were then turned in the direction of Strachey and Rothenstein. Both had indeed the unfashionable reputation of being friendly with the other sex; Strachey had even been seen on a motor bicycle, for instance, with girls such as Hester Chapman, who was considered 'fast', and Elizabeth Ponsonby, who was very wild and beautiful, and it had been to their beautiful friend and his cousin, Julia Strachey (who had acted in John's one-act plays), that he had already confided his belief, while passing the Chelsea hospital, that he had 'Napoleonic capacities', which would soon be put to good use to save the country. His performance, indeed, as Napoleon in Shaw's *Man of Destiny*, produced by the Magdalen Dramatic Society in May 1921, had been described as 'excellent' by one spectator.

A man perhaps should be judged by his company. At the Carlton dinner, at which Chamberlain spoke, Strachey was sitting

[1] *See* Stuart MacIntyre's unpublished M.A. thesis, *John Strachey, the development of an English Marxist* (Monash University), pp. 10–11, for discussion.

next to an old school friend and one who was to become his closest friend all his life, Boothby, the 'Viscount Lympne' of the college play. Strachey had first heard of Boothby when the latter, a choirboy with a beautiful alto voice, was singing *O for the wings of a dove* in an Eton concert.[1] Perhaps it is in one of Boothby's articles of this time that the best picture of these young men's ideas becomes apparent: in an essay entitled 'The Next War' he wrote: 'the British Empire and the U.S. could dominate the world . . . is it not eminently desirable that the great white English-speaking races should be in a position to shape the world's destinies?' Churlish though it may seem to recall such intemperate thoughts, after so many years, they were doubtless shared not only by Strachey but by many young Conservatives present at the dinner: by, for example, J. C. Maude,[2] son of the famous actor Cyril Maude, who, at the dinner, had proposed the 'toast of Princess Mary and Lord Lascelles, with the felicitous tact and self-effacing brevity for which he is becoming well known', and by Ralph Assheton, the president of the club;[3] by Charles Petrie,[4] who had founded the Carlton Club in 1919, and by Viscount Hastings;[5] by Viscount Castlereagh;[6] and Victor Cazalet;[7] and William Teeling;[8] and by the brilliant Edward Marjoribanks.[9]

Strachey's academic qualities were as yet untested. The President of Magdalen, Sir Herbert Warren, was 'anxious that', as he put it in a letter to Strachey's father (who had gained a First in History at Balliol in the 1880s), 'if he possibly can, he should follow in your steps, and secure a First Class at the end of this year or when he goes down. A First Class is not everything . . . but it is a great deal to lose, or miss. I think very highly of his natural

[1] *See* Strachey's review of Boothby's autobiography, *My Yesterday; Your Tomorrow*, in *New Statesman*, 21 October 1962.
[2] Now a judge.
[3] Afterwards chairman of the Conservative party and Lord Clitheroe.
[4] Afterwards Sir Charles Petrie Bt, historian.
[5] Afterwards Earl of Huntingdon, a Labour peer, and Under-Secretary of Agriculture, 1945–1950.
[6] Son of Ramsay Macdonald's Lady Londonderry.
[7] Afterwards M.P. and killed in the aircraft in which Sikorski also was killed in 1941.
[8] Afterwards M.P. for Brighton.
[9] He died by his own hand in 1930, having written a biography of Marshall Hall.

capacity, and his unutilised gifts, and I feel sure they will come out well in the end, as yours have done. But I should like him to achieve this success at this point. I do not want him to buy it too dear, and, of course, it cannot be made absolutely certain, but I do want him to take all the natural steps.'[1] Benign and snobbish, Sir Herbert Warren naturally liked his undergraduates to be a credit to him, and to Magdalen. 'What does your name mean?' Sir Herbert once asked Prince Chichibu of Japan, then an undergraduate. 'Son of God', was the reply. 'Ah we have the sons of many prominent men here,' answered Sir Herbert, absently.

Such were Strachey's ideas, friends and tutors. His family was unusual, and conscious of it. They were one of the most prominent of those post-renaissance English families which, becoming country gentlemen in the late sixteenth and seventeenth centuries, were distinguished as administrators of the Empire in the eighteenth and nineteenth. The fertile imagination of nineteenth-century genealogists once, in a very unStrachey way, arranged for a Strachey descent from Boreslaus, younger brother of St Wenceslas of Bohemia. But the fortunes of the family reflect those of England. Several generations of Stracheys, brought up in Somerset and the family home of Sutton Court, went to India or to the Americas, had great adventures, and returned, knighted and prosperous. One Strachey travelled to Virginia in 1609, was wrecked, and wrote a book about it, thereby, it is believed, influencing Shakespeare in writing *The Tempest*. Another Strachey was a friend of Locke. The most eminent of the Stracheys had been secretary to the immortal Clive in India and an oral tradition in the family had suggested that Sir Henry Strachey had been playing cards in Clive's house the night that he had cut his throat.[2] In the twentieth century, the lives of the Stracheys have been more diverse; and the two most distinguished members about the time of the First World War were, on the one hand, St Loe Strachey, editor of the *Spectator*, and Lytton Strachey, the historian and critic. (St Loe was so named after a family which had married into the Stracheys in the sixteenth century.)

St Loe Strachey was the epitome of the patriotic, respectable,

[1] Sir Herbert Warren to St Loe, 21 September 1922.
[2] *See* John Strachey's *The End of Empire*, p. 45.

informed journalist; and Lytton Strachey was the scourge of successful men represented by his family, and particularly by St Loe, his cousin, even though his own early articles had all appeared in the *Spectator*. The St Loe branch of the Strachey family was a subject for derisive laughter on the part of Lytton Strachey: St Loe being so worldly, confident, and dashing; and Lytton being so withdrawn, tentative and sceptical. They had quarrelled in 1917, appropriately, over Lytton's treatment of the proconsul Lord Cromer, in his essay on Gordon in *Eminent Victorians*. Thereafter, Lytton's name was seen no more in the *Spectator*. For Cromer, who had died only the previous year, was one of St Loe's heroes and friends; they corresponded almost weekly. His son Evelyn John was, indeed, called after him and Cromer had been his godfather.

Evelyn John Strachey had been born on Trafalgar Day, 21 October 1901. At Oxford, he was known as 'Evelyn'. In the family, however, he was always 'John', or 'Johnnie'. In 1922, he was the heir of the family, since his father's eldest brother, Sir Edward Strachey (created Lord Strachie in 1911, when Asquith wanted his long-held parliamentary seat in South Dorset for another purpose) had only one son, much older than his cousin, who seemed unlikely to have a family. Thus this Oxford Conservative would presumably inherit the baronetcy, such family wealth as there was, and the pictures, as well as the marvellous old house of Sutton Court, in Somerset, with the great lime avenue stretching towards the Mendips. He had already inherited some Strachey characteristics: long sight, a beaked nose, a tendency to gout, dry skin, and hairy backs to his hands. 'It is both an advantage and a disadvantage to be born in the purple,' Sir Herbert Warren once wrote to St Loe, but John Strachey never regretted his ancestors.[1]

St Loe Strachey, a shorter man than his son, had taken over the *Spectator* when aged thirty-eight, in 1898. He was almost self-taught, since, before going to Oxford in 1878, he never went to school but, with the help of tutors, educated himself from his father's library at Sutton Court. At Balliol, he had been unpopular

[1] Sir Herbert Warren to St Loe, 21 September 1922.

with Jowett, but had gained a First Class degree, and a reputation of having read everything:

> I am Strachey, never bored,
> By Webster, Massinger or Ford;
> There is no line of any poet
> Which can be quoted but I know it.

At the *Spectator* he had the reputation of misquoting everything. Like his son, he had written sonnets as a young man. Though called to the Bar, he had been a journalist all his life and had been, for a time, editor of *The Liberal Unionist*, and afterwards of the *Cornhill*. From 1898, until ill-health forced his retirement in 1925, St Loe issued to the world an unending stream of orthodox, though vigorous, editorials, providing intelligent rationalizations of conservative attitudes to the Empire (above all to India) and, more unusually, to the U.S., where St Loe Strachey had many friendships, particularly with Theodore Roosevelt – whom he somewhat resembled in his openness, energy and generosity of spirit. He hated tariff reform and hated socialism. He made a success of the *Spectator*, and became quite rich in consequence. His volume of autobiography, *The Adventure of Living*, is pompous but not stuffy, and lively and fluent. He was a kind, charming, energetic man but contemptuous of novelty. 'I have no subconscious' was one of his favourite remarks. His wife, in her memoir of him, says that he was heading leftwards when he died.[1]

St Loe was an ex-Liberal Unionist and a Free Trader. That was a difficult combination because, since the 1890s, the Union and Free Trade had been championed by different parties: thus, in 1906, the normally conservative *Spectator* had advised its readers to vote Liberal. In 1921–2 St Loe was trying to break up the coalition government and was busy seeking to persuade Grey, or McKenna, or even Winston Churchill to lead an alternative ministry.

St Loe's character at work was well described in a reminiscence

[1] Amy Strachey, *St Loe Strachey and the Spectator*.

by James Strachey, Lytton's younger brother and a psycho-
analyst, who worked as his private secretary and who for a
time was also a frequent contributor to the *Spectator*: 'numbers of
contributors called on him in the early part of each week; leader-
writers. . . . Eric Parker, who wrote the nature article, the clergy-
man who wrote the weekly sermon, and, later in the week, the
various reviewers. To all of these, indifferently, the same treatment was applied. St Loe was a tremendously fluent talker,
producing floods of remarkable ideas and amusing anecdotes –
many of which would have startled the vicarages. These he poured
over the heads of his visitors at top speed, interlaced with detailed
instructions about what was to be written in the leader, the sermon
or the review concerned. The visitors had hardly a moment for
breathing before they were whirled out of the room. . . . On
Thursday afternoons, silent perhaps for the first time in the week,
St Loe sat back comfortably in a chintz-covered armchair with a
pencil in his hand, and read through the galley proofs of the whole
of the forthcoming issue. He altered a word here and there, he
scribbled a fresh sentence in the margin, he struck out a whole
paragraph and replaced it by one of his own.'[1] St Loe regarded the
Spectator as the 'watchdog of the nation'. 'He was the last of them,'
Clement Attlee once remarked, a little cryptically;[2] by which he
meant, presumably, the last of those eminent Victorians – St Loe
was over forty, after all, when the old Queen died – whom his
cousin Lytton portrayed with such malice. Lytton Strachey's
biographer, Michael Holroyd, suggests that, in his quarrel with
St Loe over Cromer, Lytton was 'clearly flaunting his freshly won
independence' from the Strachey family, an institution of its own,
and one even stronger than the *Spectator* (though in a sense the
two were synonyms, as can be seen from the number of Stracheys
who contributed to the journal).[3] This quarrel happened at a
specially critical time during the First World War; any attack by
a conscientious objector, such as Lytton, on a recently dead
patriot, such as Cromer, must have seemed sacrilegious to St Loe,
who supported the war with vigour, having argued, as early as

[1] James Strachey, *Spectatorial Essays* (1964), introduction, pp. 8–9.
[2] Attlee to the author, January 1964.
[3] Holroyd, *Lytton Strachey*, I, p. 388.

1915, that it was the duty of employers to dismiss young men from their employment unless they joined the army. Even before the war, St Loe had followed Lord Roberts's exhortations, and himself trained volunteer 'Surrey guides' in rifle shooting on Saturdays. (St Loe got his own back on Lytton Strachey by remarking in an autobiography that Lytton Strachey and Cromer were the two best reviewers whom he had ever had.)

The material for St Loe's responsible attitudes was gathered by an immense correspondence and by conversations with ambassadors, politicians, men of the world at, for example, dinners and lunches at his own houses in Cornwall Gardens, Chester Square and Queen Anne's Gate successively, and in Surrey at Newlands Corner, a large house built at the worst period of Edwardian grand taste in a then agreeable, convenient, but isolated, stretch of high land near Guildford. His wife, Amy, was a hostess in the Edwardian style, who took upon herself to perpetuate the legend of the Strachey family, and its tradition of public service; '*une matronne*, in blue silk, with amber necklaces', Lytton Strachey described her when calling at Chester Square in 1907.[1] She was the daughter of Charles Turner Simpson, an able and shy lawyer who was Counsel to the Post Office, and of the lively daughter and, for years, the housekeeper of the distinguished early Victorian economist and author, Nassau Senior, from whose Sephardic Jewish ancestors young Strachey, presumably, inherited his swarthy looks (Nassau Senior was the great-grandson of Moses Aaron Senior, a merchant settled in the Barbadoes)[2] and perhaps some other Jewish characteristics: 'the habit of persistent cerebration typical of Jewish intellectuals', as Douglas Jay put it. But, if Strachey were, perhaps, one sixty-fourth Jewish, as seems likely, that scarcely made him more semitic than the King.

Amy Strachey herself, nicknamed 'Gigi' in the family, also sometimes looked un-English, being mockingly referred to by Lytton Strachey and his brothers as 'Oriental Amy'. Julia Strachey

---

[1] Holroyd, *op. cit.*, p. 302.

[2] Moses Aaron Senior's son, Nassau Thomas Senior, was a prominent West Indian sugar planter, slave trader and, for a time, governor of Cape Coast Castle, in the Gold Coast (Ghana), then a big slave centre. A biography of Nassau Senior (*Nassau W. Senior, 1790–1864*, by S. Leon Levy (Newton Abbot 1970)) traces the Senior family back to its Spanish origins before 1492.

thought of her as 'that extraordinary Portuguese' and remembers her as like 'a huge block of flats, in tweeds in the day, in brocades at night, with some extraordinary object, like holly, stuck on her head on special occasions'. Harold Macmillan, whose family lived not far away in Sussex, recalled her as 'formidable' and 'very large and over-bearing'. Perhaps, however, these impressions were exaggerated. She was unpretentsious, serious and probably shy. She wrote a biography of her husband and a 'Masque of Empire', performed at the Stracheys' house in Surrey in 1908. She also contributed to the *Spectator* from time to time, writing novel reviews in 1900 and an article on 'Socrates and the Revelation of God' in 1909. She was a theatrical woman, whose natural desires for a dramatic life were perhaps not satisfied by her marriage to St Loe who, despite his ardent political passions, may have been cold in his attentions to her.

The childhood of John Strachey was thus passed in what seemed on the surface to be the secure world of pre-1914 English upper-class society. Religion played virtually no part. The Stracheys were Anglicans, and conventionally compliant. Both St Loe and Amy were fond of the Bible, and St Loe once edited an anthology entitled *Practical Wisdom of the Bible*. They rarely went to church, though, like all good Whigs, they regarded the Church of England as a useful department of state. They lived comfortably. Lytton Strachey recalled being met at Guildford Station by a 'most gorgeous newly painted scarlet motor car' and being lent one of St Loe's 'numerous fur coats'.

John Strachey was St Loe's and Amy's second son, but the much older brother, Tom (Thomas Clive, the second Christian name being one more act of imperial *pietas*), had died of pneumonia in his first year at Balliol, aged eighteen, in 1907. Since his sister Amabel was seven years older than he, Strachey's childhood resembled that of an only son. Perhaps, however, his memory of his elder brother was greater than might be imagined, even though he was only six years old when he died; for, as an adult, Strachey looked for substitute elder brothers in political life. It is possible that his mother's affection for Tom was such that she could not repeat it for John. Amabel in consequence became something of a third parent.

It is sometimes supposed that the keys to curious personalities can be found in their childhoods; but, if so, in this case, hints only are available: thus Strachey's wife, Celia, says that 'Amy Strachey gave him no affection at all as a child', though Amabel would dispute that judgement. Doubtless, anyway, he saw little of her as a child, though he often used to go riding with St Loe. Strachey himself recalled later that the day that Lloyd George's Old Age Pension Act was passed was greeted by St Loe and the whole family as one of intense mourning, for he regarded this limited concession to welfare as a real evil.[1] No early letters from Strachey to his mother or *vice versa* have survived, and, indeed, few references to her remain in his papers; once, in 1922, when Strachey was almost twenty-one, he is found expressing satisfaction that she has 'once again shown her qualities of dash and decision' in purchasing a new Lagonda motor car.[2] Amy Strachey herself wrote, in the biographical study of her husband: 'the Stracheys are most strongly the children of their fathers, not of their mothers'.[3] She might have added that the English upper class, at that time, were very much the children of their nannies, not of their parents (Strachey's nanny was a certain Nurse Holland, and he was extremely fond of her: 'Good gracious, if it hadn't been for Nanny Holland we should have died,' he once said to Amabel); and that she personally much preferred boy children to girl ones. Unfortunately, however, Strachey did not profit from this prejudice. His relations with his mother (though physically he resembled her) were, in after life, in the word of his wife Celia, 'appalling', in the sense that their communications, though frequent, were formal, cold and grey. As a small boy, Strachey once threw a tennis ball at his mother's face in the garden of Sutton Court. This offence was not forgiven. Unloved as a child, he reserved his warmth later for ideas – an attitude which he learnt from his father who combined a respect for ideas with *joie de vivre*.

Strachey probably owed more to his father than he himself supposed. When in the 1930s he was analysed, Strachey was brought to accept that he had been 'close to him'.[3] His prose

[1] *Spectator*, 3 November 1928.
[2] Letter No. 2 from Le Mans, summer 1922, undated.
[3] *See* below, p. 121.

style, if more lucid and witty that St Loe's, was equally authoritative, fluent and cultivated.

The other members of the family did not have much influence on the young Strachey. His paternal grandfather, Sir Edward, died the same year as he himself was born. His Strachey grandmother, daughter of John Addington Symonds, the critic and historian, had died in the 1880s. His uncle, Lord Strachie, was chiefly busy with agricultural projects at Sutton Court and, though a member of parliament and, for a time, a minister under Asquith, rarely appeared in St Loe's house. Another uncle, Henry, a bachelor artist, was seen more often, for he contributed many articles to the *Spectator*, as did St Loe's sister, Aunt Frances, who married the Sutton Court family doctor, Dr Shaw, and lived in Somerset. On his mother's side, John Strachey had few surviving relations and, indeed, his mother had identified herself so much with the Strachey family as to have almost forgotten such of her Simpson or Senior relations as survived.

John Strachey went first to an undistinguished private school, Edgeborough School, Guildford, and then to Eton, in the summer of 1915, to R. S. de Havilland's House. He had until then been a day boy at school and had lived almost all the time at Newlands Corner, riding being his main exercise.

Strachey 'hated Eton' and he was not popular. He did not fit in well with the somewhat idle but clever and sophisticated world of Eton: the Stracheys had always taken ideas seriously, and jokes could not be made of them. He dressed and behaved oddly. He afterwards said that, at that time, he blamed his family for having neglected to teach him how to behave. Sir Alec Douglas-Home recalled him as being 'unwashed'. Perhaps the fact that St Loe had himself never been to a public school exacerbated his son's reluctance to be disciplined by Etonian conformism. His housemaster, R. S. de Havilland, was a rowing coach and generally an enthusiast for games: his house was somewhat philistine, and perhaps St Loe chose wrongly to send Strachey there. Nevertheless, Strachey was good at cricket and, so Boothby recalled, 'rose in consequence. He was, I think, a little disappointed that he didn't get his Eleven.' Thereby, indeed, hangs a tale, since, in after life, Strachey frequently said, as a joke, that he became a socialist, or even a communist, because he had not got into the Eton Cricket XI. 'I have a stock answer to dear old ladies who ask me "And why, Mr Strachey, did you become a communist?" "From chagrin, madame," I reply, "from chagrin at not getting into the Eton Cricket XI." '[1] Perhaps this paradox has more to it than one would suspect, since Strachey apparently thought that it was his unconventional behaviour and unusual appearance that thwarted his ambition, rather than lack of cricketing ability. But Strachey was, as it happens, a bowler at a time when there were many good bowlers at Eton – G. O. Allen, C. H. Gibson, and three others who played first-class cricket afterwards: 'he was, as far as I can remember, quite a good bowler,' recalled Ronald Aird, the captain of the side, 'but as he never played for the XI, or did anything very remarkable for the Second XI . . . I can see no reason why he should have had any great disappointment. . . .'[2] At all events, unlike many socialists of his generation (who customarily later affected an irritation with team games), he remained interested in cricket and played it often, though he was never an outstanding player. Still, he very much liked to be successful both at it and at other ball games, for which he had a good eye. 'A keen and hearty player who is often too keen, kicking the ball when he ought not,' was a comment on Strachey's performance in the Eton Wall game on St Andrew's Day (30 November) 1919.[3] Oddly, when Strachey arrived at Oxford, and before his aesthetic 'decadent' time, he seemed briefly to have affected 'an almost aggressively public school manner' – and one 'not particularly Etonian', in the recollection of John Rothenstein.

The most important intellectual influence on Strachey at Eton was not his housemaster, de Havilland, nor, needless to say, the pious headmaster, Dr Alington, but Henry Marten, history master, afterwards Provost of Eton, and tutor in history to Queen Elizabeth II.[4] For Marten, Strachey, a 'history specialist', wrote a series of historical essays, which for the first time suggested his

[1] 'The Education of a Communist', *Left Review*, December 1934.
[2] Letter of Ronald Aird to the author.
[3] *Eton Chronicle*, November 1919.
[4] Sir Henry Marten (1872–1948). Knighted 1945 for his services to the Royal Family. Author of a famous schoolboy history, with Townsend Warner of Winchester. He addressed the Queen as 'Gentlemen'.

intellectual strength, his skill at writing and his versatility. Strachey had always much love for Marten. It was obvious, during his last year or so, that when he went to Oxford, as seemed inevitable for him in view of the family tradition, he would read History. But he did, unlike many boys of his time and class, have some scientific education under a master known as 'Piggie' Hill. This did not affect him fundamentally, nor did the presence at Eton, at that time, of Aldous Huxley as a temporary English master, and M. R. James, Provost from 1917 onwards, though Strachey was associated with the *Eton Review*, a journal concerned to talk about new writers, under the editorship of Lord David Cecil and with Huxley an inspiration in the background. Strachey left Eton at the end of 1919 and went for the first half of 1920 to a tutor's in Guildford, in order to be able to pass 'responsions'.

The war lasted most of the time that Strachey was at Eton. This cast a shadow over all activities. Newlands Corner became a hospital. Amy Strachey was matron: Amabel served as a nurse, and her husband, Clough, fought in the Welsh Guards and took a tank course. St Loe championed the patriotic cause with energy. The whole family knew many wounded men well, while at Eton 'every week, we went to college chapel to hear the tragic list of names read out in gathering gloom'.[1] Nevertheless, neither pacifism nor, until the end of his life, much concern with the avoidance of war played a part in Strachey's intellectual life. The publisher, Victor Gollancz, for example, afterwards an intimate, regarded him as a different sort of socialist from himself in the 1930s, when he, Gollancz, was primarily a pacifist.[2] Perhaps this was a recollection of St Loe's attitude; for St Loe remained to the end of his days convinced that the First World War was righteous.[3]

John Strachey was, afterwards, one of an important minority within the English system – namely, a public school man who had hated his public school. Still, he received, towards the end, good reports. His father wrote to his housemaster in early 1919: 'I need

[1] Boothby, *I fight to live*, p. 7.
[2] Gollancz, *Reminiscences of Affection*, p. 131.
[3] St Loe Strachey, *The Adventure of Living*, p. 457.

not tell you that I was delighted, though not surprised, to hear such a good, and such an improved, report of John. I do think he is a very satisfactory product of the Eton system. I find him not only a most delightful companion, but a person of quick intelligence and one who can use his knowledge. . . . In spite of his apparent dislike of, or rather, inability to cope with the classics, he and I seldom have a ride or a walk together in which something of the classical curriculum does not bubble out. . . . Here I really find myself now in the position of the English working man who is . . . taught by his children.'[1]

Strachey at Oxford, in contrast, seemed a contradictory figure. An aesthete, actor, active University journalist, and playwright, he was also obviously a politician – though not a University one; a poet, he prided himself as a man of the world and, indeed, Lord David Cecil remembers him at Oxford as seeming already a part of the wider world, beginning on a public career through his journalism. He had an easy, witty manner with friends, though with acquaintances he was distant. Reports of him at this stage, as indeed through much of his life, are very contradictory: Julia Strachey, his cousin, and an extremely observant writer, found him almost excessively amiable to nearly everybody; others found him haughty. Preoccupied by ideas, he played cricket seriously and racquets well. He was not then a good speaker: the *Isis* described him at the Union as speaking in a manner suggestive of 'a dejected penguin', and addressing the house in 'a chilly mournful manner, which was far from persuasive'.[2] But what he said, however, was admitted to be 'distinctly interesting'. Arthur Ponsonby, the Labour politician who was the father of Strachey's friend Elizabeth, thought, in August 1920, that Strachey was a 'curious boy, very precocious and argumentative, clever and self-assured, apt to be rather pontifical, like his father's *Spectator*, but with a sense of humour'; and then, a year later, 'most intelligent and wonderfully mature [but] I rather wonder if he is not lacking in some fundamental male characteristics'.[3] At this stage, the Ponsonbys were perturbed at the influence which Strachey

---

[1] St Loe to R. S. de Havilland, 22 January 1919.
[2] *Isis*, 19 May 1921.
[3] From a Diary, MSS, for 20 August 1920 and 8 August 1921.

seemed to have over their reckless daughter, Elizabeth, and Arthur Ponsonby was perhaps not the best judge of Strachey's character; but even he was forced to admit that a village skit upon Shakespeare, which Strachey had organized at the Ponsonbys' with Julia Strachey and Tom Darlow, a Magdalen friend, was highly entertaining.[1]

[1] Darlow, son of a nonconformist minister, was fat, jolly and easy with money. He died in a car crash after being on the *Daily Herald*.

Chapter 2 / VIENNA

At the end of March 1922, three weeks after the Conservative dinner at which Austen Chamberlain had spoken, Strachey, accompanied by Rothenstein and Eddie Sackville-West, who were respectively the literary and the music critics of the *Oxford Fortnightly Review*, embarked upon a journey to central Europe; they went first to Vienna.

Vienna in early 1922 was distressed. There was still, three years after the end of the war, a shortage of food so acute as to have recently caused political upheavals. Nor had the country found any political self-confidence.

In Vienna, Strachey began to move away from the romantic, well-intentioned and public-spirited conservatism of his father towards a form of socialism. The reasons for this first, critical change in his opinions were various, and the process was not complete until a few years later. Perhaps Strachey's dissent from the received attitudes of the politically conscious English upper class would soon have led him anyway into a minority position. Could a true blue Tory really play cricket with a reticule?

Still, these attitudes might not have matured from affectation into renunciation had it not been for Vienna. Strachey expected, after leaving Oxford, presumably in 1923, to join his father on the *Spectator*, with a view to becoming its editor eventually, when St Loe's health, damaged by overwork during the war, should force his retirement. Strachey's conservatism had recently been even reinforced when one of his Oxford contemporaries, Arthur Reade, was sent down for preaching communism: the case had created a stir, but Strachey was hostile to Reade, and announced as much in the Ponsonbys' drawing-room at Shulbrede Priory when they both were present.[1]

The only letter which survives from Strachey's stay in Vienna indeed suggests how both he and his father imagined the future would be: addressed from the Erzherzog Karl Hotel, undated, Strachey wrote: 'Three rather good subjects for articles seem to have come my way. . . . The first is a movement you may have heard of called "The Land Settlers Movement", which is really an attempt, spontaneous in origin, to get some part of the huge Vienna population out of the town and back to an at any rate semi-self supporting state. . . . The second subject is the position of Hungary. This town is full of exiles from Count Karoly's "Liberal Socialist" Government and Bela Kun's communist one both of which Horti (sic) has proscribed.[2] I have met some of them and heard a good deal both of recent history and of the present position. I hope next week to get on to Buda (probably by the river) for a few days and collect some more stuff. It is all rather a picturesque story. . . . The third subject would be general artistic and literary activity here. . . . Do let me know what you think. . . .'

A few days later, the news came of the death of the Emperor Karl, in Madeira, on 1 April. 'The streets [of Vienna] were impressively draped with long black hangings,' recalled Rothenstein, 'some of them stretching from upper windows almost to the ground. We all of us were oppressed by the sense that this magnificent city was slowly dying.'[3]

[1] Arthur Reade became disillusioned with communism, later joined the Labour party and afterwards Mosley's New Party (see below, p. 96). He stood in 1929 as Labour candidate for Abingdon.
[2] Karoly took over the government of Hungary after the armistice in 1918 and formed a coalition, in which the socialists played the main part. These were displaced by the communists led by Bela Kun in 1919. Admiral Horthy at the head of an army of 'white' Hungarians drove out this government, assisted by the French and Roumanians. Karoly and his wife Catherine afterwards became friends of Strachey.
[3] Rothenstein, op. cit., p. 88.

St Loe replied to his son in a letter which well indicates his cast of mind. 'My dear John,' he began, 'Thank you for your delightful . . . letter, which amused us all tremendously. . . . I should like some of the articles for the *Spectator*, but I think you are perfectly right in preferring somewhere else. I know you don't like *The Nineteenth Century*, or otherwise I should suggest that, for it is a much better forum than you suppose. Again, there is the *Cornhill*, which is very friendly, and I was only talking about you to Huxley the other day and could easily propose the article. I could also propose one of them to the *Morning Post* and another to the *Westminster*. If you sign them, by the way, sign EVELYN STRACHEY, and that will distinguish you from all of your tiresome relatives.

'I am thrilled by the idea of your going to Buda Pesth. Make many notes about its physical beauties. I should think the buildings were hideous and Hun-like, if not even Mongolian, but interesting. Beware of spies and *argent*[1] (sic) *provocateurs*, who are as tiresome as they are silly. The fact that you are sublimely innocent of any revolutionary movements or intentions don't matter at all to such gentry. They always think that an Englishman has got some deep game when he is merely trying to find out what are the facts. If Hohler is still our Minister . . . be sure to call upon him. He knows me very well indeed and would be very pleased to see you.[2] He was under your godfather, Lord Cromer, in Egypt. I should also let the Legation in Vienna know whether you have gone in case you are held up by passport troubles – always possible in these days – and have to wire to them. Then they will know it is really you.'

Strachey and his Oxford friends were accompanied by a young French journalist, Yvette Fouque, 'plump, fair, with beautiful eyes, and a wonderful complexion, a kind of musical comedy peasant,' in the words of Strachey's sister Amabel Williams-Ellis, the wife of a much older Colonial servant in Casamance, in French West Africa, but now independent, intelligent, radical and, to the young Englishmen, alarmingly well read. She was a member

[1] Presumably a misspelling, perhaps a joke.
[2] Sir Thomas Hohler (1871–1946), Minister in Budapest 1921–1924.

of the French intelligentsia, older than the undergraduates, and had been mistress to the politician Caillaux. Her sister later married the rationalist Julien Benda, famous as author of *La Trahison des Clercs*. Yvette had been several times to Casamance, and spoke affectionately of *mes chers noirs*, but was already thinking of a separation from her husband. She played an important part in the intellectual development of John Strachey. For she was a determined character, as well as being politically alive. Strachey later wrote to her: 'any decency I may have achieved, any possibility of getting on with people and getting a chance to use my brains for what they are worth, I owe to you. It was your effort to break up the vileness of my British bourgeoisdom that gave me a chance.' Of course, these remarks were extravagantly put, and Strachey was not always to regard the 'British bourgeoisie' as vile.

Nor was Yvette's influence only, or even, at the start, mainly political. Rothenstein, Strachey and Sackville-West dined with her at a music hall, and they began to talk of Henry James. 'I find,' said Yvette, 'that I read him with less interest since I began to read Proust.'

'But who,' asked one of those present, probably Strachey, '*is* Proust?' Yvette's eyes opened wide, and she set to work to repair this ignorance.

Admittedly not everyone agreed with this favourable assessment of Yvette: 'she was a terror,' one of Strachey's English girl friends said, 'a real terror. We used to say – if you must take out a French girl, you might take out one that is well-dressed.'

For Strachey, however, Yvette became for a time a passion; so far as it is possible to see from his letters, so did he also for her, for a longer time. They travelled to Budapest together, they visited the Castle of Durnstein, and, though Boothby (who, of course, was not present) believed that the friendship was physically unrewarding, they returned to Vienna in love. Strachey later described the days on the Danube as 'the only 3 days in which I was ever young'.[1]

After visiting some of Vienna's homosexual bars (Lytton Strachey, on their return, asked Strachey in his high voice, 'Oh, do you like that sort of thing?') the undergraduates returned to

[1] In a letter of 7 December 1924.

Oxford for the summer term; Yvette remained in Vienna.[1]
Strachey wrote an article for the *Oxford Fortnightly Review*.
'Hungary,' he began, in the tones of St Loe, 'must be entered by
the Danube. . . .'[2] Strachey reserved his more interesting comments for the Hungarian exiles living in Vienna, members of
Karoly's cabinet; and for the legitimist party in Hungary, run
by the 'big Magyar landowners' who, his readers gathered, 'are
not necessarily bitter reactionaries', but more often men brought
up in the 'fine traditions of their race'. At the same time, he
remained in touch with Yvette. She must have written to him
soon after he left Vienna for, on 8 May, he wrote in reply:[3]

You ask me to be frank: My God if I were frank; if I could,
for one moment, really show you the emotions, the, to me,
strange and tremendous blasts and currents of feeling that beat
upon me and sweep over me. If, by some miracle, you could,
in a moment, know all that is going on in me (far more, of
course, than I know) then I think you would see one whom
you have always seen, at any rate, with some elements of self-
possession – or, at any rate, possessed only by the most soft
and tender of passions – in so strange a state that he, for one at
any rate, feels utterly unable to recognize himself. But, to be
frank, that would be to tell you all that [I] feel, and, if I told
you all that I feel—— But, at every new second, I feel a new
sensation, beyond anything, utterly and incomparably unlike
anything I have ever felt before. . . .

I had waited for your letter for so long, that, when it did
come, I was utterly unable to realize it. People were in the
room, I could not read it then, it lay in my pocket. When they
went, I did not begin to read it. Not that I was in [the] least
afraid to. Fear, at any rate, has never been with me. But my
mind was simply numb; I went on mechanically doing other
things. When at last, still unconscious, I did open it, nothing
happened. I did not read a word. Then suddenly, like some great
flood gates opening, I realized what was in my hand. . . .

[1] Strachey so says in his letter of 13 April 1928.
[2] Issues dated 12 May and 26 May 1922, respectively.
[3] I am indebted to Madame Julien Benda for kindly making available to me
Yvette's papers.

Monday

I wrote these last two pages on Saturday just after getting your first letter. Since then, I have read and reread it very often, and it has made me very happy – and, even compared to the state I was in then, very calm. It was far the most wonderful letter I have ever had – wonderful for what it told me – in that it took me from the depths of an unquietness, I hardly realised to a sort of strange wistful happiness which I am now in – but most wonderful for what it did not say, most wonderful for all those *mots inutiles* about the Hungarian liberals, most wonderful when it was most irrelevant, most terribly and overwhelmingly moving when it was most commonplace. I can bare [*sic*] it when you tell me that you love me, but when you write to me about the Hungarian liberals, or the decorative arts – that is too much, and I feel a mad unreasoning impulse to rush straight out of the house, and ask the nearest policeman which is the way to Vienna. . . . But I meant to start out by apologizing for those two pages I wrote on Saturday. They *are* bad. They're *tellement littéraire*, if you like. And yet, I think I shall send them to you. They were the only way I could say what I felt at the moment of opening your letter. They read very oddly and stiltedly don't they? – rather like a novel of 15 years ago – oh, do forgive them – they are mine – and they hold in their . . . formal hands all that I call my heart. . . . I know . . . that we shall both get more pain than pleasure from our love . . . fate will not always be kind . . . .

I have read *Adolphe* and loved it. A character such as his is the only kind that I can really conceive of – much more understand – although, of course, I am quite aware that they are a tiny minority. As Constant writes in his diary when he reads his '*roman*' to his friends '*le caractère du héros les révolte. Décidément, on ne sait pas me comprendre.*'[1] A good entry, that? I think it should be the epitaph of every *évolué* nature who has been born into this world: *Décidément, on ne sait pas me comprendre.* I love its calmness and comparative lack of interest. He had no Yvette! As a matter of fact, did you send me *Adolphe* with any

---

[1] Constant, *Journaux Intimes.*

'ulterior motive' – any *arrière pensée*? It was charming of you if you did – I wonder. [Yvette had written '*Ce Triste Adolphe*' on the flyleaf.]

For the next few months, Strachey's friendship with Yvette Fouque was the most important in his life, despite the intermittent nature of their meetings, and despite the existence of other attractions for both of them: thus Strachey continued his friendship with Elizabeth Ponsonby and others, while Yvette had other friends including another Englishman, Nigel Thornton, about whom Strachey wrote from Magdalen: 'You're sure you love my absence better than his presence? That is the comparison you know: But that is an unworthy thought. I know, by all that's passed between us, that you do. I cannot bare [*sic*] to think for one moment of the possibility of doubting you. . . .'[1] Still, he seems not to have been very happy. He wrote to Yvette of the 'vile triviality' of Oxford life and, in the summer of 1922, longed to escape from it to the maturity of France or of Vienna.

[1] Undated letter from Strachey to Yvette, Magdalen College, 'Saturday night'– probably May 1922.

Chapter 3 / LONDON

In June 1922, at the end of the summer term, Strachey handed over the *Oxford Fortnightly Review* to Henry Scrymgeour-Wedderburn,[1] with Evelyn Waugh as Business Manager (the *Review* soon adopted such unorthodox policies that the Conservative party withdrew the subsidy which it had paid to it). Strachey himself went off to stay in France with Yvette; or, rather, in the same hotel at which she and her mother were staying in Le Mans.[2] He wrote to his father several times: 'I feel I ought to be able to get a good deal done here. You will send me Philip Guedalla's book on the Second Empire,[3] won't you? . . . I will review it at once if you will send it. I'd like to do it at fair length, if I may. If you could also get hold of Bolton King, *Making of Modern Italy*,[4] I should be awfully obliged;' and then, 'It is very pleasant here, and I really hope I'm learning some French – I certainly talk it a good deal . . . .' A little later, Strachey sounded alarmed, lest a new arrangement which his father was planning, with G. M. Trevelyan, to review historical books should jeopardise the chances of his own review of Guedalla.

[1] Scrymgeour-Wedderburn was Strachey's Conservative opponent in Dundee in the General Election of 1951. He became Lord Dundee and a Conservative Minister.
[2] Pension de Famille, 5 Rue Sainte Marie, Le Mans.
[3] Philip Guedalla, *The Second Empire* (London 1922).
[4] Bolton King, *The Making of Modern Italy* (London 1922).

There were several other letters about the *Spectator*. The paper was going through a difficult time, and St Loe was looking for investments for it. A businessman named Cochrane had offered St Loe an investment of £8,000 and, with that backing, he was proposing to reduce the selling price. In late July, St Loe wrote to his son explaining that 'certain overtures have been made to me for the purchase of the *Spectator* at a very large sum of money'. He added that he would think seriously about it, if he could get a capital sum which would 'give an income of about the same amount as the *Spectator* gave in its prosperous years'. The reasons which he gave for this were that a financial crisis might ruin the paper, and he was alarmed for his health. But also, with the money that he hoped would be at his disposal, St Loe felt that he would be easily able 'to find plenty of opportunities for you to practise, what I am sure is your gift, public writing. I have,' he added, 'several ideas in my head for securing a pulpit, or rostrum, for both of us, or rather, one for each.'[1]

Meantime, John Strachey had been giving his views on recent issues of the *Spectator* with candour for one who was not quite twenty-one: thus, in a letter at the end of July, he wrote to his father: 'I have read the last issue from cover to cover and *deeply congratulate* you on it.[2] It strikes me as a *great* improvement on anything there has been for some time. . . . The Reviews I thought started brilliantly. . . . The Santayana simply perfect, do congratulate Amabel (I suppose it was hers).[3] . . . I am so glad you have been having good reports of the *Spectator*, and I'm sure its prestige in certain circles, *and for certain things*, is very high. But, all the same, I think that you should remember that all the nice things your friends have said are reported to you, and none of the nasty ones. . . . It is extremely difficult to get at people's real attitudes in a case like this. I think the *Spectator* has a rather unfortunate reputation in some quarters. *Please* excuse all this unfortunately rude discourse – but so few people will criticise freely, that I think somebody should. Ever your loving son. . . .'

St Loe replied: 'All your criticisms of the *Spectator* are interest-

---

[1] St Loe to John Strachey, 4 August 1922.
[2] The issue of 29 July 1922.
[3] A review of Santayana's *Soliloquies in England*. Amabel was then Literary Editor.

ing and valuable, though I don't agree with them . . . if I took any of your favourite newspapers and put them under a microscope, as you very properly put the *Spectator*, I could show, from my point of view, plenty of poor, bad, pompous, and pretentious writing. . . .'[1]

Yvette's husband, Edouard Fouque, was with her and John in Le Mans, at least for a time, and, indeed, gave some advice about the route which Strachey should follow, when, later in the year, he was to go on a motoring tour of France with his parents: 'M. Fouque, who is a *Provençal* by birth, and a man of some discernment, states that Avignon is probably the most comfortable town to stay, Arles the best centre for excursions, and Nimes unpleasant . . . in all respects. But, of course,' added Strachey tartly, 'I can't say whether he has the same standard of relative values as you.'[2] Monsieur Fouque's presence did not prevent Strachey and Yvette from travelling together to Tours and staying there for four days, though he later mentioned the 'joys of Tours', as having held 'the seeds of agony in them'.

After this visit, Strachey returned to England, stayed a few weeks at his parents' house in Surrey, saw old friends, such as his cousin Julia, and set off with his parents, as planned, in mid September for the motor tour of France. The main incident of the journey was a near-disastrous one, since having followed the advice of Monsieur Fouque, and put up at Avignon, John Strachey was hit by appendicitis and had to be operated upon on 21 September in a small clinic run by nuns. For some days his life seemed in danger. Amabel, as befitted a nurse in the war, came out to help and found her brother needing it: '*Nous avons beaucoup priés pour Monsieur*,' one nun said to her. But they seemed to have done little other than pray. The St Loe Stracheys were, understandably, alarmed lest their second son should follow their first to an early grave. They eventually took him back to convalesce in England, by train. Yvette met him in Paris as the train went round the *ceinture*.

On return to England, Strachey had to have a second operation. While recovering, he wrote to Yvette from a nursing home (98

1 Letter of 4 August.
2 Strachey to Yvette, 1 November 1922.

Baker Street). After a series of protestations of affection ('you are
the most beautiful, the happiest – in a word, the best thing in my
life. Only when I am with you do I feel fully satisfied with life.
Your wonderful spirit can evoke in me anything that there is of
value'), he wrote: 'let me be utterly frank [and say] that I have not
got what one reads of as physical passion for you. I think the
physical understanding and sympathy we reached at Tours
transcended anything that we could have reached by mental
contact alone, as heaven transcends earth. But that is not this
strange consuming passion which I have never experienced, and
do not even know if I am capable of experiencing.'

He went on nevertheless, after this brave declaration: 'I hope
we shall go on meeting each other very often. . . . Then we can
only see. The obstacles to our ever permanently living together in
the sense of continual physical presence in the same house certainly
seem, both for you and for me, very great. But how can we tell?
If we care enough, who shall say what will be possible, what
impossible. I am just twenty-one, what could be more childish
for me to try and decide what I shall be like at 25? What more
disastrous for us both than to try and tie the illimitable future in
a net?'

What are we to make of this curious statement? Did Strachey
feel a strong intellectual attraction for Yvette but no serious
physical one? Was he writing the truth? Did he really wish to
free himself of her powerful influence? Whence, above all, does
this mature candour derive which seeks to be honest, even in the
devious frame of a protestation of affection? Why should he, if
he has these affectionate thoughts, feel that it would be so difficult
for them to live together? Why, indeed, if he loved her, did he
not persuade her to come to England?

The truth no doubt is partly social and, partly, from occasional
remarks which he later lets slip, moral. No one of Strachey's age,
self-consciousness and background, at that time, would wish to
saddle himself with the responsibility of looking after a married
woman, of becoming, no doubt, the occasion, if not the cause,
for the final disintegration of her marriage, and of dealing with
the lawyers of the 'discriminating' Provençal, Monsieur Fouque.
Consciously or unconsciously, Strachey's family's views looming

in the background must also have been relevant, as were his own political ambitions. Perhaps, in fact, he did not love her completely: both he and Yvette were extremely elusive characters in private matters.

Meantime, Strachey had made the fundamental decision to leave Oxford, and to start there and then to work on the *Spectator*. He did this to please his parents, who had been severely shaken by his illness at Avignon, and feared that the dank air of Oxford in winter might, indeed, lead to a repetition of the illness which had caused the death of his elder brother. Sir Herbert Warren was displeased, and said: 'of course, that is a blow personally to me, and I venture to think it is a loss to him . . . he might have gained a great deal from a couple more terms here.' He begged St Loe to reconsider the matter.[1] St Loe, however, was anxious that he should not do so. Many of his thoughts were now bound up in his son, whom he described in a letter at this time to his cousin, Charles Strachey, as a 'very able boy, and has not only intellect but character; and best of all a real desire for justice, and to do the right thing'.[2]

When John Strachey eventually recovered from his second operation, he joined the *Spectator*, and began to work on occasional editorials, reviews, and some signed articles. By this time, the political situation had changed. For the coalition had fallen in October, and Bonar Law had formed the first post-war Conservative administration. Strachey's first problem, however, was his new relationship with his father. He adopted a fairly strict line, as a letter written from his friend Boothby's parents' house near Edinburgh[3] suggests, *à propos* of a collection of articles which his father wanted to publish as a book: 'of course,' wrote John Strachey 'there is a great deal of *absolutely necessary* work to be done on them in eliminating the inevitable repetitions and contradictions of a series of newspaper articles. . . .' He suggested that either he and Boothby should do the work, or that St Loe should get down to it himself: 'could you let us have a line *by return*

[1] Sir Herbert Warren to St Loe, 21 October 1922.
[2] St Loe to Charles Strachey (Colonial Office), 27 November 1922.
[3] Beechwood, Murrayfield, Midlothian. Boothby's father, Sir Robert Boothby (1871–1941), was a banker and insurer.

saying *definitely* which you would like done?' (To this letter there was a postscript: 'Millar has failed to pack me any white waistcoats. Catastrophe! Could 2 be sent up by post?'[1])

St Loe wanted his son and Boothby to do the work, in this particular case, since he said that that would 'make the book appeal more strongly to the people I want to convert, that is, the younger and not the older generation. My object is . . . to show . . . that there is cause for regarding Political Science not as the dismal Science but the science to overcome the economic tragedy of the world. . . . It will be great fun if we knock something out to take the town,' St Loe added with typical enthusiasm, 'I envy you the stimulating intellectual air of Edinburgh,' and added 'of course you will look at the Raeburns in the National Gallery.'[2] The book was eventually published as *Economics of the Hour*.

Yvette and Strachey did not meet again, meanwhile, until February or March of 1923, and then only fleetingly. After that, there was no further meeting until the summer. Strachey was beginning to regard his own part in the affair as a 'long story of gradual failure on my part to be what you had hoped I was'.[3] It is evident from a later article by Yvette that in January 1923 Strachey became suddenly 'francophobe': '*vous fourbissiez votre grande sabre pour envahir Calais quand nous "envahissons" la Ruhr*'.[4] On this point they differed. Yvette, while detaching herself more and more from Fouque and trying to embark on a literary career, continued in love with Strachey, while he stayed affectionate towards her, sometimes possessively so.

Soon, Yvette went off to Berlin, where she remained many months writing and inspiring others. Strachey wrote to her there a little later: 'I have just got your letter. . . . I can't say how impressed I am with it . . . it ought to be of the greatest help to us. I shall make my father read them regularly . . . [But] you mustn't spend too much time on them when you might be writing either your novels or articles for those Americans [i.e. U.S. journals and periodicals] . . . Oh, my dear,' he added, 'I do

[1] Strachey to St Loe Strachey.
[2] St Loe Strachey to his son, 18 December 1922.
[3] Strachey to Yvette, 9 December 1924.
[4] Letter de Londres 29 Juin 1936, by inference, in a French newspaper.

hope you aren't unhappy in that great windy Berlin. We *did* do something rather wonderful while you were here, didn't we? We did build something worth building, something to live on. My dear, I *do* think of you very often, and you make everything seem very flat and dim, if I think of it without you, and very interesting and rich if I think of it in your way. . . .'

In the same letter, he writes of Proust: 'I am reading the second part of Swann's love affair with perhaps more exquisite pleasure than I have ever read any book before. But that is hardly so much because of itself as because it makes me think of everything in your way, it makes me see the world with your sense of relative values, with something of your wisdom and maturity. Unlike literally everyone else who has ever read Proust, I do not find myself like Swann but really, in many ways, extremely like Odette.' After this surprising confession, he went on, 'You, of course, *are* Swann – to the very life – or perhaps to the very death. . . . You may have been Adolphe, but you are now certainly Swann. However, I have one distinct advantage over Odette, that I can read about myself. . . .'[1]

The unresolved situation between Strachey and Yvette thus lingered, mostly through letters, during 1923. At the beginning of the next year, Strachey's sister, Amabel, wrote to Yvette, who was still then in Berlin:

Dearest Yvette. How nice to hear from you . . . and what wonder from Berlin! You are too sympathetic to remain in such a place calmly, even if you had been more tranquil when you went there. . . . You know [she went on, the mantle of the elder sister coming upon her] Evelyn is too young and undeveloped to love anybody for long. He has grown up irregularly. His head is extremely mature but, in his affections, he still has, at bottom, all the self-protecting coldness which lies under the enthusiasms of adolescence. He won't have a heart for years yet, I expect. It is almost terrifying to realise how cold he is. He doesn't, of course, realize it, nor do I believe it's permanent, but he really is heartless, for all he is so

---

[1] Letter of Strachey to Yvette dated 'Monday night', with Yvette's note, 1923, added. In later life, Strachey found Proust impossible to re-read.

genuinely affectionate, and sympathetic, and means so very well. You see it in all his relations with people, and no effort of his can change him. . . . I thought so much about you and have always been so sorry for a situation which, I'm afraid, has brought you a good deal of pain. I did not, of course, care, and thought only of Evelyn's side until I met you.[1] After that, when I found a person so delightful, and whom I admired and liked so much, I thought perhaps as much of you. . . . I don't like your *mort intellectuelle*, your head is one of the cleverest I know, and I often wonder if you don't take its portion, and give it to your favourite, the heart. I believe you are too civilized, and complex, and developed to neglect your brain, and that you would be happier if you worked it hard and really set it tasks . . . books I mean, I don't count articles, especially if you kept away from theories and politics, except as incidental expressions of the human spirit, and wrote about men and women of whom you already know more than I probably shall if I live to be 80. . . .[2]

In London, meantime, Strachey continued a mixture of political experiment and social gaiety. He wrote many of the *Spectator's* leading articles in the next few years, particularly about foreign affairs. But he was equally likely to be found drinking green beer at the Gargoyle Club as with politicians. He spent a holiday with Boothby in Italy on Lake Como and 'educated' him, as Boothby recalled, in monetary policy; and had his third operation within a year, for tonsils, in July. Carrington, the heroine of Bloomsbury, wrote to Lytton Strachey in late 1923 of a party at which she met a 'terribly *funeste* group of young men, friends of Julia [Strachey] and Hester [Chapman]. A very tall, monstrously fat Jew, a Beardsley character, you remember the drawing of the fop in *Under the Hill* by Beardsley. Unfortunately, I found he was merely John Strachey. . . . Then John Rothenstein . . . and another very Balliol snobbish young man who I didn't know. They pretended they were very superior, and upper class,

[1] They had met when Yvette came to the train in which Amabel was carrying John back to England in 1922.
[2] Letter from Amabel, dated by Yvette 6.1.24.

and stood in a group and sneered at the rest of the party.'[1] Once, when walking in Hyde Park with Julia Strachey, Elizabeth Ponsonby (with whom he was then having an affair) and some others, he tried to explain to those 'bright young people' a complicated point of economic theory: 'couldn't we all have postal orders?' asked Julia Strachey inconsequently. 'Of course, that's exactly what I was trying to suggest,' said Strachey. One girl who at that time knew him well described him as 'charming then, really charming. I was never in love with him, but he was such fun. Tremendous fun. Very gay. He couldn't keep away from me, and, of course, I went to bed with him. He was very interested in that. Very. I did so because I thought it the polite thing to do. What would have happened if we'd married, I can't think. . . . His family were terrified lest we should get married. They were dead against it, or, rather, Amy and Amabel were. St Loe and Clough were charming. But they kept out of controversies. But I can't possibly tell you what went on between us, and, apart from that, I knew nothing. I wasn't interested in politics. I'm afraid we thought politics a very mediocre activity. . . . You should say, though, that he was a darling, a perfect darling.'

Strachey, meantime, joined the Labour party in 1923, presumably at the very end of it since, in November, in an article entitled 'The Labour Party's Aim', in the *Spectator*, he is found still criticising socialists for their ignorance about 'ordinary men'.[2] Bertrand Russell once asked Strachey: 'why are you a socialist? Did you hate your father, your childhood, or your Public school?' Strachey replied, honestly or dishonestly, 'a bit of all three'. One old friend, Richard Hughes, said 'wasn't it to annoy his father?' Amabel said, 'do you think it was Yvette?' His wife Celia (who did not then know him) said that she thought it was 'Vienna'. John Rothenstein believed that it was 'sheer brain power'. Strachey himself, as noted previously, said often, as a joke, that it was because he did not get into the Eton XI. Such apparently trivial

[1] Carrington to Lytton Strachey in *Carrington, Letters and Extracts*, from her Diaries, chosen by David Garnett (London 1970), p. 265.
[2] *Spectator*, 24 November 1923. The exact date of Strachey's joining the Labour party is impossible to establish.

explanations as these may contain a grain of the truth. Also, the desire for novelty was always strong in Strachey's breast. In 1923 he had, however, met the Webbs; asked by them to dine at their house on Millbank, Beatrice Webb peered at him quizzically and asked, 'Now, on which side of us are you young people coming up now? We notice that first a generation of young socialists comes up well to the left of us and then the next generation comes up well to the right of us. Now, where are you, Mr Strachey?'[1] Strachey did not exactly know, but he soon began to desire anyway to 'come up' with the Webbs. In October 1924, he explained himself in the theoretical journal of the I.L.P., the *Socialist Review*, in terms which suggest that he had found in socialism something for which he must have been looking for a long time: 'for any young man with an as yet vague and undefined interest' in politics, he wrote, and who hoped to be of 'practical service, however small, to the country', the choice was between three parties. The Conservatives were selfish, believing in the established order. The Liberals had no cause. The Labour party aimed to 'change the whole configuration of society, as we know it, and to inaugurate a society based on the conscious cooperation of every single man and woman in society. . . . Man must have something in which to believe. He must rest his ignorance of whither, which and why upon some rocks in which he can have faith. Too many such rocks have lately crumbled to dust before his troubled eyes. But at last there looms up a new object for the exercise of the great human faculty of belief.'[2] But Strachey accepted socialism precisely for other reasons: it offered, as it seemed, Reason, or the chance of its introduction into human affairs. For Reason indeed Strachey had a paradoxical but passionate enthusiasm.

Strachey also, during the winter of 1923-4, began to take for the first time a serious interest in economic problems. At that time, there was controversy as to whether Britain should, or should not, return to the Gold Standard. In several articles in the *Spectator*, Strachey took a negative view of this idea, agreeing

---

[1] Strachey, *The Strangled Cry*, p. 186. The Webbs had then just finished their *The Decay of Capitalist Civilisation*, their most hostile critique of society.
[2] *Socialist Review*, October 1924.

with Keynes, primarily then known for *The Economic Consequences of the Peace*, that the fundamental cause of the country's economic stagnation was insufficient demand. His almost visionary article in the *Socialist Review* was thus balanced by an economic one in the *Spectator*, in September 1924. There, under the signature 'I.L.P.', he accepted Marx's 'destructive Critique of capitalism', and added that he thought that 'only a Socialist government could redistribute resources more equally, and generate sufficient demand'. But, beyond that humdrum reflection, he went on: 'the united army of mankind must march onward to the glorifying of the human spirit. Man must learn to put away all his dark and dreary past. All his primaeval fears and suspicions of his fellows, his utter and all too well-founded lack of trust in the goodwill of others, must be eradicated. He must move forward as far from the point of view he has now reached as he has already come from the amoeba. . . . This, then, is the basic belief that can make me work for the Labour party – the faith that the realization of the socialist ideal is only the first step in the realization of man's ultimate destiny. . . .'[1]

The actual leadership of the Labour party in the mid 1920s seemed, however, to high-minded and ambitious young men to be unexciting. Ramsay Macdonald, Clynes, Henderson and J. H. Thomas were ignorant of practical economics, while Snowden, Chancellor in 1924, though well versed in nineteenth century political economy, was closed to new ideas. The amateurishness of these men who had, after all, founded the modern Labour party, basing it on good-natured humanism, low church public spirit and the generosity of attitude associated with the old Liberal party, had little appeal to younger and more impatient men. The magnitude of their achievement – namely, the creation of what has been after all the most resilient and effective social democratic party in Europe – was obscured.

More exciting in 1924 seemed the Independent Labour Party (I.L.P.), whose leaders, though collaborating with the leaders of the parliamentary Labour party, regarded themselves as a 'ginger group' for radical thinking, untrammelled by the bondage of trade unions. Many of the ideas later adopted by Keynes (and

[1] *Spectator*, September 1924.

hence referred to today as 'Keynesian') were being thought about by the I.L.P. in the mid 1920s. Clifford Allen, the new, charming, magnetic and omni-competent (if usually ill) chairman and reviver of the I.L.P., had not only found new sources of finance from philanthropic individuals, but had gathered around him many intelligent men such as Frank Wise, an ex-civil servant, and H. N. Brailsford, whose cast of mind was exploratory and lively. Brailsford became the well-paid editor of the party's beautifully produced and well-written journal, the *New Leader*, which soon acquired a large readership of 50,000. It was then possible to join the Labour party and the I.L.P. at the same time. Strachey did both, like many others.

Clifford Allen himself believed that it was he, always on the look-out for intelligent young men, who introduced Strachey to the I.L.P. But the Webbs probably played a part, while it was certainly Arthur Ponsonby, himself a convert to Labour from Liberalism, in 1918, who introduced 'an ungainly young man' to the I.L.P.'s new Organizing Secretary, Fenner Brockway, at their new 'impressive premises in Great George Street' and told him that 'here is a young man, son of the editor of the *Spectator*, who wants to do something for socialism'. It turned out, Brockway said, 'that he was good at writing. We found his spelling very bad, we couldn't understand why someone who had been through Eton and Oxford could spell which "wich". But, still, he could write all right.'[1] Strachey worked with Brockway in the I.L.P.'s information department and, after that, on the *New Leader* under Brailsford. He shortly contributed a series of articles entitled 'What Youth is Thinking', in which he described, with some freedom, his own libertarian views on love and morals. These views outraged nonconformist members of the I.L.P., one of whom argued that their advocacy of what seemed to him to be 'free love' would lose the next election for the Labour party.[2]

Arthur Ponsonby's role in pushing Strachey towards the left may have been a determining factor, for the former had been trying to loosen the hold which Strachey had over his daughter. In August 1923, for instance, Ponsonby noted: 'serious talk with

[1] Brockway, *Inside the Left*, p. 145 ff.
[2] *Ibid.*, p. 146

J.S. about E and her friends and his influence'. Neither Ponsonby nor his wife wanted Strachey as a son-in-law, though apparently he had no desire for such a relation either. Ponsonby's fatherly chat to Strachey on this occasion in 1923 must have strayed into politics, and Ponsonby perhaps pointed out the possibilities now opening to Labour as a party of government, rather than simply of protest.[1] At all events, Strachey soon did embrace Ponsonby's opinions and he soon drifted away from his daughter: they did not meet much after 1924.[2]

Both St Loe and Amy Strachey were distressed when their only surviving son, whom they expected would inherit, and edit, the conservative journal the *Spectator*, became a socialist. There was, however, 'no row', as Boothby put it: St Loe 'took it very well and interested himself in his son's doings'. Vague indications only survive of St Loe's reactions: 'Geoffrey Cox,'[3] St Loe wrote to John in January 1924, 'had told Clough [Amabel's architect husband] on the phone yesterday that he had heard that, owing to John Strachey, the *Spectator* had gone completely Labour. I need hardly say that I am not frightened by gossip of this kind. It was sure to be. At the same time, it is a warning that we ought to be a little careful, and I have told Clough industriously to spread the news that you only take part in the literary and business side and not in the political side.'[4] He added, in a later letter, for the first Labour government had then just taken office, 'I have lots of amusing, and all of them pleasant, and generous, stories to tell you about the actions of the new Ministers . . . but I cannot put them on paper. They seem, one and all, to have acted with great good breeding, as I, personally, was sure they would.' This letter ended with a statement of dissent from John Strachey's admiring views of Lenin, who had died the week before.[5]

Another occurrence at this critical time was that, in early 1924, Strachey set off on his first journey to Germany, theoretically to

[1] From a Diary, 27 August 1923.
[2] Perhaps it would have been better for her if they had met more. Elizabeth Ponsonby had a tragic life, and died of alcohol poisoning in 1940.
[3] Probably the then Assistant Adjutant General of the London region, afterwards Sir Geoffrey Cox.
[4] Letter of 24 January 1924.
[5] Letter of 30 January 1924.

study 'the situation' from a political point of view, but with the thought of visiting Yvette in Berlin evidently not far from his mind.

Germany was then beginning to recover from the crisis caused by the French occupation of the Ruhr a year before. This was of interest from a journalistic point of view. Strachey, writing to his father from Munich, believed that 'Germany is modifying distinctly my point of view on the Franco-German situation. Not exactly towards Poincaré-ism, but yet away from indiscriminate support of Germany – of what Germany? She is almost unbelievably split up, both horizontally and vertically. I think the class split is the fundamental one, and that the socialists have, finally, been beaten by the great industrialists, who will henceforth rule. I have got rather interested in the situation, so I think I shall go on to Berlin. Yvette Fouque is still living there, and she can introduce me to a lot of people of interest, all the social democrat leaders. . . .'[1]

Yvette, in fact, came to Munich to see Strachey, and Strachey himself went to Berlin, at the beginning of February 1924;[2] of what transpired there, the only evidence is a letter from him to Yvette, written from Cologne on his way back to England. It included an attempt to parody what he fondly hoped might be the style of his biographer, whom he, Strachey, imagined would 'leniently condemn the irregularity and handsomely commend the humanity' of what, ironically, he described as the 'softer, private, intimate side of the great man': 'but it must not be thought,' this piece of self-mockery continued, 'that Strachey had, at this time, no other interests than politics and literature. In the spring of 1924, he took a holiday in Germany and it seems tolerably certain that he again met Marthe le Bas, or, as she was then called, Madame Yvette Fouque, and renewed that intimacy which was so important, if so unusual, a feature of his youth. Whatever may be thought of the moral issues involved,' Strachey mockingly went on, – 'several sentences from the original edition have been deleted at the request of the family, and of the Le Bas Society of Le Mans, and the subsequent edition reads "But for this side of

---

[1] Letter from Regina Hotel, Munich, undated.
[2] Strachey to St Loe Strachey, from Dom Hotel, Cologne.

Strachey's life the student must be referred to the earlier and less well-known novels of Le Bas".'

Strachey continued: 'But, indeed, it is far more important that you should become great than that I should. It is a horrible confession of my disgusting weakness, but I *need* you to be great as a prop to my weak imagination of you.' The letter ended 'Best, best love in all the world (my ? own ?) Yvette, Evelyn.' To the two adjectives 'my' and 'own', Strachey added a footnote: 'Professor Grumpkins considers that this must be a textual error, as Strachey was, at this time, still quite sane.'[1]

Yvette also came to London either that same spring or summer of 1924, while Strachey went to Paris in the summer. In September, they spent several 'quiet, beautiful days at Geneva. As if we, war-worn like Europe, but wiser than her, had referred our troubles to the League of Nations, and had been given the mandate of quietude.'[2]

In the course of these meetings, politics was, of course, discussed, as much as, or even more than, anything else. They had, for example, one long political argument at lunch at Versailles, in which Yvette declared her commitment to socialism: 'you said that after all you *had to be* on the side of the workers'. Strachey later wrote, 'You know that means very much to me? Although you are too old – in thoughts – too steeped in France, to be a socialist in the dogmatic sense of the word (that I realise is for simple-minded people, of whom in many ways, I am one), yet you are with us – of us – in that far more important, indefinable sense, inevitable sense.'

These remarks must have seemed patronising from one who had himself only recently become a socialist, but, then, they are not dissimilar in tone from his remarks to his father about how to edit the *Spectator*: once Strachey had made up his mind, he automatically began to lay down the law, even if the decision had only happened the previous day.[3]

1 Letter from Dom Hotel, Cologne, Tuesday. Yvette added the date and the month.
2 Letter dated 9 December 1924, from Flat D, 45 Cromwell Road, SW7. He shared this with Eddie Sackville-West.
3 The letter in which these remarks occur is not dated. Yvette added 1925, and her sister 'or 26', to the text. The letter is on paper headed 76 Chester Square, SW1,

Soon after returning from Geneva, Strachey became embroiled for the first time in active politics. One aim of Ramsay Macdonald's first Labour government had been to restore relations with Russia. In February, this had led to diplomatic recognition of Russia and, in August, while Strachey and Yvette were in Paris, to a commercial treaty. This gave British goods most-favoured-nation treatment in Russia, and promised Russia a loan, when, and if, the debt to Britain of the old Tsarist government were settled. The Liberals, as well as the Conservatives, opposed this measure, and Macdonald's frail minority government, which depended on Liberal support, was thus endangered. The Labour party managers therefore decided to go to the country in October. In this election Strachey was nominated and stood for the Aston Manor division of Birmingham. 'So there I am,' he wrote to Yvette, '*lancé* on a political life! No one knows better than yourself how deeply unsuitable I am to it. But still it is Life, and I really find I care for little else. The Socialist movement is the first thing I have ever found in which I can begin to sink myself – so you may imagine how I need it! I hope it may alter me – who knows but that Marx may finish what Yvette began!'[1]

---

where Strachey had moved with his parents. Thus the conversation may not have described events in 1924 but later. But we know from Strachey's letter of 9 December 1924 that he was in Paris in mid 1924 and there is no other sure reference to one of his visits there. At all events, a conversation of this sort certainly could have occurred then, and at Versailles.

[1] Letter of 9 December, 1924 – i.e. actually later than the election, which occurred on 29 October.

Chapter 4 / POLITICS AND MOSLEY

'You have now got your neck well into the political collar and you will never get it out again, or want to. That is a safe thing to say of anyone who voluntarily goes into politics. It is the most attractive and exciting thing in the world. My last advice to you is, try and make a mixture of urbanity on one side and vivid fighting on the other. That is the best kind of candidate and the one who is in most request. The acrid and bitter fighter, though he may win a good many cheers, is never really liked as a candidate – at any rate, not when the excitement of the General Election is over and people choose quietly.'[1]

These were St Loe's words of advice to his son before the general election campaign of October 1924. They were the, as usual, hectically dictated, but much considered view of a man who had been many years on the edges of the political life, who had once ventured himself to the very brink (as an unsuccessful candidate for a university seat in 1906) and who had comforted himself with the thought that, as the editor of a famous weekly, he had influenced decisions more than most back-benchers.

By this time, Strachey had acquired a new influence over his intellectual development; one who would replace, during the next seven years, the influence of his father and of Yvette. This

[1] Letter of St Loe to Strachey, 15 October 1924.

was Oswald Mosley, 'Tom', as he was known, the outstanding young politician in the House of Commons, who had recently abandoned the Conservatives and, after a spell as an independent member for Harrow, had been a member of the Labour party since March. Mosley had left the Tories over the Irish question and the Peace Treaty. Mosley, being five years older than Strachey, was a member of the war generation and had been wounded. With great audacity, he was now proposing to challenge Neville Chamberlain for the Ladywood, or central, constituency in Birmingham and was hoping to extend this to a challenge of the whole longstanding Conservative control of the city. No Labour member had previously been elected for any Birmingham constituency (except one Lib–Lab, and he more Lib than Lab). About the time that the two met – probably at the Webbs – Mosley had been adopted as candidate in Ladywood and had already flamboyantly asked Birmingham to 'overthrow the false gods of reaction which have dominated the city for the last generation at the cost of so much suffering'.[1]

Mosley at that time deserves careful study, in respect both of his friendship with, and influence over, Strachey and of his part in Labour politics. He was eloquent, young, resolute, handsome, witty, masterful and, as it seemed, a lover of humanity: 'It is his ambition to serve his fellow men . . . a gentleman in the highest sense of that abused term . . . more truly socialist than many Labour M.P.s', wrote the commentator 'Watchman' in the Birmingham socialist paper, the *Town Crier*, in June 1929, in a profile. He danced beautifully, despite a lame foot. He had married the beautiful and delightful Cynthia ('Cimmie'), Lord Curzon's daughter, 'the most Curzon of his three daughters', as Curzon himself had thought.[2]

Everything seemed open to Mosley. The Webbs thought him 'the most brilliant man in the House of Commons . . . the perfect politician, who is also the perfect gentleman [and] . . . an accomplished orator in the old style'.[3]

Mosley's obvious capacity for political leadership had not yet

[1] *Town Crier*, 12 September 1924.
[2] Lady Curzon, *Reminiscences*, p. 106.
[3] Beatrice Webb, *Diaries*, 1918–1924, p. 242.

exhibited any flaw. He seemed in fact a meteor. It is true that some thought him cruel in his jokes and ways, while others considered him a little frightening, if attractive. Allan Young, the new Borough organizer of the Labour party in Birmingham, had already observed that Mosley had been 'bullied by his father and spoiled by his mother'. But to most people, Mosley seemed a great political leader in the making. It is foolish to comment on Mosley's promise in his twenties from the standpoint of knowledge of what happened to him in his forties. Indeed, the ruin of the latter years would not have occurred, had it not been for the sparkle of the early ones. It was understandable that John Strachey should attach himself to Mosley's star, though he himself still seemed to Mosley more a man with 'a lily in his button hole', than a revolutionary. The attraction must have been mutual: if Strachey welcomed a leader – perhaps had often looked for one – Mosley needed a man of ideas. Both men were socialist converts, refugees from the upper class. Both were comparatively well off, Mosley more so than Strachey, but Strachey knew nothing of poverty. They were both tall and dark, but Mosley was very good-looking while Strachey's looks were odd.

Soon after they met, Mosley helped to secure Strachey's adoption as the Labour candidate in Aston Manor, a constituency next to Mosley's, then held by the Conservative Sir Evelyn Cecil, nephew of the great Lord Salisbury and a man old enough to be Strachey's father.[1] Strachey agreed to this proposal with enthusiasm. Strachey went to a Sunday morning selection meeting in Ruskin Hall, Aston. Then, after being adopted, he was pushed onto a soapbox by his supporters at the Barton Arms.[2]

Strachey's election address proclaimed: 'The issue before you is clear: Shall this great Constructive Work [i.e. of the Labour administration] go on, or will you allow the Unionists to wreck it all? Rally to Ramsay Macdonald, our great Prime Minister. Do not fail him in his hour of need. If you put Labour into Power,

---

[1] Afterwards Lord Rockley. Mosley, *My Life*, p. 185; this is confirmed by Frank Moody, then Chairman of the Aston party. The 1923 candidate was an alderman due to become Lord Mayor in May 1925.
[2] Letter of Albert Jordan to Strachey, 29 May 1946, when he became Minister of Food.

you can transform England. I myself stand for the complete transformation of Society into a socialist commonwealth, as rapidly as possible. To that end I advocate the immediate national-isation of mines, railways, agriculture, banking, electric supply and the total abolition of food taxes as a measure of elementary justice ... only *our own Labour Votes*, your own efforts, can bring you *Freedom*. Birmingham must lead England in the march of Labour and not lag behind – and Aston must lead Birmingham. I am, Ladies and Gentlemen, Your Obedient Servant, John Strachey.'[1]

The Aston Manor constituency was wholly working class in character and included some of the worst slums, and toughest districts, of the city. It was characterized by long rows of back-to-back, or terraced, houses separated by little ill-lit courts. But Aston was still, with Sir Evelyn Cecil, under the influence of the Tory Chamberlains. For, often, these ragged-trousered philan-thropists would vote Tory.

Aston, with its headquarters at the well-established Ruskin Hall, had, however, by 1924, one of the most active Labour parties in the city, while the first Labour Guild of Youth in Birmingham had been founded there. Still, it seemed a hard nut to crack.

In the campaign the issue of the Russian treaty loomed large, and the Zinoviev letter played a part in the result. To both Strachey and his sister Amabel, the election was a revelation in more ways than one: this was the first time that either had seen these, or, indeed, any, slums. At first, Strachey presented a very odd impression – a man 'who had never got into the slops' – but he was quick to learn, and, in the course of the election, endeared himself to the local party, and, to at least one member, he was still in the 1970s remembered as 'Jack'.

Sir Evelyn Cecil had had a majority of 5,750 (13,291 (Tory), 7,541 (Lab), 2,846 (Lib)). Against this, Strachey campaigned hard. We hear, from the *Town Crier*, of 'brilliant short speeches', delivered, as always in days before widespread use of micro-phones, with increasingly croaking voices. But there were also big meetings, at the Theatre Royal in Aston, or in the amphi-

[1] Strachey election manifesto, October 1924.

theatre at Aston Park. 'Record public meetings' were reported, and the candidature of Strachey was described as 'being received with great enthusiasm'. In the end, Strachey cut Cecil's majority to 2,385, gaining 11,859 votes against Cecil's 14,244. This increase in the Labour vote, though common to the West Midlands, was against a substantial Conservative victory in the country as a whole, mostly at the Liberal's expense. Strachey wrote to Yvette: 'Like most Labour people I did not get in, on the other hand I am considered, I believe, to have done well and am sticking to the constituency, and I really think that I should be able to pull it off next time. . . .'[1] Mosley himself nearly achieved the impossible; he failed to defeat Neville Chamberlain in Ladywood by only 77 after two recounts; perhaps in truth he won: a Tory teller was seen disappearing towards the lavatories with a pile of votes in his pocket.

As early as 7 December 1924, Strachey was re-adopted Labour candidate at the Theatre Royal, Aston. Stirring speeches were made by Allan Young, the new political organizer of the Birmingham Labour party, a young Glaswegian of capacity, intelligence and culture;[2] Frank Moody, of the local party; by Cynthia Mosley; and by Robert Denison, the newly elected Labour member for Kings Norton. Strachey made a vigorous speech, saying that Labour's aim was to end the class war, to apply the principles of socialism to industry, and also to build a new world out of the ruin of the old.[3] For the next four and a half years, Strachey was active nursing this constituency, getting thereby to know well countless people whose lives he would otherwise never have been able even to imagine.

After his readoption, he went off to Hurtwood to spend Christmas with the Clifford Allens, and to 'hunt' Kenneth Lindsay, a fellow Labour candidate, in a game devised by the Trevelyan family in the Lake District. The visitors' book at Hurtwood

[1] This was the letter of 9 December, previously quoted.
[2] Allan Young (b. 1894), born in Glasgow, had been apprenticed to a cabinet maker at 15, educated to socialism on Blatchford's *Clarion* and Tolstoy. His father gave him and his two brothers a book every Friday. An agnostic. Served with R.A.M.C. in the First World War. Labour Agent in Chippenham before Birmingham.
[3] *Town Crier*, 12 December 1924.

shows him signing himself 'Evelyn John Strachey', perhaps a sign of indecision as to who exactly he now was.[1]

In the year following the general election of 1924, while the Baldwin government was settling itself in with its comfortable majority, Strachey's intellectual life developed largely under Mosley's influence. For Strachey, while continuing to write regularly for the *Spectator*, now wrote his first book, *Revolution by Reason*, which was dedicated to Mosley, 'Who may one day do the things of which we dream'. The dedication was appropriate, since Strachey and Mosley worked closely together over its preparation.

Mosley, like Strachey, had announced his intention of remaining in Birmingham for the next election, and (after a journey to India in the winter of 1924-5) was busy searching for an intellectual basis for his own already idiosyncratic political position. How far the ideas contained in *Revolution by Reason* were Mosley's and how far Strachey's is difficult to say. Mosley did not have time, or did not permit himself to have time, to read much, and his speeches, as reported in the Press, were brilliant, political creations, though not very philosophical. Strachey had been interested in banking and monetary problems before he met Mosley and it seems more likely that Strachey was the thinker, and Mosely the interpreter. Mosley, however, would not agree with this judgement.

At all events the ideas contained in *Revolution by Reason* were first put forward by Mosley at the conference of the Independent Labour Party at Gloucester in April 1925, also attended by Strachey. They were repeated by him in speeches in Birmingham in May 1925 ('The Banks for the People') and, in a series of letters to the *Times*, in answer to the banker Robert Brand, at about the same time. They were developed in greater detail by Mosley on 10 August at an I.L.P. summer school at Anley Castle, on the Severn. (These schools had been reborn under Clifford Allen: high-brow lectures were given by expert individuals to middle-class socialists in comfortable surroundings. Allen himself was usually in the Chair.) They were described by Mosley as the

[1] From Clifford Allen's visitors' book. Though he now signed himself 'Evelyn John', it is worth noticing that the Ponsonbys referred to him as 'John Evelyn'.

'Birmingham policy for dealing with the finance and banking system in the transition to Socialism'. Mosley next published a pamphlet summarizing his ideas, under the title *Revolution by Reason*, and Strachey expanded the thinking in the book of the same name.

Boothby recalled visiting Mosley in Venice during the summer while this was being written; 'Every morning Tom Mosley and John Strachey , . . discussed *Revolution by Reason*, a book which they were writing together, and which I then thought the height of political audacity. . . . This was the period when Mosley saw himself as Byron rather than Mussolini; . . . to me, it was infinitely preferable. He was, certainly, a powerful swimmer, and used to disappear at intervals into the lagoon to commune with himself.'[1] (Boothby had been elected to parliament in 1924, as Conservative member for East Aberdeenshire, and was regarded in his party as 'a coming man'.)

Revolution by Reason, published at the end of 1925, is Shavian in flavour, quoting, early on, Shaw's reflection that the 'evil to be attacked' is 'simply poverty'. (Shaw was an acquaintance, and admirer, of Mosley.) The main theme was that the 'poverty of the poor' prevented them from buying enough things either to satisfy their own wants or to absorb the products of modern industry: 'almost any manufacturer in our basic industries could tell you that he could double or treble the amount he produces', as had occurred during the course of the war, and that men 'cannot get work because there is no demand for the things their work would produce'. What was the reason for this defect in the economic system? A maldistribution of wealth, as the orthodox socialist views suggested? Or was it, perhaps, that, as Keynes and some U.S. economists were saying, 'we do not produce enough since we have inadequate money'.

The choices ahead were, therefore: revolution in the Russian manner; gradualism; or some new formulation, such as had been sketched by Mosley in the Birmingham proposals. The Russian method involved, however, the conscription of labour. Quite apart from the 'fatal barbarities of such a course, there are very grave economic objections to it. In the first place, terrible damage

[1] Boothby, *op. cit.*, p. 24.

is apt to be done to the productive machine.' There were also great disadvantages to the idea of conscripting men in peacetime: 'It is all very well to say that you are only conscripting men to free them. They may not believe you.' Furthermore, it was 'almost impossible to believe that either a violent upheaval of society or the subsequent conscription of labour can ever be realized in this country'.

So, what about gradualism? But that would mean that a socialist government would 'be urged to take over those industries which are just becoming obsolete. No, real socialism, if it is to be quickly effective, must come over the whole productive field simultaneously.' On all sides, since 1919, 'socialist' governments had been thrown into 'power'. But everywhere they had failed to put their hands on the keys of the economic machine.

The alternative suggested by Strachey was that based on the Birmingham proposals. This would include a 'banking system capable of giving' such accommodation to industry as would enable it to increase the purchasing power of the workers, so that a new home market could absorb industry's real productive capacity. There would also be an economic council for the co-ordination and control of that productive capacity. Lessons could be learned from the emergency socialism of the war years, for it was then discovered that it was not necessary to nationalize . . . that is, to acquire the capital of an industry in order to make it work. All that was necessary was to control the supply of raw material. The economic council would increase money paid to workers by sponsoring a minimum wage law. There followed a description of the working of this council, which would have to be staffed by virtual supermen, to ensure that 'the industrial omnibus' was not jerked too violently out of the two great parallel ruts of Poverty and Unemployment. Thus, the minimum wage would have to be approached in the most stealthy fashion. The council would control money as 'a magnet controls steel filings'.

The book reads today like a generously presented amalgamation between Labour 'pragmatism' of the 1960s and fascism. But it was urbane, and witty, with occasional flashes of rhetoric.

Among letters received by Strachey in consequence, two stand out: one from Hugh Dalton, the Reader in Economics recently appointed at the London School of Economics who had got into parliament in 1924; the other from Keynes, from whom some of the ideas in the book certainly derived. Dalton, who reviewed the book in the *Labour Magazine*, made a number of minor criticisms. He thought *Revolution by Reason* 'weak on the international side', and he, like Hobson, wondered how Strachey would find the 'supermen' to run his Economic Council: 'To go off gold again isn't practical.'[1] Keynes doubted Strachey's arguments that the surplus income of the rich could be described as ineffective demand; and, he added, 'a good deal of your argument is addressed to the particular type of unemployment which exists at the present time, rather than to various other conceivable types which have come to pass in the past and might again in future. You do not face the fact that it is precisely the industries which cater for foreign trade which are under-employed and not those which produce for working-class consumption.' But, he concluded: 'It is scarcely to be expected that we should agree all through on all the very complicated monetary points which arise, about which no one has ever yet written clearly. I am still too confused in my own mind to know exactly what I want to do. But my sympathies and expectations tend to march in the same direction as yours.'[2]

There was also a note from Ramsay Macdonald, addressed from Suez, on board a P & O liner en route to India: 'We are not thinking enough of ways and means of bringing about socialism, and are contenting ourselves by talking loosely about two adventures: a general act of Nationalization and unlimited public charity. You might assure yourself on one general point about your scheme. The literary composition is good. Your name ensures that – but, is its construction all right? don't you assume results? . . . A ship, however, is not a good place for quiet thinking . . . with kindest regards. . . .'[3]

In the autumn of 1925, Strachey also began a series of broadcasts on the newly founded B.B.C. in conjunction with his

[1] Dalton to Strachey, 3 January 1926.
[2] Keynes's letter of 5 January 1926.
[3] Ramsay Macdonald to Strachey, 29 January 1926 (misdated 1925).

increasingly close friend, Cyril Joad, 'to introduce the great broadcasting public to some of the problems of philosophy'. The conversations, afterwards published in book form, were provocative and amusing.[1] Joad dominated the talks with his cynical hedonism. Strachey played the butt. There was little discussion of politics. The talks were deliberately low-brow; thus, in the fourth dialogue, Strachey says: 'I've been reading some of this new psycho-analysis stuff – Dr Freud and the Unconscious and all that . . . it's rather exciting to discover how wicked one is at bottom.'[2] There were discussions of the nature of truth, or progress, ending up with Strachey reading aloud from *Alice through the Looking Glass*.

Meantime, there had been further 'spectatorial' problems, to use the mocking adjective invented by the evil Cousin Lytton. St Loe went for a holiday, following further ill-health, in November 1925, and left his son in virtual control, along with Evelyn Wrench, who had become the political major domo of the *Spectator* in the past year or two. Wrench, a powerful journalist of Irish origin, had worked with Northcliffe and, in 1912, 'gave up all outside work so as to devote himself to the Overseas Club movement and other imperial activities'. He was a good business man, and had founded both the English-Speaking Union and the Overseas League. He was, however, more open-minded than St Loe, and 'very nice to look at', as Celia Strachey recalls. He now wished to be the controlling influence on the *Spectator*, but this made things difficult for both the Stracheys, father and son, who were coming to rely upon his managerial skill. John Strachey soon wrote, 'the present regime is unsatisfactory. . . . It is neither the old personal control by yourself, nor yet a vigorous management on more ordinary lines.' He, therefore, proposed to his father that he himself should become a leader and review writer, and leave the whole of the business side to Wrench, who would 'keep to that side', except for such advice as he might give on Friday mornings. He concluded: 'It was you yourself that convinced me of the unsatisfactoriness [of the present position]. You have the real control. I exercise it. Such a system cannot and does not work

---

[1] C. E. M. Joad and John Strachey, *After Dinner Philosophy* (London 1926).
[2] *Ibid.*, p. 55.

well. I am not a suitable person to run the *Spectator*. Obviously that person should be you, but if, for reasons of health, and happiness, you do not want to do so, then I think it should be Evelyn Wrench, advised by me and Ewen Agnew [of *Punch*].' (*Punch* had been thinking of buying the *Spectator*, and remained interested.)[1]

It is perhaps surprising that Strachey, now a fully-fledged socialist, should make no bones about handing over, for political reasons, the *Spectator*, to so strong an 'imperialist' as Wrench, but he preferred Wrench on business grounds. He certainly had no desire to run the *Spectator* himself, at that moment: doubtless a sadness to St Loe, for John Strachey might have been a good editor.

At all events, Wrench became chairman of the *Spectator*, and remained as such for many years. St Loe went off to write books and, indeed, within a year, had published a historical novel about the Risorgimento (*Madonna of the Barricades*), as well as a further autobiographical study (*The River of Life*). He also sold Newlands Corner to a hotel company, keeping most of the land, upon which Clough Williams-Ellis built for him and his wife a smaller house, Harrowhill Copse. John Strachey remained as a director of the *Spectator*, and received £440 a year, in return for an article or review per week. At the same time, in February 1926, he became, through his I.L.P. connections, editor of the revised I.L.P. theoretical monthly, the *Socialist Review*. The question of this appointment had led, in the autumn, to a quarrel in the Independent Labour Party.

Clifford Allen had wished to re-appoint Ramsay Macdonald himself to this editorship, in order to confirm the relationship between the I.L.P. and the parliamentary Labour party which he, interested in the practical implementation of his ideas, was anxious to maintain; it was a position which Macdonald had held up till 1924. Macdonald and Allen had been particularly close during the first Labour government. In this design, Allen was foiled by his own managing committee, the National Administrative Council (N.A.C.), led by a group headed by James Maxton, John

[1] Letter from John Strachey, undated, addressed from 45 Cromwell Road. The context suggests a November date.

Wheatley and Elijah Sandham, who, at the head of the I.L.P. members who were actually in parliament, hoped for a more revolutionary approach to politics than either Allen, so aristocratic, cool and disdainful, or Macdonald, seemed to represent. The two groups had had other disputes during 1925. The clash came to a head during the Labour party conference at Liverpool on 30 September 1925, when, during a discussion of the *Socialist Review*, Allen walked out and refused to continue as chairman. He was temporarily succeeded by F. P. Jowett of Bradford, who had been First Commissioner for Works in the Labour Government of 1924, though it became clear that Maxton and his 'Clydesiders', as his followers became known, were poised to take over the party, and impose their more revolutionary, if rhetorical and unpractical, programme. It was, therefore, strange that Strachey, one of Allen's young men, should have been able to capture the job of editor of the *Review*. This was because, despite his background, he seemed as radical as any of the Clydesiders in his writings; and he was prepared to do the work competently for no salary. He was not a great admirer of Clifford Allen despite the latter's help to him. His first leading article in the *Socialist Review*, in February 1926, said that, henceforth, the I.L.P. would offer 'uncompromising resistance' to those forces, 'both powerful and insidious, which seek to turn Labour from its purpose, or to water down its drastic proposals'.[1]

Mosley, meantime, was in the U.S. on a tour of discovery of labour conditions and economic questions generally. As usual, he preferred to learn his economics from experience, rather than from books. In one letter written to Strachey, he explained, indicating how his education was proceeding: 'We found men on wages of $20 a week living in two rooms and paying a rent of $20 a month. . . . It seems as long as rent and interest survive, the proportionate toll is taken of the workers whatever wages they may draw. They are, of course, better fed and were all cooking excellent meals. . . . You might draw a moral on the rise of rent to take the due proportion of the increased wages.'[2] During February, Mosley wrote, heading his letter 'the South

[1] *Socialist Review*, February 1926.
[2] Mosley to Strachey, 15 January 1926.

Seas!' 'You are a rotten correspondent, but forgiven because the *Socialist Review* must be weighing heavily upon you, to judge from your note in the *New Leader* – We are at Peace at last far away in a houseboat with Franklin Roosevelt fishing for ferocious and enormous reptiles which have not yet materialized – Our host is a very charming and remarkable person who was assistant Secretary to the Navy. . . . They say he will be next Governor of New York, and may eventually be President.' He concluded 'I hope soon to hear from you on general situation, notably coal. The owners seem to have made consummate fools of themselves – we sail on 20 March and expect to have a week before the conference . . . must close now, would you kindly tell Sutton[1] I can take no meetings before the 26th and will then do Gorton and East Manchester only – could you take the Cumberland conference? . . . Florida was a delightful rest. . . .'[2] These letters, however, do not give the impression of the extent to which Mosley was influenced by his U.S. experience; for he reached the conclusion there that Britain alone could no longer compete industrially – and henceforth became an advocate of imperial preference; and he was much impressed by the Federal Reserve Board's new financial resourcefulness.[3]

The early part of 1926 saw some discussion within the I.L.P. about Mosley's (and Strachey's) ideas, though the critical issue at the Whitley conference of the I.L.P. in April concerned Maxton's challenge – he was, in the event, elected Chairman – and the party's proposal for a living wage included in their policy statement *Socialism in Our Time*, a document produced largely on the basis of work by Brailsford and J. A. Hobson. Strachey, speaking at that conference, argued that the policy included in Mosley's Birmingham proposals was essential to the 'living wage', but neither he nor Mosley pressed the I.L.P. to accept their whole project.[4] The I.L.P. continued to be dogged by personal as well

---

[1] Mosley's secretary, sometime Chairman of North St Pancras Labour party, research assistant to Mosley, Strachey and Allan Young in the 1920s, later still Director of Research in the British Union of Fascists.
[2] Mosley to Strachey, 15 February 1926.
[3] Mosley, *op. cit.*, pp. 185–6.
[4] *Town Crier*, 9 April 1926.

as ideological disputes between Maxton's and Allen's followers, with the latter in disarray.

These theoretical discussions were interrupted by the drama of the general strike. Before the strike began, Strachey, at a meeting at Aston, had argued for full support of the miners in their proposed challenge to the government.[1] He spoke strongly again to this effect in a May Day speech, on 2 May, accompanying, as usual, Mosley and other Birmingham socialists. During the strike itself, Mosley set up a printing press in the Labour party headquarters in Crown Buildings, Corporation Street, brought down from London Leslie ('Dick') Plummer, manager of the I.L.P. paper *New Leader*, to work the press and, with Strachey as editor, organized, on behalf of the Birmingham Trade Union Emergency Committee, a Strike Bulletin running to nine daily numbers.[2] (Plummer had been brought in from Fleet Street by Clifford Allen to run the *New Leader* at the then princely salary of £750 a year. He became an intimate friend of Strachey's with unforseeable consequences.)

During the course of this publication, Strachey wrote an article saying that the government had been defeated, by 316 to 75, on a motion by the Scottish M.P., Tom Johnston, ending arrest without warrant. Strachey; Allan Young, the borough organizer; Plummer; and seventeen other members of the Strike Emergency Committee were arrested, and later brought before a Magistrate for committing an act 'calculated to, or likely to, cause disaffection'.

'All the men are of excellent character and standing?' asked one J.P., Mr Ladds.

'I would not go that far quite,' replied Chief Superintendent Burnett.[3]

All these men were remanded and later fined. Mosley, who chanced to be away in the Potteries at the time that the police pounced, was furious to miss arrest and 'gave himself up'. But he was not arrested. Strachey wrote to Yvette: 'I have been here

[1] *Ibid.*, 23 April 1926. See *New Leader* article by John Strachey, 1 June 1926.
[2] Strike Bulletin published by Birmingham Trade Union Emergency Committee, 5–14 May.
[3] *Birmingham Mail*, 14 May 1926.

in Birmingham all through it and we have had great excitements. I thought very often of you and your wise and tender eyes. I thought that you would say I had done right in throwing myself wholly onto the workers' side – in going with them all the more in their foolishness and mistakes than in their victories and wisdom. Of course, the working people are always fundamentally right and it was – and is – great peace of mind to me to be wholly and irrevocably with them. I must tell you all about it when we meet. It was, as you would say, *du cinéma*, pure and simple. Tom [i.e. Mosley] was superb – half the hero of melodrama – half laughing at himself!' About his arrest, Strachey wrote: 'I was arrested – for a curious, muddled mistake – and very nearly went to prison. However, in the end, I was only fined £10! You, I am sure, will say that prison would have been ideal for me. I'm so sorry I missed it – but I don't pretend I was looking forward to it. . . . The hour is not ours,' he added. 'We may have to live through a long period of domination. But, at least, I not only know where I am, but know who are my true friends.'[1]

Mosley, at this time, seemed a man of many talents. Thus, in a typical 'home movie' made about now, *Stephen's Drama*, he showed himself an original film-maker. In this semi-surrealist film, Strachey, looking fat, plays the part of the juvenile lead, carrying off the heroine (Cynthia Mosley) to the discomforture of a mysterious madame (Cecil Beaton, in false nose and feathers), and to the surprise of the beautiful Stephen Tennant, who plays a blind girl. This period-piece well evokes the odd world at Denham, where the Mosleys, in an elongated, expanded and comfortable cottage, lived a divided, perhaps ominously divided life: one day the Labour party, J. H. Thomas and Ramsay Macdonald, the next Oliver Messel and Cecil Beaton. Strachey was the only one of those who, apart from Mosley himself, successfully straddled the two groups.[2] His brother-in-law, Clough Williams-Ellis, had redesigned and modernized the house, previously an old Buckinghamshire manor. Marjorie Allen, Clifford Allen's wife, and a landscape gardener from the University of Reading, designed the gardens.

[1] Letter to Yvette, dated, by her, May or June 1926.
[2] See *Stephen's Drama*, in the possession of Nicholas Mosley.

After the strike, Strachey began, in collaboration with Brailsford, to edit *The Miner*, a weekly of the N.U.M., which he did well and professionally, though again without a salary. The mineworkers were still on strike, despite the return to work of the rest of the unions. The purpose was to put the miners' case, 'in view of the gross misinterpretation to which they and their leaders were being subjected'. Strachey obtained this new job through the I.L.P., which, to begin with, jointly controlled the paper with the N.U.M. (the I.L.P. and Brailsford dropped out after November 1926, but Strachey remained editor).

The Miner was managed, like the *Socialist Review* and the *New Leader*, by Plummer, Strachey's collaborator in the General Strike, by now a friend and a man who seemed, like Strachey, also certain to play a big part in Labour political life. *The Miner* was an immediate success, selling 60,000 copies of its first issue, and the second and third 80,000 and 110,000 respectively.

With *The Miner*, as well as the *Socialist Review*, Strachey now had two time-consuming and unpaid jobs. Both he approached and dealt with professionally. This meant an editorial a month, of several thousand words on issues of the day, in the *Socialist Review*, a short leader in *The Miner*, and the main editorial business of securing articles in both, consulting others: above all, A. J. Cook, who gave Strachey what he thought appropriate for the leader in *The Miner*, and the I.L.P. leaders on the *Socialist Review*.

Strachey wrote some bloodcurdling articles in *The Miner*. Thus, in September 1926, he was proclaiming that 'the handful of cruel, stubborn and dull-witted reactionaries, who today have the audacity to claim that they "own" the great coalfields of Britain, will be deprived of every vestige of power which they have so terribly abused.'[1] Doubtless this was A. J. Cook's opinion in Strachey's words. It is difficult, indeed, not to draw the conclusion, that, despite their political collaboration, Mosley and Strachey were intellectually drawing apart in these months. Strachey seemed more and more interested, judging from his articles and reviews in *The Miner* and in the *Socialist Review*, in Marx, Mosley more and more interested in 'saving capitalism' by some modern

[1] Editorial in *The Miner*, 11 September 1926.

U.S. method.[1] At this time, Strachey seemed a 'ruthless intellectual' and 'a convinced apostle of class-consciousness'. So at least he appeared to Geoffrey Elton, one of a group of Labour parliamentary candidates who met regularly for dinner at Henekey's public house in Whitehall. Strachey, wrote Elton some years later, 'could scarcely conceal his impatience when I enlarged on my own idea of a party of all classes united against the Profiteer'.[2] Soon afterwards Mosley was returned to parliament at a by-election in Smethwick, on the borders of Birmingham.

[1] *See* discussion of this in the dissertation by Stuart McIntyre, ch. V.
[2] Lord Elton, *Among Others* (London 1938), p. 214.

Chapter 5 /INTIMATE RELATIONS

About a year after the General Strike, Strachey was writing to Yvette: 'There is something at once exhausted and hysterical about the Labour movement here. I cannot tell whether it is going up or down. I get more and more francophil. . . .'[1] But he was, nevertheless, at this time, the epitome of the coming young man in the Labour movement – almost Marxist, prolific in output, speaking incessantly. In July 1927 Strachey was writing in the *Socialist Review* of the Arcos raid.[2] In August he was complaining in that journal of Mrs Webb's argument that the Russian Revolution was 'the greatest disaster in the history of the Labour movement' and might 'keep back the advent of economic democracy for half a century'. In September, he published, as *Notes of the Month*, his lecture to the I.L.P. summer school at Kiplin Hall, near Catterick, on the I.L.P.'s financial policy, proposing 'heavy direct taxation, coupled with a reform of our banking policy along modern lines' as the key to socialism in the future, rather than nationalization.

Strachey remained in touch with Yvette, though he at this time had several other friendships, including one with Nancy

[1] Strachey to Yvette, letter dated, by her, 20.4.27.
[2] In May 1927 the police raided the offices of Arcos, the Soviet trading organisation in London, in the hope of finding incriminating evidence against the communists. They found nothing, and broke off relations with Russia almost in spite.

Cunard, the spirit of the 1920s, who was in Venice in 1925 when Mosley and Strachey were there also. Strachey was intoxicated by the free world in which Nancy Cunard lived: he was delighted by the endless breaking of conventions, the relentless desire to experiment, and the heady mixture of racial and sexual freedom which she administered to her admirers. Many years later, Nancy Cunard wrote to a friend, Solita Solano, that Strachey was 'one of mine – Ah! So very much.'[1] Even so, writing to Yvette in 1925, from his parents' house in Chester Square, after a visit from her, Strachey says 'My dear, I feel as if I have rediscovered the sweetest and best thing that I have ever known. It is, perhaps, your sanity . . . that moves me most.'[2]

In one later letter, he wrote: 'I suppose I still fear you, I cannot, do forgive me, come close to you with the deepest subconscious part of myself, as I do with my mental conscious part. . . . And, whenever I have been particularly happy with you, this subconscious part of me, which I have refused to consider has its revenge and drives me further than ever from you. It is a kind of madness. What is the cause of it? Can it be that *Nationality* which I had thought mattered less than anything, really matters more than anything?'[3] Again, in a letter in late 1925, written from Liverpool during the Labour party conference, Strachey said: 'whenever I am feeling timid, afraid, rooted in security, unwilling to trust in life's current, it's the remembrance of you which makes me ashamed. It sounds silly and melodramatic to say it, but quite literally you seem to act as a sort of judge viewing rather sternly my inadequacies and turnings back. . . . And I know that, like Peter, I *must* betray you not thrice but many times. Of course, you may very well retort, that you don't in the least want to rise again for me. Ah . . . have patience . . . I am growing up very very slowly. But still *ca marche.* . . . My book [i.e. *Revolution by Reason*] . . . at last is in the publishers' hands. Unfortunately, I fear that I have committed almost every blunder of the youthful

[1] Letter from Daphne Fielding, Nancy Cunard's biographer, to the author, 1 March 1972, recalling a letter to Solita Solano now in the Library of Congress.
[2] Letter undated but dated 1925 or 1926 by Yvette. This letter talks about the conversation at lunch in Versailles previously described.
[3] Letter dated Autumn 1925 to Yvette, since it ends with Strachey sending her his book which must be *Revolution by Reason.*

beginner. Of course, the book is clever. I have no difficulty in being intelligent. But I feel that it is wrongly toned. . . .' A little after this, Yvette wrote back to Strachey: 'Dearest, it was hard to part so short. Will you not let me hear from you from time to time? Will you not try to manage my coming to England some day in October? It would be extraordinarily helpful for my book, which is coming well but lacks "atmosphere". I suppose I could pay a board, if my smiles and wits are not considered enough to get me mince-pie and jellies. (Is it right?) You are well on the road and I love you very much indeed and feel very grateful. O my dear! Our past, our common past is not at all bad, to be sure. I am rather moved by all these letters I read. It *was* quite good – but we never fully realized it. Must we have no future, no better future even? I am writing nonsense. Just the very direct and tender emotion which fills me when I think of our last meetings, all so perfect. Why not more? I do hope that you no longer fear me. *I* no longer fear England, do you see? Do try and write a few lines. Give my love to Celia and to Tom [Mosley]. I do so need him for my book![1] Love, dearest – which in French is not only "*amitié*" – much better. Y.'[2]

Strachey was to reply, in this case on the back of the letter itself, 'Ah yes, of course, it was good. But we didn't know it. We, the kind of people we are, never do. As a matter of fact, does anybody? The desperate looking back, summing-up, wasn't it Proust's idea that that was all there was in Life? But, yes, let us have a future. Naturally. Of what kind? Well – And I *will* do something about your coming over. . . .'[3]

But by 1927 Yvette clearly had begun to wean herself away from Strachey and indeed was divided as to whether to marry the promising Senator Millard Tydings,[4] on the one hand, or go to live in Moscow with a Russian journalist, Jan Lvovich Arens.[5] She hesitated between the two exciting worlds that these two

[1] She did not finish the book.
[2] Undated letter from Yvette. Celia is Celia Simpson. *See* below, p. 67.
[3] Letter on reverse side of Yvette's.
[4] Senator Millard Tydings (b. 1890). Lawyer, Senator for Maryland, 1927–1951.
[5] Strachey introduced a character called Aarons in his book *Post D* (*see* below, p. 202 and Yvette introduced a man obviously modelled on Arens in her own *Le Mariage de Moscou*.

seemed to represent. The Russian, in fact, eventually won, and Yvette went to Moscow, though still in touch with Strachey, who confided to her his troubles at the time of his father's fatal illness and other matters. She remained there until the atmosphere became too terrifying to stay.

The main problem for Strachey during 1927 was the pernicious anaemia of his father. 'I often wonder how he got on with old St Loe,' Attlee once remarked;[1] and the truth is that, by this stage, Strachey looked on him with disapproval, as a very old-fashioned intellectual. But, when only a little younger, their relations were warm, though Strachey had a tendency to patronize his father. The prospect of his father's death caused another flow of emotion, as suggested by the following letter to Yvette: 'I blame myself . . . for not having written before. I have been putting it off from day to day, half subconsciously expecting to be able to say something definite one way or the other about my father. . . . I have been through very unpleasant emotional reactions. I think I can confess to you, with the assurance of being wholly excused, for I can't excuse myself, what I can tell no one else, perhaps. And that is the terrible passion with which all the fundamental, and till now, subconscious part of me wishes my father to die. Poor man, I wonder if he too feels about me, as I do about him. I rather fancy that, in his case, utterly subconsciously, of course, he does. But I may wrong him utterly. But this discovery about myself has hit me rather. I am shocked at the weakness of it. And the fact that it reveals that, even now, I am not really *free* of my parents. I must still have a highly emotional attitude to them. When I do not love, I, very foolishly, hate. This is the other side, of course, of my emotional failure and impotence towards the outside world. . . .'[2]

St Loe died about six weeks after this letter, on 26 August 1927, aged 67. Whether or not this enabled Strachey to escape from the influence of his parents is debatable. He seemed unmoved at the time. His mother lived on to a great age, dying in 1957, less than ten years before Strachey himself. St Loe Strachey left

[1] To the author.
[2] Strachey to Yvette, written on the train from Birmingham, Sunday, dated by her 8.7.27.

£30,000 – a sum less than might have been expected, considering the great success of the journal for so long. But much of his money had been spent in his last years of illness.

All St Loe's money went to his widow but his *Spectator* shares went to his son. Strachey, however, was in a scarcely better financial position after the death of his father than he was before. He continued to live at home.

By late 1927, the combination of mixed emotions caused by the death of his father and the loss of Yvette to Arens caused Strachey, then twenty-six, to feel an acute depression. In November he wrote to Yvette a somewhat desperate letter: 'My dear. I've been feeling *so awful* about you: so bad that I've carried your last letter about with me for two whole days unopened; taken it out of my pocket each evening and put it back in again in the morning! There's a sort of grandeur about cowardice on such a scale. . . . Why, why, why, haven't I written? . . . Each week every thought about you became more and more painful. I became to myself Nieztsche's "paid criminal", ready in self-contempt to inflict as much injury as he could. . . . Truly, it is remarkable that my psychological reactions to you are just as violent as ever. I love you, and yes, when in the reverse position, fear you, in a sort of wretched way, just as much as ever. . . .' And then, as so often in this correspondence, comes a quick change to more practical matters: 'I'm so glad you like what I wrote about Dutt' – the outstanding English communist intellectual of that time, editor of the *Labour Monthly*. 'A great book,' Strachey goes on, talking about Dutt's *Socialism and the Living Wage*, 'I will send it to you.' He continued 'I am writing some more about it this month. You seem the only person who has understood a word of what I tried to say. But no one in this vile land ever begins to be interested in world politics. This little British village of gaping provincials! So it is just a dialogue between you and me and Dutt (who is half Indian and half Swede – and dying at that).[1] But I'm so glad we have an audience of one, in Paris, at any rate.' He ended up, 'Write and say again those things which redeem us.'[2]

In early 1928, meantime, Strachey and his sister Amabel went

[1] Dutt still lives (1972).
[2] Letter of November 1927.

to Russia by train. Strachey had been invited, as editor of *The Miner*, to visit the Russian minefields in the Don basin. This was a favourable moment to go there, since the commotions of the founding of the Bolshevist state were past, and the troubles of Stalinism scarcely visible. Both Strachey and his sister returned enthusiastic, especially in respect of Russia's medical advances, though, for the moment, the visit had no direct effect on his politics. During the journey, Strachey fell ill, at Baku, and had to be cupped. On his return, he wrote a short impression of the Russian mining industry, published by the *New Leader* as a pamphlet, with a short and enthusiastic introduction by A. J. Cook,[1] The pamphlet is descriptive and gives little impression of what Strachey or Amabel themselves saw, save the bare fact that they studied mining conditions in the Don Basin at Tcherbinovsky and at Vlasovska. Because of the good housing, clubs, wages and so on, Strachey concluded that he would prefer, if he had to choose, to be a miner in the Don Basin than in South Wales, Durham or Lancashire.[2]

Also on his return, on a spring weekend in 1928, Strachey wrote what seems to have been the last of his attempts at self-analysis, to Yvette. Guilt at his untenable position made this letter especially maudlin. Writing from the Williams-Ellis's marvellous manor house at Plas Brondanw, at the foot of the Snowdon valley in Merioneth, where he was staying, he said

> My dear, your note sounded ill and unhappy and that makes me unhappy too. Perhaps guilty too. But I don't think I ought to feel guilty about you, ought I, because, if one does, one couldn't really regard you as a human being at all, but only as something to be faced? . . . I have never regarded you for one moment as I have regarded anyone else. And that simply and solely because you happened to be the first woman I ever slept with! How childish and how horrible, because childish. You, indeed, were sacrificed, if ever anyone was, to the false and disastrous morality in which I, and everyone else like me, was brought up. You were sacrificed, and all the infinite joy we

[1] *Workers Control in the Russian Mining Industry* (London 1928).
[2] *Ibid.*, p. 35.

might have had together, simply because, for me, sex was a great black mountain which had to be climbed and crossed – was something in itself nothing to do with you! Vile, vile, English puritanism, how deep into us it has gone! Deepest of all, perhaps, in me, who did not think I had it at all. And, here it is spring weather again – as it was at Durnstein – and is there now this year again, I suppose. . . . [But] even if I found Venus herself, she would not have that divine flame – that strange, inconvenient, hopeless, bitterly moving something, that final touch of your genius – or madness, that you have so supremely, and that makes you always, and eternally, beyond comparison. . . . Next time I see you, it must be differently. What I mean is that I mustn't come over to Paris and meet in railway stations and go alone driving in cabs through the woods. We must meet with people, with a background, not *en l'air*. . . . My dear, the measles is *too* bad. I know it can be a simply vile disease. . . . What about your books?

At this stage, however, Strachey's ambiguities so far as his personal life were concerned were soon diverted by a new star on the horizon. This was Celia Simpson, daughter of a Sussex Vicar, whom he had met, but not known well, at Oxford, and who, since the end of 1925, had been working on the *Spectator*, in theory as secretary to Alan Porter, the literary editor, in practice as literary editor herself after Porter's dismissal. Celia had been a socialist even at Oxford, that is, longer than Strachey had. She reached the *Spectator* the week that *Revolution by Reason* was published. Her job was to arrange for reviews in discussion with the Editor, and also to arrange with John Strachey what his weekly article, under the terms of his arrangement with Evelyn Wrench, should be about.

Strachey seemed immediately attracted to Celia and took her out to lunch at the Ivy on Fridays, the day when he did his article. He expressed surprise that there could be a socialist secretary on the *Spectator*. She, to begin with, found him, despite his proclaimedly extreme socialism, snobbish, being rather under the 'social influence of Mosley'. He seemed also immature; on the second time they met, he asked her who her father was and what was his income. For two years, their friendship remained distant. Their relation was primarily political. They would meet at the 1917 Club, a club founded by Keynes, Leonard Woolf and Ramsay Macdonald as a social centre for younger sympathizers with the Russian Revolution. Here, in a house in Gerrard Street, Soho, 'young Bloomsbury' would meet, dine or play ping-pong, and discuss social revolution.

Celia also went to Russia in 1928, alone, by air – an adventure at that time. Celia was, if anything, more impressed than Strachey had been. She gave her comments to an admiring Canadian journalist: 'I was there a fortnight,' she said. 'Food is a little cheaper than in London, but there is a constant drift of the peasants too from the land to the city. Housing is the greatest problem. They are working feverishly, but they cannot cope with it. Moscow is a strange city – there is only one class. Everyone looks alike, dresses alike, there is no difference in manners, or customs. If there are others, you do not see them.'

Celia Simpson was a girl of spirit. Thus, when the Shakespearean scholar G. B. Harrison wrote a review of Lytton Strachey's *Elizabeth and Essex*, Celia re-wrote a sentence which seemed less enthusiastic than she desired: Harrison complained, saying Strachey's scholarship was deficient. Celia replied defiantly 'Scholars exist to provide material for people like Strachey.' Celia did not come from a conventional vicarage, since her mother came from a distinguished Irish intellectual family, the Pursers of Dublin, and she was herself witty and intelligent.

On her return from Moscow in May, Celia was whisked off by an Oxford friend of Strachey's, Alex Spearman, who had become a stockbroker, to North Wales, in a Bentley, with 'Dor', a girl-friend of Cyril Joad, also being present – for Joad, like the others, was staying at the Williams-Ellises. Strachey and Celia thereafter entered on a long friendship which was, in the end, the most important one in both their lives.

Joad, the philosophical publicist, was particularly friendly with Strachey at this time, his immediate influence being that of a jester, or stimulant, his long-term one being to excite Strachey's interest in nature more than it had been previously awakened, particularly in the sea and the mountains. Joad, who was active in the I.L.P., was vain but lively; Amabel Williams–Ellis recalls walking with him, about this time, and, seeing that he was making notes during their conversation, expressed herself flattered to have her remarks written down. 'But,' said Joad, 'I'm writing down my conversation, not yours.'

It was, however, with Boothby that Strachey remained on the closest terms. Indeed, among his Eton and Oxford acquaintances there was no one to whom he was so close, though Boothby was now, as it seemed, the hope of the Conservative party, since he had become parliamentary private secretary to Churchill as Chancellor of the Exchequer, and though Strachey was heading leftwards. A letter written by Strachey after both of them had been staying with the Mosleys at Antibes, gives a good idea of their friendship:

Dear Bob, Your letter: found on coming home this evening; and awakening all those things which alone I think matter. But one thing, especially about Cim [i.e. Cynthia Mosley] and also me sometimes, and often in the future, I daresay. Please remember that we are all jealous of you; that our heads are full of envy of you: that every upper class socialist is a neurotic, on edge, 'up against it' and so guilty. This is no particular excuse for us. But, *tout comprend*. . . . As to politics: you sum it up very well, I have faith. You have not. I am very sorry – not for you – for us. It is all right now – but, someday, it may be pretty terrible for us. All the more reason to live now to the best. As to being an opportunist: God knows, you are far less of one than most. As you say, you have 'outbursts'. But you must – if you can – forgive our outbursts too. After all, you do serve, more skilfully than most, the British bourgeoisie; which, to my mind, is a very filthy master. Indeed, you don't seem altogether to care for it yourself. But thank you many times for writing that letter. You – oh hell – you are alive! And that's pretty well unique.

You have embraced 'no faith'? . . . 'selfish, superficial, cowardly, self centred, dishonest, egoist'? Well, yes, of course, you are all that and more, and so am I, and Cim Mosley, and some 45 million others. But I rather think that is no excuse for any of us: which you think is a perfect excuse. John. . . . P.S. You know how I think we feel about you at the bottom. At least I do. That, at a pinch, you would always and necessarily fail one. That you, and your family, and public opinion, would always win against us. Don't think that this is in any way a complaint. I have realized this fully for some time now. But inevitably it has some effect upon us. Very little on me. You are one of the very few people in the world who I have *felt* about – felt in a way that no rational consideration affects at all. But you have taught us never, in the things that count, to hope or expect to have any title, or influence, over you. And, alas, that must mean something. But, believe me, if you become king of the cannibal islands, I shall still have, until I die, the same depth of feeling towards you.

It was indeed true that Strachey's feelings were rarely aroused by anyone, or anything, as much as they were by his friendship with Boothby. But still, at this time of his life, Strachey was evidently attractive. Thus, he went to stay during 1928 with Harold Nicolson, who was then at the Embassy in Berlin. They went boating together at Potsdam, accompanied by a girl of impeccable social background, who was a friend of Nicolson's. While crossing the lake, the girl became faint, turned white, and insisted on making for the shore from where she got a taxi back to Berlin. Afterwards, she told Harold Nicolson that her fit had derived from the overpowering physical attraction which she had immediately conceived for the, to her, previously unknown Strachey.

In the autumn of 1928 Strachey went to visit the U.S. He was encouraged to go there by Mosley, who had drawn such information from his own journey. His mother also encouraged him, perhaps in the hope that he would meet people who would divert him from Celia, the 'daughter of the Vicar of Fittleworth', and his English socialist friends. He had been invited by Joe Brewer, the Oxford friend who had been with him both on the *Oxford Fortnightly Review* and in Paris in 1922. The Birmingham Labour organizer, Allan Young, saying goodbye, commented sharply, 'I suppose you're going to the U.S.A. to look for a rich wife'.

This remark was prophetic. For, soon after he arrived in the U.S., Strachey met Esther Murphy, an Irish American and a Catholic, daughter of Patrick Murphy, the owner of Mark Cross, the large New York department store specializing in leather goods. Esther was a part of American Bohemian literary life. Her brother Gerald was the original of Scott Fitzgerald's Dick Diver in *Tender is the Night*, and they were all great friends of the Fitzgeralds. After a short friendship, and although Celia was, by that time, in love with him, Strachey decided to marry Esther. Celia heard this news by an announcement in the *Evening Standard*. Although she had no expectation at that stage of actually marrying Strachey, and no explicit desire to, she was dumbfounded.

Strachey's motives in proposing this marriage were complicated. He was drawn to the international Bohemian world of which Esther was a bright star; and, of course, many marry for worlds, as much as love. He was attracted by Esther's money which, he believed, might launch him successfully into the sort of adventurous politics now apparently available to him. Esther was also a Lesbian. This apparently presented to Strachey a special sexual challenge, of the sort sometimes offered to a woman by a male homosexual. Esther was admittedly proud, loyal, warm-hearted, generous and extravagant and Strachey was obviously genuinely attracted to her. But her other characteristics were such as to make it surprising that Strachey should have married her. She was, in Boothby's word, 'hideous'. She squinted. She was very tall. She drank like a fish. Though witty in conversation, she never drew breath – a 'non-stop conversationalist at age nine', as Calvin Tomkins, the memorialist of her brother Gerald, put it in his *Living Well is the Best Revenge*. Her memory was full of information about obscure passages of French eighteenth-century history – she was for years working on a life of Madame de Maintenon – but her mind was quite undisciplined.

In February 1929, nevertheless, Esther and Strachey became engaged. Strachey insisted on a handsome dowry from P. F. Murphy, which he obtained. He wrote to Yvette:

My dear, owing to the fact having leaked out in the English press, it is just possible that you will hear of the news that I'm engaged to be married to an American from some outside source. *Of course*, I should feel terrible about it, if it were not from me that you heard it. So I write at once to tell you that the news is true. I'm going to marry a girl called Esther Murphy – New Yorker, Irish descent, extremely intelligent, not pretty, 6 feet tall, 30 years old, with some money and a very, very good person indeed. She, I think, loves me very much. This, my dearest Yvette, is if you will believe me, not foolishness, not mere *lachété*, or resignation to the lure of the dollar, but a deeply felt, and absolutely necessary, development of my life. *Of course*, the fact that she has money is vitally important to me – ah, you know me well enough to know that – but please, please believe that I have not foolishly rushed at the money, sacrificing too much for it. She is a deeply civilized, deeply and passionately intellectual person, to whom the cultural heritage of man is life itself. She knows French literature and history, I really believe, as well as you do, and English literature and history far better than I do. She is the only other woman I have ever met whose intellectual equality I could never question. She knows England very little, but France very well. (She goes to France every year.) I know that this marriage will inevitably strengthen and help my life. It will give me the objective ability to go in wholly for politics and also a certain inner strength to do so.

My dear Yvette, as to us, what is there – what need there be to say? For I know that, at length, you know that, however miserably inadequate what I have given you has been, yet it was all I had and that it is yours forever. Our profound attachment will outlast, I fancy, more than love affairs, or marriages. It has outlasted even separation, that cold insidious enemy. Actually, this marriage will mean both the possibility and the necessity of my being in Paris much more: and, so, our worst enemy – I think the really formidable enemy – which our Love (if I may still use that word, I know of no other to describe what I, at any rate, feel) has had to fight – I mean, of course, the Channel, will receive a blow.

I saw Tydings [i.e. the young Senator] several times and liked him enormously. But I'm glad you didn't marry him. It would have been a great adventure but, *après tout*, a painful one. Please write me a word, telling me how you are, and wishing me well. . . .[1]

It is not known what reply Yvette made, if any, to this curious letter. She already had other interests. It was not so with Celia, who refused to see Strachey again. Strachey had, on the other hand, taken it for granted that Celia would go on seeing him when it suited him. Despite this setback, Strachey went ahead with his plans and, on 24 April 1929, at the Catholic church of St Mary's, Cadogan Square, married Esther, his last act as a bachelor being to consult a dietician (photographs of the time suggest it was necessary). Amy Strachey seemed pleased: she thought before meeting Esther that she sounded 'exactly the sort of girl John ought to marry'.[2] She apparently did not mind that Esther was a Catholic.

Mosley was best man. Amabel's daughter, Susan, present as an unofficial bridesmaid, remembers the latter's sudden appearance behind herself and her sister, on the steps of the Carlton Hotel, where the reception was held. Mosley, with his smiles and moustachioes, seemed to the girls to be a villain of melodrama. When rice to throw at the bride was produced, Mosley whispered to them: 'Throw it upwards. It hurts more.' The remark did not seem a good omen.

A month later, there was a general election, on 30 May 1929, the first in which there was universal adult suffrage. By this time, the signs were that Labour was at last going to make a big break-through in Birmingham. In Aston, Labour had already elected several councillors, and members of the board of guardians. In the campaign, Strachey was assisted by his new wife, who sat on the platform and, for once, was not very talkative. Even Mrs St Loe dropped her antipathy for socialism and sent a 'Mother's Message to Mothers', encouraging them to vote for her son. The campaign was enlivened by slanders by the

[1] Letter of Strachey to Yvette dated 22 February 1929, from 39 St Leonard's Terrace, London SW3. The letter ends 'There is one terrible . . .' One can only guess what might have followed.
[2] Amy Strachey to Joseph Brewer, 12 February 1929.

£5 Reward!

DESPERATE TORIES WILD LIE.

Mr. JOHN STRACHEY writes:

"It has come to my notice that Tory Canvassers are making the outrageous mis-statement that I am a foreigner. This is a most serious allegation which the Aston Tory Party, utterly beaten in political argument, has fallen back upon as a last desperate throw. **I was born in Guildford, Surrey, and my family has lived over 400 years in Somersetshire.**

I offer £5 Reward to anyone giving me the name and address of anyone spreading this lie and leading to the issue of a writ for Slander."

(signed) JOHN STRACHEY.

STRACHEY IS BRITISH

Conservatives that Strachey was a foreigner. Strachey issued a broadsheet offering £5 reward to anyone 'giving me the name and address of anyone spreading this lie and leading to the issue of a writ. . . . STRACHEY IS BRITISH!'

In the event, Strachey defeated his Conservative opponent, J. P. Whiteley, by 1,558 votes (18,672 to 17,114). Other Labour victories were in Deridend, Duddeston, Erdington, Ladywood, and Yardley (Kings Norton being surprisingly lost). Both Mosley and his wife won in Smethwick and in Stoke respectively. Sir Austen Chamberlain scraped home by 43 in West Birmingham. Though Allan Young lost in Sparkbrook, the old Chamberlain directorate of the city was thus lost. The future seemed golden.

In a speech at Aston Park on the Sunday following the election, Strachey explained that he was looking forward to the swift 'transformation of society into a Socialist Commonwealth', though, without a clear majority, there were, he realized, limits to what could be done. The Tory Citadel was breached, however, 'we have them on the run. Let us see to it that we go forward from strength to strength.'[1] Some months before, in the *Socialist Review*, he had described how a new morality would 'inevitably follow from a socialistic society: men would become either savages or socialists'.[2] But, in fact, Strachey's and Labour's freedom of action was, in 1929, small. With 287 seats in the new House of Commons, Labour had a majority of seats over the Conservatives (who had obtained 260) and so could form a government; but the Liberals had 59 and held the balance.

Note – The future of Yvette

Yvette, after her return from Moscow, was herself married again in 1932, to Raymond Guyot, professor of the Sorbonne. But her life with him was short, since he died in 1934. Thereafter she remained in Paris as an inspiration to those who knew her but in many ways unfulfilled, her life a 'perpetual struggle against poverty', until she died of cancer in 1964. When Guyot died in 1934, Strachey wrote her a letter, a little egoistical as usual,

[1] *Town Crier*, 14 June 1929.
[2] 'The New Generation. The Necessity of Socialism', *Socialist Review*, 15 February 1929.

which ended: 'I do not think that I should sign myself Evelyn for, for better or worse, Evelyn no longer exists.' Strachey remained in touch with her. She had many friendships. She often came to England in the 1930s and later, staying with either the Stracheys or with Boothby. Her novel, *Mariage de Moscow*, based on her association with Arens and the communist world, was published in 1964 in Paris.

Chapter 6 / MARRIAGE AND WESTMINSTER, 1929-31

After his marriage and election as member for Aston, Strachey went to live with his new wife at an attractive eighteenth-century house in Lord North Street, Westminster, then known as North Street, in the preferred quarter for politicians because of its proximity to parliament. Here, he and Esther started to entertain in a manner befitting their status as a most promising couple. Strachey also, while giving up the *Socialist Review*,[1] and then, in December, *The Miner*, received the minor accolade of becoming a parliamentary private secretary to Mosley, who, though not in the cabinet, had been asked by the new prime minister, Ramsay Macdonald, to be Chancellor of the Duchy of Lancaster and to coordinate the government's policy on the most difficult problem facing the administration, namely Unemployment, then standing at 1,164,000 and increasing monthly. If, a few years previously, Strachey could write that everyone was jealous of Boothby, because of his successes, it could now be held that it was Strachey who was enviable.

But this, however, could only have been a surface impression. Both in his personal life as in politics, Strachey was on the brink of crisis.

To consider the first matter first: he and Esther fell out quickly.

[1] The *Socialist Review* was soon afterwards sold.

She talked endlessly, and primarily about the politics of the U.S., which, as Boothby said scathingly, 'didn't interest people very much then'. One member of parliament, George Strauss, who became a friend of Strachey's at this time, described her as a 'female policeman'. He could not 'understand how someone so sensitive as Strachey could have married someone who would have so dominated him'. She would talk, he recalled, for the whole evening with Strachey in 'second place'. Strachey told Allan Young that she was so drunken that she would be unable to have children; and he, Strachey, desired a family. In consequence of this, Allan Young secured a promise from Esther to give up whisky, but she was soon after found drinking a bottle of gin a day. One evening at the Mosleys, Boothby recalled, Esther was going on about Senator this and Senator that, and Strachey said: 'if you go on about that any more, I can't stand it'. Esther left the room in tears. Mosley recalled that, when Strachey first brought her to his house at Denham, there were many talkative Englishmen to lunch, and Esther, after being silent a long time, wept. Strachey later told Mosley 'that was because, in America, everyone listens to *her*'.

In the first summer of the marriage, the Stracheys went to France. On 13 August, from the Hotel du Luxembourg, Nîmes, Strachey wrote the following desperate letter to Yvette:

I wonder where you are. I am motoring about France with Esther. We shall cross Paris about the last day of the month or the first of September. Will you be there? If so, let me have a word to the Villa America (!) Antibes.[1]

It is not going well. I am still too young and foolish to have undertaken this. Perhaps in ten years' time. Unfortunately, I live my life backwards or, at any rate, all out of step and time. However, there it is, and, no doubt, it will all solve itself, sooner or later – and sooner, rather than later.

She is so *spoilt* – how could she be anything else? It is not her fault, of course, it is money, America, everything. But that doesn't make it any better for me. Isn't it *awful*, the poor people are the *only* possible ones – and they are, well, poor! At

[1] This was, in fact, Gerald Murphy's famous villa on the Cap d'Antibes.

present we are held up at Nîmes, with a motor breakdown. And how she takes it! They cannot even show enough decency, calmness, niceness to get over the tiny contretemps which the pursuit of their pleasures bring them. And yet, we, the poor, are helpless, impotent, cringing before them. God forgive us, we go to the lengths of marrying them!

Is not the Revolution as much a moral necessity as it has become a political improbability? My dear – how nice even to think about you, for a little while. Evelyn.[1]

After their return to England, Strachey and his wife drifted quickly apart. Esther went to the U.S. in the autumn. Soon, on Strachey's insistence, he was seeing a good deal of Celia again. In the middle of the year, after parliament had risen, they even went to Russia together with two other new Labour members of parliament, Aneurin Bevan and George Strauss. Celia at this time was becoming increasingly interested in communism and that fact, and the fact of her strong character, had a certain influence over the course of Strachey's political trajectory during these months: what exact effect, it is impossible to know, and perhaps even Strachey himself would not have been able to tell exactly had he lived to write this book as an autobiography.

During this time, despite the twin influences of Esther and Celia, and perhaps the residual one of Yvette, Mosley's remained the strongest. Mosley's role during this second Labour government, with the personal assistance of Strachey almost to the very end of it, and until well after Mosley had left, was dramatic.

Mosley had written and talked so much about unemployment before 1929 that he was the obvious person to attempt to work out a practical policy with regard to that problem when Labour finally got into power. He tried to work out a radical policy deriving from *Revolution by Reason* and the Birmingham proposals. Unfortunately, Mosley was placed under the overall direction of J. H. Thomas, the railwayman's leader, who became Lord Privy Seal. Perhaps this was, as the Scottish Labour leader, Tom Johnston, suggested, a scheme to 'keep some potential

[1] Letter from Strachey to Yvette, 13 August 1929. This seems to have been the last time Strachey signed himself thus.

troublemakers quiet'.[1] If so, it failed. Thomas was economically illiterate and old. He left economic questions to be considered by his permanent secretary, the orthodox Sir Horace Wilson. Thomas was the last person to be impressed by new ideas such as those which Mosley, George Lansbury and Johnston, then respectively first Commissioner for Works and Under-Secretary for Scotland, together with Strachey, Allan Young (now Mosley's private secretary) and other private helpers, worked out during the autumn of 1929. Consequently, Mosley ignored Thomas when he was putting his ideas together in final form. He knew that Thomas would ask for Wilson's opinion, and that that would be negative: and, then, Thomas would say 'I agree with 'Orace 'ere.' Mosley and Thomas grated on each other in several ways: Thomas seemed to Mosley to be a prejudiced Labour politician of the 'old gang' and to drink too much. Mosley seemed to Thomas an adventurer.

At all events, Mosley showed his proposals outside his office, notably to Keynes, before he consulted Thomas. Then Mosley asked Macdonald to place his memorandum before the cabinet – again without consulting Thomas. A controversy ensued. Thomas offered his resignation, which was refused. Macdonald privately rebuked Mosley.[2] Strachey took a copy of the document home to his house where, at a dinner party, it was seen by journalists. An accurate account of the Mosley memorandum duly appeared in the *Manchester Guardian* of 7 February. This leak caused further fury to Thomas, particularly since the Press generally did its best to suggest that the three unemployment ministers involved – Lansbury and Johnston, as well as Mosley – were involved in a mutiny. Naturally this was damaging to Strachey, who, according to Mosley anyway, had already allowed his 'intellectual contempt' for many of his colleagues to show only too vividly.

Strachey's maiden speech, meantime, in the House of Commons had been on 5 November 1929, on the subject of 'Relations with Russia'. By then, however, he had already expressed the view in both *The Miner* and the *New Leader* that the Government

[1] Johnston, *Memories*, p. 103.
[2] Thomas, *My Story*, p. 174.

was neglecting the question of unemployment.[1] He deplored that the collapse of the champagne trade between France and Russia should be considered a reason for not trading with Russia. He argued that Russian exports could be increased to some £40 million. He ended: 'therefore, let the government, which is doing so well, tonight take this the first step in a really constructive Russian policy'.[2] Then, in the winter of 1929–30, he went to the U.S. again, and returned even more gloomy about the general unemployment situation in the 'capitalist' world, as he told the House of Commons on 3 February 1930.[3] He spoke again on the subject of trade with Russia on 5 February, speaking more critically of the government attitude and of Thomas, Lord Privy Seal, and suggesting that 'the catalogue of human suffering is being added to every hour, while there is no true relationship between this country and Russia'.[4] He also made speeches on the government's mining bill on 11 March and on 2 April.

Mosley, in his memoirs, wrote of Strachey at this time in his career that he 'had the necessary robustness of physique and character [for political success] but nausea overwhelmed him when his cold intellectual eye surveyed a familiar spectacle: the Labour leader engaged in keeping his party together by importing to high office a strange assortment which was quite unsuited to any place in the government of a great country'.[5] This may not have been quite accurate, since Strachey had more tolerance than Mosley had for the idiosyncrasies and personal failings of the first generation of Labour leaders: but he did undoubtedly have a 'cold intellectual eye' which caused him all his life to believe that human beings could be rational if only things could be explained to them clearly.

The Mosley memorandum itself today reads less like a proposal for a new economic policy than one for governmental reconstruction of the type introduced rather ineffectively by Churchill in 1951; there would be overlords and a serious attempt would

[1] *New Leader*, 4 October 1929; *The Miner*, 19 October 1929.
[2] Hansard, 5 November 1929, Vol. 231, Cols. 957–61.
[3] *Ibid.*, 3 February 1929, Vol. 234, Col. 1591.
[4] *Ibid.*, 5 February 1930, Vol. 234, Col. 1950.
[5] Mosley, *op. cit.*, p. 235.

be made to rationalize transport, to modernize industry along U.S. lines, plan the export trade and so on. Mosley was concerned with the centralization of decision-making, more than with policies or men. The Cabinet discussed Mosley's memorandum at the end of January, and appointed a sub-committee to consider it further. This group included no friends of Mosley, and they procrastinated, refusing to publish it. In the meantime, the annual I.L.P. conference pronounced firmly against the Labour government's attitude to unemployment: only a minority of 53 to 357 pronounced in favour of the government. Almost all pro-government I.L.P.ers who were also M.P.s were absent. Probably this exacerbated the course of events, though the cause of the I.L.P.'s split with the government was less unemployment than the question as to how to achieve 'Socialism in our Time'.

When it became gradually clear that the Cabinet would reject the memorandum, Mosley resigned. Macdonald tried to keep him in the government. He refused, though the other two unemployment ministers, Lansbury and Johnstone, who agreed with Mosley in principle, stayed on. Lansbury thought of resigning, but he did not.[1]

Mosley then attacked the government at two meetings of the parliamentary Labour party, and in the House of Commons. Mosley's speeches on these occasions were exceptionally eloquent, but were unsuccessful in persuading more than a very few Labour members to support him. (At the parliamentary Labour party meeting of 22 May he only got 29 votes against 210, with a number of abstentions.)[2]

Strachey was with Mosley throughout this time, though he had spoken in favour of the government's budget on 1 May in the House of Commons: and, on 4 May, in a Labour Day speech in Birmingham, had spoken judiciously of the need of the I.L.P. to provide criticism, and defending what the government had already done for the unemployed.[3] But he did not speak specifically on the Mosley memorandum in the House of Commons. Doubtless, though, Strachey was one who was, at this time,

[1] Postgate, Life of George Lansbury, p. 256.
[2] These details are discussed by Skidelsky, Politicians and the Slump, p. 188.
[3] Town Crier, 9 May 1930. See Hansard, Vol. 238, Col. 415 ff.

pressing Mosley to make a break with the party rather than one of those who, like Trevelyan and Arthur Henderson, attempted to restrain him, by not pressing ahead for a vote at the party meeting in May. For Strachey's articles and speeches were then increasingly hostile to the whole 'system' and to the 'game of politics'[1] and Mosley had already, even before resigning, begun to contemplate the formation of a new political grouping; thus, at dinner with the Webbs on the day before his resignation, Mosley had said that, if he resigned, he would 'lead a new group who vote solidly to keep Labour in, but would be critical. . . .'[2] For the moment, though, Mosley, like Strachey, was still a member of the Labour party and a member of parliament. Neither had given up hope of persuading the party as such to adopt their plans. The Webbs, though still sympathetic to Mosley personally, were not impressed by his ideas: they were, as Strachey later pointed out, more sociologists than communists, and saw unemployment more as a passing phase of the trade cycle – at least at this time.[3]

On 6 June, the *Town Crier* carried an article by Strachey explaining why he had voted for Mosley at the party meeting. 'We came to the conclusion,' he said, 'that, however serious the step might be from a personal point of view, it was Mosley's duty to resign from the Government and lay his case before the party. . . . There will be no split in the Labour party.' Strachey added: 'If I had thought that Mosley's action was in any way intended to divide the Labour forces, or even that it might have that effect without there being any intention to do so, I would never have given it my support. . . . In this way, we have taken up a position entirely distinct from that which has been assumed by certain members of the I.L.P.'[4]

The reaction in Birmingham was, to begin with, favourable. The Aston Labour party backed Mosley, as did the Perry Barr I.L.P. Guild of Youth. Much more important, the Smethwick Trades and Labour Council gave Mosley 'unabated confidence'.[5]

[1] *See* summary in McIntyre, pp. 126 ff.
[2] Beatrice Webb, *Diaries*, 19 May 1930.
[3] Strachey, *The Strangled Cry*, p. 187.
[4] *Town Crier*, 6 June.   [5] *Ibid.*, 13 June.

Both Strachey and Mosley maintained close and friendly relations with their constituencies. Thus, Strachey wrote a harsh criticism of the rent acts in the *Town Crier* of 18 July, and both he and Mosley spoke at a big fête in the Botanical gardens in Birmingham on 26 July. Meantime, the real issue in the Labour movement to most people seemed less the future of Mosley than the future of the I.L.P. For most of the I.L.P. members had become estranged from the parliamentary Labour party during the past year, Macdonald had resigned from it in February and, despite efforts by I.L.P. moderates, such as Emanuel Shinwell, was vigorously criticising the government's graduation at the same time as was Mosley. But the I.L.P. leaders were wary of Mosley, and he did not court them.

In the summer of 1930, and before the next Labour party conference, Strachey paid his second visit to Moscow. Of his male companions, George Strauss and Aneurin Bevan, the latter was among those sympathetic to many of Mosley's ideas and had probably voted for Mosley in the parliamentary party. He was still unmarried and, being still in his early thirties, was living in London for the first time. He had immediately made friends with Strachey in 1929, and they had spent a great deal of time arguing and talking since then. George Strauss was less sympathetic to Mosley, and his friendship with Strachey began chiefly because, in the Labour party, there were then 'very few non-working-class members'. (Strauss was the son of a Conservative M.P. and rich.) He was, however, at that time, and for many years afterwards, on the left of the Labour party. The three were accompanied on the boat to Russia by three women: Jennie Lee, who was on her way independently to the Caucasus and, at that time, not particularly friendly with Bevan, whom she later married; Magda Gellan, a girl friend of Harry Pollitt's; and Celia who, still on the *Spectator*, was, according to Strauss, 'far the most enthusiastic and uncritical supporter of the Soviet Union' of the group. The sun, she herself recalled, was in her eyes. She, Strachey and Bevan had earlier that year gone on a long walk through the Dorset downs and then had driven up to Tredegar to stay with Bevan's relations. Their conversations in Russia consisted of, on the one hand, much bantering between Strachey and Bevan, and, on the other, violent condemnations of Ramsay Macdonald for betraying socialism, in which Strauss played the part of an ineffective dissident.[1]

The journey began ominously: on arrival at Leningrad they went up onto the deck to look at the view. While they were watching, the light faded, and, in the gathering gloom, a barge drifted across their path. Their vessel continued on its way and cut the barge in half, many Russian sailors being killed before their eyes.

They spent three weeks in Russia, principally at Leningrad, Moscow, and Kiev. They saw, they thought, 'everything we wanted: not necessarily what the Russians wanted to show us'. They visited the dam and power station at Dneprovskoye, a huge enterprise then being constructed by special Komsomol units of Soviet workers under the direction of the U.S. firm of Cooper Brothers; they looked at an engineering plant in Leningrad; they visited the Shakhty coal mining area and went down the Artem pit, where Bevan, with his 'nine years' practical mining experience underground', was able to give an expert opinion that the safety equipment was much below British standards. They also saw a factory for the production of agricultural machinery at Selmasch-troi, in a suburb of Rostov. Nearby, they went to three collective farms, 'still roughly and badly organized', with their methods very crude, but, nevertheless, 'much better than the individual peasant farmers', and also 'State Farm No. 2'. Strachey, who had 'travelled over much of the same ground in 1928 was greatly struck with the change in the very landscape since that time. In 1928 the whole steppe, as far as eye could see, was cut up into the tiny peasant strips which formed the only method of agriculture. Today, it consists of vast fields stretching to the horizon.'

In all these enterprises, Strachey and his friends were, they later wrote, 'impressed by the keenness and intensity of labour'. This 'we believe to be due to two causes – the payment of piece rates and the genuine enthusiasm of the worker.' They ate a 'satisfying lunch' at a factory kitchen in Leningrad, and went to a workers' club at Kharkov. Strachey was impressed by the lack of beggars and wild children orphaned in the civil war (*Besprezornii*) who, in 1928, had seemed to constitute a serious problem. They thought

[1] Strauss memorandum, p. 1.

that 'the people in the streets of the towns we visited looked little different in the matter of health and clothing from the people in any working-class area of any industrial town in England'.[1]

Finally, Strachey (and here he obviously reflected some element of the thought of Mosley) argued that Russia, a primary producer, had a great future as a market for Britain – 'the one great opportunity remaining in the world today. . . . No foreign trade operations are unaccompanied by risk, but the risk of allowing our heavy industries to continue in their present devastating condition seems to us infinitely more serious than the risk of cooperating in large scale trading operations with Russia.'

Reading this pamphlet, *What we saw in Russia*, forty years later, it is clear that these ardent travellers saw little of the reality in Russia in the late summer of 1930. Yet Strachey did think that the estimates for future production from the Artem coal mine were 'ridiculously optimistic'; he did know that a textile factory in Leningrad was running at about one-third capacity (owing to shortage of raw material) and that shoes and boots were rationed, while no one knew whether it was true or not that the reason was the increased demand for footwear by 'new classes'. The new housing in Moscow had 'ill-fitting' joinery and 'inefficient' plumbing. They appreciated that, with communications being bad, food supplies varied greatly. One woman told Strachey that she had 'grown to hate the sound of the words Five Year Plan', and it was obvious that prices were 'enormously high . . . for anything but the bare necessities of life'. Finally, Strachey and his comrades appreciated that the agricultural revolution had involved a 'policy of coercion' – even if they wrongly believed that it had been abandoned the previous March – and a 'great cost in social conflict: not only were whole sections of peasants bitterly alienated, but it is calculated that one third of the country's livestock was slaughtered during the past winter, by peasants who were unwilling that their stock should be pooled with that of their less thrifty or less successful neighbours'. Thirty years later, and in a different mood, he described 'seeing the most ghastly food shortages in the Russian towns' on this journey.[2]

[1] *Ibid.*, p. 25.
[2] Strachey, *The Great Awakening*, *Encounter*, pamphlet No. 5, p. 33.

The booklet indeed compares well with many writings about Russia at that time. The authors sympathise but they remain cautious. Nevertheless, it is still remarkable how successful the authorities were in 1930 in disguising the fact that that time was the toughest in the whole dark history of Soviet agriculture. The central committee of the Soviet communist party had then decided to embark on the complete collectivization of the more important agricultural regions by the autumn of 1930 or, at the very latest, by the autumn of 1931. The consequence was that there was, in much of the Russian countryside, open civil war in the course of 1930, with the peasants fighting back against the collectivizers with 'the sawed off shotgun, the axe, the dagger, the knife'.[1] Either by starvation or by actual shooting, several million Russian peasants died in the course of the changes, whose benefits Strachey and his comrades somewhat took for granted.[2] It was also the time in the Soviet Union when the last breath of opposition from within the communist party itself was being effectively silenced. An early show trial, with confessions of sabotage, was already being prepared for November 1930. Trotsky was already in exile.

Admittedly, the atmosphere seemed to Strachey more tense than in 1928. Thus, at their first lunch in Moscow, their Leningrad guide who had accompanied them arrived late: the Moscow guide showed surprise. Strachey said 'the G.P.U. were asking for him'. The Moscow guide did not take this as a joke, turned white, showed great distress, and demanded further particulars.[3] Then, when leaving, the travellers thought that it would be hospitable to offer a supper party to those whom they had met. They took a room in the hotel, ordered the appropriate amount of food and drink, and invited thirty guests. When, an hour after the planned beginning of the party, no one had arrived, they thought that this was just an example of Russian unpunctuality. When, an hour later, still no one had come, they appreciated that the

---

[1] Conquest, *The Great Terror*, p. 21.
[2] In a conversation with Churchill during the war, Stalin suggested that ten million peasants were killed. Probably he exaggerated in order to impress Churchill. He probably succeeded.
[3] Strauss memorandum.

guests, who had all accepted, had decided, presumably each separately, that it would be dangerous to visit foreigners.[1] They then returned to England, but not without incident, since they had neglected to get exit visas, were turned off the train, spent the night in a brothel at Shepetovka and suffered much inconvenience in consequence.

On their return to London, Strauss wrote a generally favourable article about Russia in *London News*.[2] Strachey not only wrote that the economic achievements in Russia were 'marvellous'; he thought that they had 'relevance' to the situation in England. Celia virtually became a communist during this journey, though less from what they saw than because of the arrival of the news (communicated by Maurice Dobb, the Cambridge economist, whom they met in the train to Kharkov) that on 14 September, in the German parliamentary elections, the Nazis had enormously increased their vote. She therefore, like many others, perhaps really became a communist for reasons of foreign policy.

Bevan, on the other hand, returned 'with his Marxist faith neither diminished nor greatly fortified'. Asked by a Welsh trade union leader what his impressions had been, he replied that, while his visit had been too short to admit any final conclusion, his impression was that, 'while Britain was a slave to the past, in Russia they were slaves to the future'.[3]

Strachey sent Bevan a draft report on their visit to Russia: 'I am far from satisfied with it,' he wrote, 'but, honestly, it has been one of the most difficult jobs I have ever had. . . . I am sure you can suggest many improvements. . . . I hear you have been writing a certain amount about Russia in the South Wales press. I am very glad. So keep the articles and let me see them when you have done with them. Do come up soon. Needless to say, this house is always at your disposal, if you want to spend a night or so up here. Things are moving so quickly just now that I rather wish you were here to talk to. Not that anything very special is happening objectively, but there does seem to be a tremendous mass of opinion on the O.M. [i.e. Mosley] lines and I am pretty

1 Strauss memorandum.
2 Reproduced in *Town Crier*, 19 December 1930.
3 Foot, *Aneurin Bevan*, p. 125.

anxious to have a hand in shaping what those lines should be, and, in that way, it is the early stage that counts, so I wish you were here.'[1]

Bevan replied in a letter which gives a good impression of the warmth, wit, and mobility of his character:

I have looked through the draft report with my usual carping mind and jaundiced eye, but regret to say that I can find nothing wrong. The best I can say of it is that I could not have done better myself. Perhaps – having had a somewhat more fastidious education – I could improve on the English, but I am afraid my over refeened style would arouse your virile disgust. Seriously, John, I think you have made a damned good job of it. For the life of me, I can't see anything to alter. It reads a bit breathless, but that is due, obviously, to constriction of space. Breathlessness is not altogether a fault. . . . I shall not be in London until next Monday and so shall not be able to avail myself of hospitality. You are very good to me John. It hurts me a little that you give so much and I can give nothing in return. So few people have given me anything that I feel a little strange and bewildered. I count our friendship as the one thing of value that membership of parliament has given me. And yet, as this friendship grows, and becomes more and more a part of me, I find myself becoming fearful. I am so conscious of bringing to our relationship nothing of value, and, therefore, am frightened of trusting so much of my affection in so ill balanced a vessel. Please forgive me for exposing so shy a feeling to the peril of words. It is your generous nature that moves me to speak, even though I know that speech would bruise where it would caress. Give my love to Esther. Aneurin.[2]

The travellers were, of course, home in time for the critical Labour party conference at Llandudno. Here, with unemployment having now passed two million, Mosley was elected (as in 1928, though not 1929) to the Labour party national executive,

[1] Letter from Strachey to Bevan, 17 October 1930.
[2] Bevan to Strachey, 20 October 1930. The pamphlet was published in 1931 by the Hogarth Press.

fourth, after Lansbury, Morrison and Dalton with Jimmy Thomas defeated. But his proposal that that body itself should go fully into his ideas was defeated. It is true that the defeat was narrow – 1,251,000 to 1,046,000 – and that, when the character of the block vote possible to the trade union is considered, the probability was that Mosley might well have had a majority in the Labour movement. It has also been suggested that, if A. J. Cook had not been delayed in a traffic jam, he would have persuaded the miners to support Mosley. Mosley's own speech on 7 October was immensely successful as a piece of rhetoric. But his ideas and his challenge were not really put again to the vote.

In the course of the winter of 1930–31, Mosley, with Strachey's help, busied himself canvassing various groups of politicians with the idea of forming a new national central party. First, he turned to what he hoped would be regarded as the left and, in a manifesto issued in December, called again for an elaborately planned economy to be directed by a cabinet of overlords, subject only to the 'general control of parliament'.[1] This would stimulate exports, control imports, and plan home consumption. This manifesto was signed by seventeen Labour members, as well as A. J. Cook. The members included Bevan, Oliver Baldwin, W. J. Brown and Frank Horrabin, the cartoonist and M.P., as well, of course, as both Mosley and his wife, with Strachey.[2] Of the others, C. J. Simmons was one of Mosley's colleagues in Birmingham, where he had been councillor and member for Erdington since 1929. Another West Midlands signatory was Oliver Baldwin, the Prime Minister's socialist son, the member for Dudley. But of special importance was the signature of W. J. Brown, general secretary of the Civil Service Clerical Association, M.P. for West Wolverhampton since 1929. He had recently become secretary of the small parliamentary group of I.L.P. rebels. James Maxton and several other I.L.P. leaders declined to

---

[1] *Daily Telegraph*, 8 December. Summarised in Mosley, *op. cit.*, pp. 280–81. In full in *Town Crier*, 12 December 1930.

[2] The complete list was: O. Baldwin, J. Batey, A. Bevan, W. J. Brown, A. J. Cook, W. G. Cove, R. Forgan, J. F. Horrabin, J. Lovat Fraser, S. F. Markham, J. McGovern, J. J. McShane, both Mosleys, H. T. Muggeridge, M. Philips Price, C. J. Simmons and J. Strachey.

sign the manifesto on the grounds that new programmes should be promoted by the party, and not by a 'weekend private conspiracy'; they disliked, too, the phraseology that the immediate question was not one of the ownership, but of the survival, of British industry. True, of the signatories, nine (Batey, Horrabin, McGovern, McShane, Philips Price, Simmons, Strachey, Mosley, and Lady Cynthia Mosley) were members of the I.L.P. But Mosley had not given much time to the I.L.P. since 1929, and their leaders were alarmed at, and distressed by, the apparent threat to by-pass parliamentary democracy. No action was admittedly taken to discipline the signatories, but they, in turn, got no more backing.

In the meantime, Strachey had spoken often in the House of Commons. On 29 October, in the debate on the address, he had made a particularly effective speech, stressing the unusual character of the economic crisis, and supporting Mosley's ideas, even though they might seem 'novel, unorthodox, and even fantastic' assertions of economic nationalization: 'we do not believe that we can get through the present crisis without national planning . . . and we do not believe that we can have national planning unless we have control of our imports.'[1] He had also advocated a commodity board to plan steel production, on 5 November.[2] He, like most of the other Mosleyite M.P.s, abstained in a critical vote on 17 December on a Board of Trade bill, stating his reason for doing so.[3] Bevan also had moved into a posture of opposition with a critical speech on the debate following the address.[4] Strachey, like Simmons, wrote an article in the *Town Crier* defending the manifesto.[5] He said that he was 'tired of sitting quietly in "the best club in the world" watching, from its comfortable armchairs, the slow decline of British industry and the rapid drift to disaster of the movement with which we are identified . . . we cannot muddle through this time. That is the essence of our message.' After summarizing the manifesto, he said: 'we recognize . . . that the present parliamentary and governmental machine is incapable of carrying out such a pro-

[1] Hansard, Vol. 244, Cols. 169–74.
[2] Ibid., Col. 923.
[3] Ibid., Vol. 246, Col. 1352.
[4] Foot, op. cit., p. 126.
[5] Town Crier, 19 December 1930.

gramme as we have envisaged. A 19th-century parliament designed for the sedate discussions of leisurely days and nights cannot conceivably look at the modern tasks . . . for parliament to insist upon the right to obstruct, to delay, to clog its own executive machine and yet not turn it out is to reduce Democracy to mere obstruction: and . . . that has to go. . . . Maybe we have committed political suicide. Who knows, and who cares?' He said much the same in the *Spectator* at the same time.[1]

Mosley and his friends were admittedly not the only ones then seeking to improve the quality, or at least the knowledge, of the Labour party. There was, for example, the group known as the Society for Socialist Inquiry and Propaganda (S.S.I.P.) founded by Douglas Cole, many young Oxford socialists, and some nationally known men such as Ernest Bevin, Clement Attlee and George Lansbury. The first meeting of this group – before it, in fact, became an organization – at Easton Lodge, the house of Lady Warwick, was attended by Strachey, and Esther, along with some others of Mosley's friends. Cole and his friends had sympathy for the ideas in the Mosley memorandum and Strachey was on the first committee of S.S.I.P. But, by the end of the year, the two groups were clearly diverging, because of the position of Mosley himself; and Strachey was not asked to come to future meetings.[2]

Mosley had, meantime, also begun talking with a group of younger and restless Conservatives (such as Harold Macmillan, Boothby, Oliver Stanley and Walter Elliot). Henry Mond and Archibald Sinclair were in occasional contact from among the Liberals. Finally, Mosley was also more ambiguously in touch at this stage with several older public men, headed by Lloyd George, who had been excluded, partly, perhaps, because they were brilliant individualists, from post-war politics. Churchill and Beaverbrook were on the edge of this *galère*. 'The failure to secure a consensus in 1930 was a tragedy,' Mosley later commented;[3] and, indeed, from the point of view of the politics of the 1930s that view is difficult to argue with. The rather ordinary

[1] *Spectator*, 13 December 1930.
[2] Margaret Cole, *The Life of G. D. H. Cole*, pp. 176–8.
[3] Mosley, *op. cit.*, p. 272.

consensus of men who eventually formed the National Government of 1931 was certainly ineffective. It is difficult to imagine, however, the diverse group formed by Mosley's contacts working together except in conditions of war.

In January, the Mosley group of Labour M.P.s formally asked the national executive of the party for a specially summoned conference to discuss the unemployment crisis. Strachey explained his reasons in the *Town Crier* in Birmingham on 30 January. Perhaps, as in the preceding year, most Labour people were preoccupied as to whether or not the I.L.P. should break away from the Labour party, though they afterwards rallied to Labour.[1] But perhaps too, if a special conference had been held under these circumstances, the rebels might have won, since the unemployment situation was worse.

A party meeting was, anyway, held. Bevan moved the resolution that there should be a special conference, though not before he had been summoned by Macdonald, who attempted to persuade him to withdraw. The Labour party, as a whole, seemed now alarmed by Mosley's challenge and seemed anxious to respond to Macdonald's appeals for loyalty. In the event, only thirteen members voted in favour of a special conference.[2] All the rebels, except perhaps Mosley himself, were distressed.

A pamphlet was put out at the end of February on the subject of Mosley's policy. This sixty-page document was drafted by Strachey, Bevan, W. J. Brown and Allan Young, though Strachey did most of the work. It described in clear terms the graphically changed situation in the world, and Britain's place in it.[3] At times, indeed, it seemed to anticipate the situation in Britain in the 1960s, without, however, seeing any prospect of a European Common Market. It did argue for a 'really large scale export of goods . . . to Russia', but that is virtually all that was left of socialism. It demanded a definite change in the political structure. Parliament must be relieved of details. 'Broadly, we

[1] See *Town Crier* article of 13 February 1931 (pro Mosley) and that of 27 February 1931 (pro Labour).

[2] Foot, *op. cit.*, p. 131.

[3] *A national Policy. An account of the emergency programme advanced by Sir Oswald Mosley* (London 1931), p. 29.

say to the Electorate: choose whatever Government you like. But, when you have chosen it, for heaven's sake, let it get on with the job. . . .'[1] It made a number of detailed proposals for cutting government expenditure – notably one for a Ministry of Defence.[2] The plan was a 'programme of disciplined national effort to meet the emergency' caused by mass unemployment, heavy wage attacks throughout industry and budgetary deficits leading to demands for reductions in social services, unemployment, insurance and so on. The pamphlet argued for the control of imports, a partnership with the Commonwealth, a National Economic Planning Council similar to that suggested in the Birmingham proposals, and parliamentary reform. The whole scheme seemed also to argue for a revival of the accidental socialism of the war.

But, by the time this document had reached the public, Mosley had decided to press ahead with the foundation of a new party, and, indeed, his plans were leaked in the *Observer* on 23 February. During the next week, there came a parting among the rebels. Bevan refused to join a new party, but Strachey was anxious to do so. Strachey tried to persuade Bevan, but Bevan, as Jennie Lee remembers, kept saying 'Where is the money coming from?', 'Who is going to call the tune?' and, even more ominous, 'You will end up as a fascist party'.[3] Mosley had already written a rather curious article in the *Week-End Review* of 31 January in which he praised 'action' as the basis of 'a new psychology of politics'.[4] In the event, then, only Strachey, Cynthia Mosley, W. J. Brown, Robert Forgan and Oliver Baldwin of the Labour M.P.s agreed to join a new party; and they were joined later by one Tory, W. E. D. Allen ('Bill' Allen) grandson of the chairman of David Allen and Son, a big Belfast firm of printers and bill-poster makers. Allen joined because he could not accept the contemporary character of English Conservatism which seemed to him run by 'solicitors with double-barrelled names' in the interests of ignorant landlords. Oliver Baldwin backed out almost

[1] *Ibid.*, p. 46.
[2] *Ibid.*, p. 60.
[3] Jennie Lee, *Tomorrow is a new day*, p. 151.
[4] *Week-End Review*, 24 January 1931, quoted MacIntyre.

immediately (and ultimately rejoined Labour) and, as will be seen, there was another, almost immediate, withdrawal.

Mosley remained hopeful of the 'brilliant' senior politicians. All, including Lloyd George, retained close relations with Mosley. But none was convinced that a new party was necessary. Mosley was. A new adventure in English politics thus began.

Chapter 7 / THE NEW PARTY, 1931

The New Party was carefully planned. Mosley had secured Allan Young as organiser. Strachey was the intellectual nerve, though he was always influenced by Mosley himself and also by Cyril Joad, who came with him from the I.L.P. into the New Party to become for a time Director of Propaganda. Mosley had secured some degree of financial backing from Sir William Morris. He also had his own fortune to fall back upon. Although the members of parliament who supported the New Party were so few, Mosley had high hopes that, once he started seeming successful, others would join: not only perhaps the Young Conservatives, with whom he had been and still was in at least social contact,[1] but, perhaps, outstanding economists such as Keynes. Perhaps Shaw would also join: Mosley was in some ways a Shavian man and Shaw had personally encouraged Mosley to begin his break. He even suggested a name – The Activists; but he drew out at the last minute.

There was especially bad feeling in Birmingham over the New Party, particularly since Allan Young was approaching members of the Labour organization there to work in it. (Speakers were offered a fiver a week to speak for the party.) Even George Morris, borough organizer in succession to Young himself, was

[1] Harold Macmillan virtually said this to Nicolson, whom he met on a train on 30 May (Nicolson, *Diaries*, Vol. I, p. 76).

approached by Young, as were one other organizer and several agents.[1] Strachey was called upon to resign his seat by his own party (as Mosley was by Smethwick).

While Mosley waited to be expelled for 'gross disloyalty' from the Labour party, his lieutenants, including Strachey, all resigned first.[2] In Aston, Strachey was quickly repudiated as its prospective candidate in a future election, but Labour's problem was peculiarly difficult there, since Strachey's agent, Dan Davies, who was also secretary of the Aston Labour party, also joined not only the New Party but its central staff in London. Most of the Aston Labour supporters believed that they had been 'nicely let down' by a 'young political adventurer'.[3] But, of course, it was Mosley's defection that caused the biggest storm: two local Smethwick men went down to Denham to plead with him and to tell him home truths, they said, 'Being met by a Rolls Royce, and going away on the bus'. The editor of the local Birmingham Labour paper, however, ended much more in sorrow than in anger in an open letter: 'we of the Birmingham Labour movement feel that you have let us down badly and justified all that your critics said when you came over to us. Had you devoted your ability and eloquence to the task of converting a majority of the people to the socialist policy of the Labour party, thus ensuring the return of a majority Labour Government at the next election, you would have been a great figure in our Movement – honoured for your service and well rewarded with office. But you could not wait. And now you are being likened to Winston Churchill. I am sorry.'

The New Party was actually launched in inauspicious circumstances. Mosley fell ill with phlebitis the night before the inaugural meeting, when it was too late to make any postponement. This illness, at this particularly inappropriate moment, may have a psychological explanation. Further, W. J. Brown, the I.L.P. M.P. who was also general secretary of the Civil Service Clerical Association and who, with Strachey, had canvassed the I.L.P. in late

[1] *Town Crier*, 27 March and 17 April 1931.
[2] Strachey resigned on 24 February (*Manchester Guardian*, 25 February, quoted MacIntyre). He left the I.L.P. at the same time.
[3] *Town Crier*, 5 April 1931.

1930 on Mosley's behalf, backed out at the last minute, apparently on pressure from his union, despite a personal appeal from the sick Mosley. He had been supposed to give the second main speech at the inaugural meeting. It therefore fell to Strachey (who had just written yet another manifesto)[1] and Cynthia Mosley to take the place of their leaders, to address the inaugural meeting on 5 March.[2]

The New Party's manifesto announced a plan to mobilize four hundred candidates in the next general election, and appealed for voluntary workers in all constituencies: 'some of us, at any rate, are not prepared,' the statement read, and this was clearly Strachey speaking, 'to continue in the idle game into which politics have sunk without an effort to rouse the nation into action. It is necessary for a few to take the risk of providing the people with an opportunity to work and to fight for a policy of action.'

'The creation of a new political organization,' the statement went on, 'is a great and difficult adventure which few politicians are willing to undertake, however much they agree with the necessity for a new policy. I expect, therefore, to be joined in this enterprise only by such few members of parliament as have decided that retirement from politics is preferable to acquiescence.'[3] 'I' was Mosley, but the words were Strachey's.

At the inaugural meeting in the Memorial Hall, Farringdon Street, Cynthia Mosley and Strachey made vigorous speeches, which were not well reported. Lady Cynthia said: 'If it comes to betraying socialism, go to the Labour front benches.' She added 'what we have done . . . has been one of the most beastly and heartbreaking things I have ever had to do'. Strachey said that the New Party 'stood definitely against trying to solve the present crisis by wage reductions'.[4] His last speech in the House of Commons in support of the Labour government had similarly been bitterly scornful of the 'unreal and ghostly procession of Measures passing in single file through this House'. While 'the slow, sure frost of economic decay tightens its grip . . . we still debate unreal measures which may hardly be intended to reach

---

[1] Comment of Mosley, June 1971.
[2] Mosley, *op. cit.*, p. 284.
[3] *The Times*, 2 March 1931.
[4] *The Times*, 6 March 1931.

the Statute Book.'[1] 'Disillusion with democracy' was one of the strongest feelings animating him at this moment, while he was, temporarily, placing his Marxian and even socialist views in abeyance.

Strachey, Robert Forgan and Cynthia Mosley undertook the series of meetings in the country in the spring of 1931 at which Mosley and W. J. Brown had been advertised to speak. They met continuous heckling and opposition, and perhaps here, for the first time, Strachey appreciated the enormity of what he had done in leaving the movement in which, as he had written to Yvette, barely seven years before he had begun to 'sink' himself with such satisfaction. Staying in large hotels up and down the country in the company of Cynthia Mosley and Forgan, he had ample time for repentance (Dr Forgan, however, recalls him recounting erotic dreams at hotel breakfasts).[2] Strachey spoke at the Oxford Union on 6 March, apparently for the first time since he had gone down; impressing his audience as 'clear and explanatory', but he 'cannot be called a sympathetic speaker'.[3]

The meeting organized in Birmingham to launch the New Party there was a specially difficult occasion. 'Have you brought your money bags?' was the first question from the audience as Lady Cynthia spoke. Strachey was listened to quietly until he said it would have been better if the Government had brought forward a bolder policy and been defeated. Then there were cries of 'we don't want another Tory government'. But the greatest opposition to Strachey was shown when he declared that Snowden stood for wage cuts and longer hours. . . . There were cries of 'liar' and considerable interruption was kept up during the rest of his speech. 'What does Sir William Morris think about wage cuts?' shouted one person, a reference to the by then known association of the future Lord Nuffield with Mosley. Then there were questions. Why did not Strachey and Mosley back the I.L.P. instead of forming a group in opposition to the Labour party? Strachey said that he thought the I.L.P. impracticable. When

[1] Hansard, Vol. 247, Col. 1551.
[2] Dr Forgan to the author, 12 August 1971.
[3] Isis, 11 March 1931. The president of the Union was the future Sir Geoffrey Wilson, later a friend of Strachey's.

asked why he did not resign his seat, Strachey said that it was the government, not he, who had gone back on past promises.[1] Strachey and his colleagues then went on to Scotland, where Strachey's Bloomsbury accent invited 'jeers and mimicry'; but at Dundee, Strachey, Forgan and Cynthia Mosley joined arms and led the audience in singing *The Red Flag*.

The New Party's first big test was at the by-election of Ashton-under-Lyne, a Lancashire cotton town with 4,690 unemployed, where, in 1929, there had been a Labour majority of 3,407. The Labour member had died. Though Mosley was convalescing in Monte Carlo, the national organization of the New Party decided to run Allan Young as its candidate, against the wishes of the local New Party committee. Dan Davies, Strachey's agent at Ashton, acted in this capacity for Young. Large meetings were held, despite the rudimentary nature of the organization. There was some criticism of the way that Mosley, Strachey and the other leaders lived at the Midland Hotel, Manchester, and only went out by car to Ashton, but both Mosley's wife and Strachey's proved themselves 'willing workers': Esther, wrote the Welsh miner, Jack Jones, in his excellent autobiography, *Unfinished Journey*, was 'by no means an effective speaker, but she could hold a crowd long enough to rest some of those whose sore throats were wearing. She had a talk about the American form of government, which lasted 12 minutes.'[2] In the end, the Labour party vote was split, and the Conservative candidate elected: the Conservative got 12,400, Labour 11,000, the New Party 4,500. The Labour supporters were naturally furious with the New Party and ugly scenes occurred at the Ashton Town Hall. Dan Davies told Mosley that, if he went out into the crowd, he would be lynched, and the crowd's face did seem to have the appearance, Jack Jones later recalled, of 'an American lynching-crowd'. Both Mosley and Young were greeted with cries of 'Judas' and 'traitor', and 'You let the Tories in'.[3] Mosley, white with rage, surveying the equally furious throng, remarked to Strachey: 'That is the crowd that has pre-

---

[1] *Town Crier*, 13 March 1931.
[2] Jack Jones, *Unfinished Journey*, p. 259.
[3] *Town Crier*, 8 May.

vented anyone doing anything in England since the war.'[1]
Strachey himself, however, was appalled. He realized that the
mass of workers were against the New Party, and suspected,
there and then, that 'we were on the wrong side'.[2] In his later
book, *The Menace of Fascism*, Strachey said that this was the time
when Mosley, in passion and personal danger, found himself
physically aligned against the workers, and when British fascism
was born.[3] All the leaders bravely pushed their way through the
crowd, however, successfully, and only Lady Cynthia Mosley
availed herself of the back door,[4] thanks to the courtesy of the
local Conservative party chairman.

For the New Party, 4,500 votes in the first by-election which it
had undertaken, with a small organization and at short notice,
seemed a considerable achievement. Keynes, Beaverbrook and
others all remained close to Mosley, and the first of these told
Harold Nicolson, another new affiliate, that he would certainly
vote for the New Party (his biographer was silent on the matter).[5]
A. J. Cook, the miner's leader, said the same. Two points, however, now troubled Strachey, in addition to his anxiety about
the marked hostility of the working class in Lancashire.

The first was the position of Russia. This had evidently been
on Strachey's mind since his visit of the previous year. Thus, on
29 May, three weeks after the Ashton by-election, Nicolson
lunched with Strachey: Strachey said, 'it will not be possible for
us indefinitely to maintain a theory that we can treat Russia as a
business firm treats another business firm without differentiating
commercial from personal relations . . . in a country where the
state is the employer, it is impossible to disentangle commercial
from political relations.'[6] Secondly, Allan Young was also beginning to have doubts, though of a slightly different kind. He was
furious at Mosley's decision to create a Youth Movement 'to keep
order at meetings'; and soon expressed his anxiety on this score

---

[1] Strachey, *The Menace of Fascism*, p. 161.
[2] Comment of Mosley, June 1971.
[3] Strachey, *The Menace of Fascism*, p. 161.
[4] Jack Jones, *op. cit.*, p. 259.
[5] Nicolson, *op. cit.*, Vol. I, p. 72.
[6] *Ibid.*, unpublished version, 29 May.

to Harold Nicolson.[1] Young had, after all, been once a 'class-conscious socialist,' who had roused an I.L.P. conference at Birmingham with a Marxian socialist speech, and was obviously in a special quandary in a role where one of his colleagues, W. E. D. Allen, could say, in answer to a right-wing critic, that the New Party meant 'no threat to the Union'. Young was also disturbed by Mosley's appointment, as 'Chief Agent', of F. M. Box, previously Conservative agent for Yorkshire. He had several furious and exhausting wrangles with Mosley lasting many hours.

From the time of the Ashton by-election, Mosley was looking around to try to find a 'defence force', as he put it, to preserve his meetings from being broken up by the Labour and communist parties. Obviously the example of what Mussolini and Hitler had done in Italy and Germany was on Mosley's mind, as was obviously the thought that he would make a good leader in their style.

Personal relations between Mosley and Strachey meantime began to be tense. Strachey later said that Mosley began to use the word 'fascism' more and more in private conversation.[2] Strachey's desire for an elder brother figure always wore a little thin in the end. Perhaps, sometimes, Mosley's clever jokes had riled him a little even in the old days: was he really pleased when Mosley told him that he was 'governed by Marx from the waist up, Freud from the waist down, but no part of you by Strachey'?[3] At all events, a rupture could hardly have been avoided after the beginning of June, when Strachey gave a speech at a 'week-end school' at Mosley's house at Denham. That morning, the *Daily Herald* had alleged, correctly, that Mosley had sent two emissaries to Germany to advise on youth movements.[4] Strachey made a 'good old-fashioned Marxian speech', to 'clear the air'. Allan Young and Joad, who were present, applauded loudly, and the latter explicitly condemned the Youth Movement.

[1] *Ibid.*, Vol. I, p. 77.
[2] Strachey, *The Menace of Fascism*, p. 162.
[3] Mosley, *op. cit.*, p. 330.
[4] *Daily Herald*, 6 June 1931, corroborated by Mosley, *News Chronicle*, 8 June 1931. Stuart MacIntyre comments interestingly.

Another party member, Peter Winkworth, redressed the balance with a fascist-style speech. Both Esther and Cynthia Mosley seemed a little perturbed, meantime, by Mosley's speech on the subject of the Corporate State.[1] Strachey, walking in the garden afterwards, saw Mosley sunk in thought on a bench in the distance: 'Behold, Rodin's *Penseur*,' he said mockingly to Bill Allen.

These second thoughts by Strachey and Joad were, in one sense, illogical, since both had recently written an article in the spring issue of *The Political Quarterly*, in which they had argued that future governments should have wide powers to issue Orders in Council, on the ground that parliamentary legislators were too 'amateur'.[2] But several reviews by Strachey in the *Spectator* at this moment in an urbane style suggested that he wished to keep open several choices.

A week or so after the meeting at Denham, Strachey and Harold Nicolson were dining with Joad at his house in Hampstead. The question was raised as to what would happen if the economic and political crisis should turn out to be exaggerated or if 'the crisis does not come or is resolved?' Would the New Party have any mission in those circumstances? Joad said that the 'young of today' were looking for some 'formula of integration'. 'What should it be?' Strachey said that it should be national socialism. Sellick Davies (a Liberal supporter of the New Party) with 'shy fervour, put in a claim for a Religious Appeal'. Nicolson, who, that very day, had agreed to edit the New Party paper *Action*, said that the longing of which Joad had spoken 'was . . . due to the inability of the younger generation to adjust its energies and ambitions to the present state concept'.[3] In an article presumably written about this time, Strachey, meantime, pledged that 'neither I nor any other of the men and women who founded the New Party would, or will ever, be connected with any organization which can be suspected of being anti-working class in character,' though he admitted that some members, or financial supporters, of it were, of course, not wage earners.[4]

[1] Jack Jones, *op. cit.*, pp. 263-4; *Manchester Guardian*, 9 June 1931, for Joad's speech.
[2] *Political Quarterly*, II, 1931.
[3] Nicolson, *op. cit.*, 16 June 1931, unpublished section.
[4] 'The Progress of the New Party', *Week-End Review*, 20 June 1931.

On 30 June, Mosley announced explicitly, in a speech in the Cannon Street Hotel, that his movement was trying to create a new political psychology, a conception of national renaissance, of new mankind and of vigour.[1] Allan Young, sitting next to Mosley, fumed with rage. He told Strachey that he was thinking of resignation. Strachey then took what seems to have been a firm stand against authoritarianism, in an address to the Youth Movement, and Mosley reprimanded Strachey, publicly, 'in terms which,' commented Harold Nicolson, 'would have caused me the most acute embarrassment.'[2] Mosley described Strachey as a 'pathological Socialist'. He then went off in the company of some of his new strong-arm friends such as Kid Lewis, the boxer; Peter Cheyney, the crime novelist; and Peter Howard, the Oxford rugger player. On 17 July, Nicolson reflected: 'I think that Tom at the bottom of his heart really wants a fascist movement, but Allan Young and John Strachey think only of the British working man. The whole thing is extremely thin ice.' On 20 July, Harold Nicolson recorded that Mosley had avoided telling Strachey and Young that he was going to talk with Churchill and Lloyd George at the house of the Liberal chief whip, Archibald Sinclair. Mosley thought that Churchill and Lloyd George might approach him for support in the event of a National Government being formed to cope with the economic crisis. That might lead to Strachey and Young severing all relations with the party. On their way to Sinclair's house at Coombe, Mosley told Nicolson that he foresaw a 'split with Strachey and Allan Young'. Rumours of this had already reached the public, since Strachey and Mosley had seemed to differ in their attitude on a recent piece of government unemployment legislation: and Strachey told the *Manchester Guardian*'s political correspondent that he thought Mosley's speech on the Second Reading of this bill was too far to the right.[3] On 20 July Strachey produced a memorandum which he called 'The New Party and Russia'. Doubtless, it did follow logically

---

[1] *The Times*, 1 July 1931.
[2] *Daily Herald*, 3 July 1931, and Nicolson, *op. cit.*, p. 50.
[3] *Manchester Guardian*, 24 July 1931, referring to Mosley's speech of 8 July, quoted MacIntyre, *op. cit.*, p. 180.

from what he had been thinking since his visit to Russia the previous year. But the occasion for the memorandum was such that, by insisting on its adoption, he was bound to provoke a hostile reaction. Mosley had not known of its contents before it was circulated, though Strachey wrote that he had been asked to prepare it – presumably by Mosley.[1]

The memorandum insisted that, instead of reaching any 'favoured nation arrangement' in terms of trade with the Dominions, Russia should be preferred. Russia and Britain, he argued, had complementary economies and both, with a New Party government in power in Britain, would have planned economies too. Britain could afford Russia long-term credits for development. Britain should make a 'progressive break with that group of powers (of which France and the USA are the leaders) . . . which is attempting to restore the pre-war form of capitalism'. The only Imperial policy remaining would be to 'assist the native races themselves to build up economic systems suitable for them'. The Dominions, however, though they 'could not agree to buy British products on a stable long-term basis, could undoubtedly, if they would, give us advantages by means of tariff preferences'.

Mosley rejected this plan, since it contradicted most of his own programme. Strachey thereupon resigned from the New Party, being accompanied by Allan Young and also by Joad, soon after. They issued a statement that, on subjects such as the Youth Movement, Unemployment, Insurance, India and Russia, Mosley was adopting 'a conservative or fascist' attitude. Before this was issued, Mosley sent Nicolson to try to prevent them from going ahead. But he could not find them for some hours, which was understandable, since they had both gone round to Celia's in Mecklenburgh Square. Eventually, Nicolson did meet both in Strachey's house towards evening. He asked them to suspend their resignations until 1 December, by which date they would be able to see whether the accusations of fascism were justified. Strachey, however, refused. He could not remain a member of a party in which he was taking no active direction. He thought that, in his absence, the party would be doing things of which he would

[1] Strachey, *The Menace of Fascism*, p. 164.

disapprove. He also argued that Mosley, since his illness, had been a 'different man'. His faith had left him and he was acquiring a Tory mind. Since Mosley now considered socialism a 'pathological condition', Strachey could not alter his decision to abandon the New Party, though he admitted that both he and Young minded 'dreadfully severing this link'. 'We were willing,' Strachey wrote some time later, 'to carry self deception very far, much too far indeed, in order to avoid a break which was very painful to us.'[1] But the break was absolute when it came. Nicolson went away, back to Mosley, who thereafter launched out on his own.[2] A recent recruit of the New Party, Osbert Sitwell, commented that 'those who know Mr Strachey are aware that his spiritual home is in Moscow rather than in London'.[3] Mosley made no published comment.

Strachey rarely referred to Mosley afterwards. Once he did so, when he was virtually a communist and Mosley a fascist, in a letter to Boothby: 'he can't break *his* heart,' he commented, 'it was broken very early, I think. . . . There was some left when we first knew him – but now, I fancy, none – or am I wrong? That's really the saddest thing about him because, contrary to general opinion, he had a heart. But you aren't, and have no desire to be a Fascist Byron carved in bronze and can suffer too much. . . .'[4] It was, indeed, Mosley's hope that he, by pure reason, could separate his emotions from his intellect, as Shaw made Caesar do, in his favourite play, *Caesar and Cleopatra*. Perhaps he did so and perhaps that was his undoing, not his making.

These developments marked the end, no doubt, of Strachey's protracted and brilliant youth. Years later he recalled that 'the sole thing that could be said for this time in his life' was that he had 'never for a moment ceased to revolt. . . . True, his revolt had been almost as misdirected as the thing revolted against had been odious. But still, to have revolted was something.'

The best epitaph on this long adventure by Strachey with Mosley was written by Bevan in a letter of 29 July:

[1] *Ibid.*, p. 182.
[2] This account derives from the Nicolson Diaries, complete version, which is slightly fuller here than the published version.
[3] Osbert Sitwell, 'Say What He Will', *Week-End Review*, 1 August 1931.
[4] Strachey to Boothby, 6 June 1935.

The news of your resignation made me very happy. It is difficult for me to explain to you how keenly I felt the impossibility of our continued political cooperation after you joined the New Party. I am now looking forward to a renewal of that cooperation in the immediate future. The break with Mosley must have been difficult for you, but if I am to be allowed to say so without the risk of being misunderstood, I am convinced that the strength of mind and personal self reliance which this decision involved means that you have reached your full maturity, in the use of your great powers. . . . I always had the feeling that your subordination to [Mosley's] superficially stronger personality was bad for you, in those subtle and self conscious directions which are most potent in the building up of one's personality. You will remember the discussion we had some time ago about the psychic basis of your relation with Celia. I am convinced, perhaps quite amateurously (sic) that your relationship with Celia in the last analysis provided you with the necessary reinforcement for your decision about Mosley. I know that you are sufficiently objective not to take offence at these remarks of mine. It is my affection for you which causes me to look so closely into the psychical rather than the superficial reasons which led you to make the decision you have. I hope that you will not commit yourself in any way regarding your future until we have had the opportunity of talking the matter over very fully.

It seems to me, looking at the political situation in this country, that the cards are not yet dealt with which the final game will have to be played. It would be a profound error for us to judge the pace and direction of these social and political collusions which exist independently of us, and with which we have to deal. It is the besetting sin of intellectuals to be too much influenced by the drive of their own minds. They are too reluctant to submit themselves to the pressure of events. In intellectuals, there is a tendency to want to dominate and shape these things arbitrarily. They can influence these events only by being moulded by them. Thus the profound difference between the typical intellectual and persons who, like myself, have the security of metaphysics on a social struggle upon which to rely in moments of doubt and uncertainty [this sentence is put in as it was written, even though it does not read very satisfactorily]. I am putting these words together very incoherently and inadequately, but I know that, as usual, your mind will come three parts of the way to meet mine. As I told you on one occasion before, I value your friendship very highly, and my thoughts are with you constantly in what must be for you a time of great introspection, if not spiritual suffering. . . . Yours affectionately, Aneurin.[1]

[1] Bevan to Strachey, 29 July 1931.

Chapter 8 / THE COMMUNISTS

When Strachey left the New Party, he was still a member of parliament. But his position was ambiguous: he had left the Labour party and the I.L.P.; he was not a member of the New Party; he was, therefore, an Independent. He was 'invited' by the *Daily Herald* to rejoin the Labour party, but refused,[1] saying that he believed that Social Democracy was now 'the deadliest enemy of the British workers'.[2]

The personal life of Strachey was also unresolved. Esther was away, and Strachey was again on close terms with Celia. At this difficult time, her dedication to the left may have been, as Bevan said, decisive. Celia was a strong character, completely devoted by this time to Strachey, his career, and to the revolutionary cause.

But neither personal nor political matters could remain static. The English political crisis broke in August. Personal cleavages, such as had divided so new and inexperienced a group as the New Party, also divided the Labour cabinet, though for different reasons. On 23 August, the cabinet divided over the question as to whether unemployment payments should or should not be cut by ten per cent. The next day, Macdonald formed his national government of 'individuals rather than of parties'. This move stupefied the Labour movement. The new National Cabinet

[1] *Daily Herald*, 29 August 1931; *see also Daily Worker*, 30 June 1932.
[2] Strachey, 'The Education of a Communist', *Left Review*, December 1934, p. 68.

included four Conservatives, two Liberals and three Labour ministers apart from Macdonald. On 8 September, parliament met and approved what Macdonald had done in its absence (by 311 to 251); two days later, Snowden introduced an emergency budget; on 7 October, parliament was dissolved, and there was a general election on 27 October.

Strachey made few contributions to the development of the crisis, apart from two or three interventions in the House of Commons which, of course, he could only do as a private member. His speeches were as full of scorn for the opposition front bench as for the government. The events of August seemed, at least to himself, to justify his own behaviour.

By the election of October he was drawing towards the communist party. He wrote virtually as much to the *New Statesman* in September, saying that communism could be quickly adopted in Britain; if this led to shortages, Russia would provide.[1] He thought that Britain had only one choice – communism (and the eternal cause of human culture, of science and of civilization itself) or the 'mental and moral suicide of fascism'.[2] Thus he wrote to Andrew Rothstein, an orthodox communist intellectual, on 10 October, that, in fighting Aston, as 'an Independent Workers' candidate, he was 'working in close harmony with your local men in Birmingham, who are most helpful'.[3] The same day, he was also writing to Palme Dutt, suggesting an article for the *Labour Monthly*, his communist theoretical journal.[4] By this time, he had talked with Harry Pollitt, the communist secretary general, about the political position in England and his own within it. So Strachey moved towards the communists fast after he had left Mosley. The communists were also beginning to think of him as a possible recruit and friend, and to treat him accordingly. Rothstein, in a letter, to which the one above-mentioned was a reply, hoped that Strachey would speak again in parliament before the House rose, and also made suggestions indeed as to what that speech might include. The communists in Aston supported

---

[1] *New Statesman*, 26 September 1931.
[2] 'The Education of a Communist', *Left Review*, December 1934.
[3] Strachey to Andrew Rothstein, 10 October 1931.
[4] Strachey to Dutt, 10 October 1931.

Strachey, though warily, on the recommendation of the *Daily Worker*.[1]

A speech made by Strachey in the House of Commons on Snowden's supplementary budget on 2 October is indicative: this was not a New Party speech, but an extreme socialist one: 'I believe that the crisis for British capitalism has become so severe that it has become an impossible task to attempt to balance the budget,' in the way suggested by Snowden, whereby nearly one-third of the National Income would be raised by taxation. Strachey thought that the 'crisis' proved the unfeasibility of 'taxation socialism'. The loss of convertibility of the pound was profoundly damaging the world capitalist system, and 'neither the export trade nor any other trade in the world will ever revive so long as we have a capitalist system'.[2]

On the other hand, Strachey had voted with the Labour opposition on 1 October (in five divisions on the Civil estimates), and on the budget, and on several other occasions on previous days. He plainly considered himself fully an M.P. Mosley also spoke in the House of Commons on 21 September – in a statesman-like manner, on the gold standard; he voted in the Conservative lobbies, while Strachey voted with Labour; he too had spoken that day, and probably this was the last time they saw each other. They passed in the lobby, nodded to each other, but did not speak.

All this suggests, probably, that there was, at the very least, a disposition in Strachey already to seek a new intellectual harbour, and that, for a variety of reasons, some personal, he expected already to find it in the communist party. The power, as well as the conspiratorial character of international communism as it was then organized, excited him: the secret messages, hurried journeys, ruthlessness and even perhaps the jesuitical argumentation of communism delighted him. But Strachey also chose communism because he felt nothing else would, or could, save what was best in western civilization. Later, at least one communist critic, Dimitri Mirsky, criticized this approach, describing it as 'the policy of the lesser evil', and attributing it to Strachey's

[1] *Daily Worker*, 24 October 1931.
[2] Hansard, Vol. 257, Cols. 721–5.

bourgeois origin.[1] In 1931, he saw the situation in manichaean colours: communism was the only chance of saving the world from fascism. Strachey had, after all, been heading leftwards, irregularly, since 1923; Mosley had always stimulated, excited, and led him, and it was loyalty to, and fascination for, Mosley personally which caused Strachey, quite naturally, to follow him over the brink into the New Party: if Bevan, a recent acquaintance of Mosley, followed as far as the January resolution in the parliamentary Labour party, it was understandable that Strachey, a devoted personal friend for seven years, should follow further, and should, in the sort of speech and article which he wrote between March and May 1931, lay aside his Marxist criticism of society. But it was only laid aside, and that only partially.

The election of October 1931 went badly for all opponents of the National Government. Mosley and Strachey both lost their seats, as did most of their old antagonists in the Labour party, except for those who supported Macdonald and the coalition. The New Party was crushed. Strachey's campaign was assisted by the presence with him of both Celia and of Allan Young as agent. He wrote and spoke virtually as a communist, attacking in his election address 'the Labour party's gross betrayal of the workers'.

Strachey, with 3,326 votes, came bottom of the poll. His Tory opponent received a majority of no less than 16,700, in place of a Labour one of 1,550 in 1929 (the official Labour candidate got only 6,212). This vote was reflected in all Birmingham. Thus, not only Aston, but Deridend, Duddeston, Erdington, Ladywood, and Yardley, were lost. Not one of the divisions won in 1929 after such a struggle remained. There were no Labour seats there until 1945. Neither Strachey, nor the communist candidate at Duddeston, nor the two New Party candidates in the city, had any effect on the votes, and all lost their deposits.

Once the election was over, a new problem arose: Esther's father became ill. Esther was fond of him. She told Strachey that she had to return to the U.S. and that she could not go back alone. This request posed a personal crisis which might otherwise have been delayed, but could not, in the end, have been avoided. Strachey put the point to Celia. She agreed that he

[1] Dimitri Mirsky, *The Intelligentsia of Great Britain* (London 1935), p. 234.

should take Esther back to New York, but elicited a promise from him that he would return on the first boat. He agreed. Strachey and Esther went to New York. When they arrived there, P. F. Murphy was on his deathbed. He soon died. Strachey left for London on the day of his funeral. Not knowing of Strachey's undertaking to Celia, Esther found this apparently callous and rude behaviour inexplicable. She was also hurt that he had refused to lunch with Al Smith, the democratic candidate in the Presidential elections of 1928, on the ground that he was 'bourgeois'.[1]

On his return to England, Strachey abandoned the house in North Street and went to live with Celia. She had just been dismissed by Wrench from the *Spectator*, on the grounds that she was too left-wing. In particular, she had organized, for the *Spectator*, an international conference on Russia, in which Wrench was interested, since he was a Russian scholar. But she had asked only people from the Russian Government, headed by Litvinov, or articulate advocates of the regime, and the *Spectator* had had cold feet. She received a handsome sum in compensation for this dismissal. She and Strachey went off to live in a cottage lent to them by the actor, Miles Malleson, an old I.L.P. supporter, at West Hoathly, in Sussex. But Strachey, though he had agreed to leave Esther, had still not decided to divorce her, much less marry Celia. A painful situation lasted on into 1932. Strachey was undecided what to do.

He was meantime in ever increasing contact with the communists. Thus, on Christmas Eve 1931, he had written from his mother's house in London, 39 St Leonard's Terrace, Chelsea, to Palme Dutt. He told Dutt, who was then in Brussels (as he had been for some years, apparently for reasons of health), that he 'wanted very much to discuss the general British position with you. Like so many other people, I have been deeply impressed by your notes in the *Labour Monthly* and the undeniable accuracy of your prognosis. I find myself unable any longer to deny the accuracy of the communist diagnosis and correctness of the communist line in Great Britain. I have discussed my own position with Pollitt, and two or three days ago with Sokolnikov [the Russian ambassador]. . . .'

[1] Boothby to Strachey, 11 November 1932.

This was a strange admission: to have a chat with the Russian ambassador as to whether or not he should join the communist party was, however, typical of Strachey's inclination always to go to the top in these matters; and Sokolnikov was an acquaintance who had dined with him at least once during 1931 in North Street.[1]

'What I am doing for the moment,' Strachey went on to Dutt, 'is to attempt to educate myself by acquiring the grounding of Marxist theory. For example, I am in the middle of the second volume of *Das Kapital*, which, I am ashamed to say, I have never read through before. A systematic reading of the first volume is certainly a tremendous experience, especially at the moment, when one sees so many of Marx's predictions being uncannily fulfilled. . . .' Then, turning to his own experience in recent years, Strachey added: 'the Communist party in Birmingham, in spite of an able man in the person of its local organizer, Ferguson, seems entirely unable, even now, to become established as a real party. It simply consists of one or two officials and a floating membership of unemployed who are entirely unreliable. I am frankly pessimistic about the possibility of the present C.P.G.B. getting any grip whatever on the mass movement, unless some other element in the I.L.P. and Trade Unions, which there is no possibility of bringing within the Party for some time to come, can be swung into line. The isolation of the Party from the workers seems to me very serious . . . and I should like your view as to how best this can be broken down. If one seeks to join the Party, there is so much valuable work which immediately becomes impossible. On the other hand, it may be that this is merely a fact which must be faced. Please excuse this long letter. You must partly blame Pollitt for encouraging me to write.'[2]

This letter does not indicate, however, that, while Strachey was reading Marx, he was also preparing his own gloss upon it. For, early in the New Year, he was already at work on the most influential of his political works. This undertaking, like many of the best works even in political literature, was begun partly out of necessity.

[1] Nicolson, *op. cit.*, for June 1931.
[2] Strachey to Dutt, 24 December 1931.

Until 1929, partly by living at home, and partly from his earnings on the *Spectator*, Strachey was never short of money. While married to Esther, and during his two years as a member of parliament, he depended on his wife's income, together with the small salary then payable to members of parliament. But now he was forced for several years to rely on his pen for a living. He retained a connection with the *Spectator*, but his own new political line was so different from that followed by that journal that his reviews were few.[1] This became even more the case when he and Celia (who left the *Spectator* in November 1931) became temporarily literary editors of the *Daily Worker*, going up to London once a week to do what was needed: Celia did most of this work while Strachey did various other jobs on the paper. Celia, it is true, had her money from the *Spectator*, and she also had just received a legacy, but this was only a short-term help to their joint funds. Strachey remained admittedly a substantial shareholder in the *Spectator*[2] and he was, of course, in an infinitely stronger position than most in that year of depression – for example, his and Allan Young's ex-agent, Dan Davies (who had followed him into the New Party), for whom he sought unsuccessfully to get a job after he too had left the New Party.[3] Still, this was a time for him of difficulty, and it was obviously this that caused him to wonder whether he should really abandon Esther and her wealth.

Esther, meantime, was in a quandary. Her view was put to Strachey in a letter from a mutual friend, in early 1932: 'Esther's distress can be in part relieved if you can manage to maintain your present situation as one of necessary experiment until you are sure, in the deepest and irreducible part of yourself, of what you must do. She *does* love you, but you must realize that she does not depend on you in any way – emotionally, intellectually or actually; nor is she, as far as I can perceive, waiting for you as the one

[1] Cf. a complaint in a letter to Wrench, dated 21 April 1932, where he says he extracted two books for review 'with the utmost difficulty', adding, disingenuously, 'Do let me know if I am not doing the right kind of stuff, because I am sure I can change it if necessary.'

[2] He had 1,017 ordinary shares in the *Spectator* in August 1932. (Note by Westminster Bank, Bishop's Stortford.)

[3] For the future of Davies, *see* below, p. 224.

hope and solution of her life. She does believe that some sort of equality is possible between you, or that, in any case, some arrangement of your lives can be made, which will prove less disastrous and ridiculous than this. After all, you *have* made it very ridiculous! I am not telling her that I have heard from you, as she would want to see what you had written, and this, because of your characteristically evasive reference to her not understanding your letter to her in the sense you gave to it, I cannot do. . . . Even *her* patience could come to an end. . . . Esther tells me you are joining the communist party. When you do, let me know, and I will send three rousing cheers from Party headquarters here.' In a postscript, the writer added that she had received a new letter that day from Strachey himself, which made 'the above inappropriate, to say the least. . . you must be very unhappy, my dear, dear John, why is it becoming so difficult for people to make the effort to know themselves?'[1]

All through 1932, Strachey still seemed reluctant either to go back to Esther or to marry Celia. Strachey and Esther continued to correspond, though their letters concerned French eighteenth-century court history. (Strachey left these letters about, presumably with the deliberate intention of allowing Celia to read them, which she did.) Celia found the situation more and more difficult. The irritations attendant on maintaining an irregular *ménage* in the heart of the English countryside were considerable. Strachey, meantime, was not at all certain that what he was doing was right. Joe Brewer perceptively wrote from America at about the same time:

John dear, I am convinced that Esther loves you profoundly. Moreover, I think she knows now very much what she wants, namely a real life with you, and she knows now what is required on her part to bring it off if it can be brought off. Whether she could ever do the things which she knows are required and which I am sure she really wants to do, depends as much upon you as upon her. She is very conscious of her shortcomings in the past, and she has a very clear view of what direction your life should take and what her part in it should

[1] Letter of 6 April 1932, from Muriel Draper.

be. I think she wants desperately to try to work it out with you. But . . . it looks very much to me as though you are trying very hard unconsciously to have your cake and eat it too, but you will have to make up your mind about it one way or the other soon. You cannot go on forever in a 'Turkey dream' and believe me, your ladies are not going to let you do [so] between them.

Your life, whether in active politics or in journalism, is bound to run its course in the main stream of British politics. Fundamentally, you are interested in your own career and you want to be amongst those who govern, and who come out top-dog in the struggle. Naturally – who of us doesn't? But you are really ambitious, and you want power immediately, and for yourself, in your own lifetime. There is no reason why you shouldn't have it, but you must recognize the desire for what it is. You are not one of the fanatical, dreaming kind, willing to jeopardize his own career and personal fulfilment for principles and causes which will only come to fruition long years from now. This does not mean that you are insincere in your beliefs, nor yet an opportunist, but simply that you have an active imagination, and you want to see things work out in your own time. Hence, however, your difficulty in deciding to join, or not to join, the Communist Party. You would a little like to see which way the cat is going to jump before burning your bridges – if I may be permitted such a luxuriant mixture of metaphors.

This quite understandable indecision appears unfortunately to have invaded your private life. It need not do so, and to my mind should not. For some curious reason which I have never yet been able to understand, you distrust your own intelligence, and you have always felt the necessity of some sort of prop to lean on – your father, Joad, Mosley – to mention only a few. If you cannot bring yourself to do without such a prop and if you continue to find some support an unconscious necessity, it seems to me high time that you found one worthy of you, one who will not prove sycophantic but who can really test your mettle, one who is capable of accompanying you into any sphere of high responsible activity to which your life may bring you, and who will also be permanently there. Who could be this kind of support to you better than Esther? And I think she is prepared to do it. At least I think she wants to try. Certainly her brains and her knowledge are good hard steel on which to whet your weapons and the fact that she would not necessarily sympathize with your views nor too easily accept your reasoning should make her the more valuable. With Esther really helping you, my dear John, what a career you can carve out for yourself! And I don't mean just financial help either, though that is not unimportant, I know....

If it is the question of sleeping together which bothers you, let me say this, that the more I see of marriage (only from the outside, I realize) the less it seems to me to depend on this. It is concerned in a curious way with quite other things for the most part. It is a way of life, a *modus operandi*, and the sex business, if sensibly and rationally handled, can be quite adequately arranged within or without its bonds. It all depends on how it is done. So far as Esther is concerned, the other phases of a joint life are clearly more important to her and I feel that if discreetly handled you could arrange this side of your life quite easily. Not, of course, with Celia, partly because of the attitude she has shown in her actions in the past, and because of the indiscretion with which you seem to have handled the whole affair. Esther's pride is involved here and, come what may in the future, you will have now to choose definitely between these two. Should you decide for Esther and a career, you will have definitely to finish with Celia. Esther could, I am sure, never brook any continuation of that, nor do I think you could reasonably expect it of her.[1]

Strachey replied at the end of the month:

As you say I and Esther parted with the understanding that we should wait a year unless either of us came to a final conclusion before. . . . As it is I came to a final decision about a month ago and at once wrote to Esther, as I was in honour bound to do. For I, who come to decision with all too much

[1] Brewer to Strachey, 4 April 1932.

difficulty, God knows, was utterly clear that I could not alas live with Esther again: that I deeply and truly loved Celia, and wanted to marry her. Esther has always said that in any case if we did not live together she would divorce me and I have asked her to do so. As you say, any life with her would be impossible to her unless I gave up Celia and that is unthinkable. While all this is profoundly decided, please don't imagine that I don't feel as strongly as I am capable of feeling about Esther. I feel the frightful tragedy of our marriage as a heavy, heavy weight which I shall carry all the rest of my life. And I am more than willing to take all the blame. . . . I realize too all you say about the tremendous possibilities that the partnership of myself and Esther might have had. You know how much I built upon it. . . . [But] I cannot agree with you on what you say as to the possibilities of marriage without sex. Alas for me at any rate it is not so . . . the thought of Esther, and of her inestimable goodness, of the startling, beautiful and so overwhelmingly moving core of purest gold that lies beneath all surface irrelevancies haunts me. . . . But you cannot think now you know how I feel that I should try to live again with Esther. I know I cannot do it. . . .[1]

But, even so, indecision remained.

In these curious circumstances, Strachey's first Marxist work was finished, in April 1932, and Celia despatched a draft of it to Victor Gollancz, a friend of hers from her days as a literary editor, at the end of May. Gollancz liked the book and telegraphed Strachey characteristically: 'DELIGHTED WITH BOOK CAN YOU LUNCH IVY WEDNESDAY GOLLANCZ.' Gollancz agreed to publish the book in the autumn. Strachey would be paid an advance of £75.

Gollancz, at this time still under forty, had been publishing on his own account since 1928; but even before, while working with Ernest Benn, he had embarked on a brilliant series of cheap books on serious themes: Benn's 'Sixpenny Library' had been a forerunner of Allen Lane's Penguins (which began only in 1936).

[1] Strachey to Brewer, 27 April 1932, written from the Old White Hart Hotel, Great Yeldham.

Arrogant, determined, philanthropic, hard-working, flamboyant and cultivated, Gollancz was already in a dominant position to carry out the political education of the young, the newly literate, and the restless generally. He was the obvious person for Strachey to send his book to.

Gollancz was sometimes a difficult man to work with. Thus, some years later, when he was organizing the famous Left Book Club,[1] he explained that, in looking for a good sub-editor for a proposed left-wing weekly, he wanted a man who 'must combine initiative with absolutely immediate and unquestioning obedience to my instructions, however foolish they may seem to him'.[2] Gollancz's political views were at that time on the far left, though he was not exactly a communist. He was, however, a pacifist.

Strachey passed the summer of 1932 revising his book. He consulted several people on details. Far the most important question was that of the communist reaction. He sent a draft to Dutt and went to Brussels to consult with him over it. Dutt's comments were made orally, but it would seem certain that his ideas were mostly accepted. Thus Strachey wrote, on return from seeing Dutt, that both he and Celia found the 'sustained discussion' which they had had with him 'one of the most intellectually exciting conversations they had ever had'.[3]

It was perhaps on this occasion that when Strachey expressed the forlorn hope that, eventually, liberty of opinion would grow in Russia, Dutt replied: 'yes, yes of course. When everything is settled and secure, we shan't have the least objection to somebody saying that twice two make five, if it gives them any pleasure to do so.'[4]

Even so, after further correspondence, it was decided that no mention of Dutt should appear as an acknowledgement in the preface to the book. Strachey wrote 'I note your point about no acknowledgement to the communists. I shall feel very ungrateful but I see the necessity.'[5]

---

[1] *See* below, p. 149.
[2] Gollancz to Tom Clark, 8 January 1937, copied to Strachey.
[3] Letter to Dutt, 25 July 1932.
[4] *A Politician's View of Democracy*, written 1958.
[5] Letter to Dutt, 2 August 1932.

During the summer of 1932, meantime, Celia and Strachey moved from Sussex to a farm in Essex, Bury Farm, at Farnham, a village near Bishop's Stortford. Neither of them had previously known that part of England, and they were drawn to it because of the friendship of Francis Meynell, with whom Strachey had often played cricket in that neighbourhood and who lived nearby at Toppesfield: and there *The Coming Struggle for Power* was finished, and despatched to the printer.

At Bury Farm, Strachey began seriously to feel the physical consequences of his undecided situation. Should he marry Celia or return to Esther? The indecision eventually made him ill. He would lie on his bed, immobile, his eyes rolling, unable to work, for several weeks, but with no obvious disease. Celia thought that he was going mad. In desperation, she took a flat in London in Half Moon Street, to seek help for him. In the end, she rang up, and then went to see, Ernest Jones, the best Freudian analyst in London, and afterwards famous as Freud's biographer. She had not met him before but, of course, knew of him. Jones listened and told her to telephone him, while sitting in such a situation that Strachey could hear what was said. She did so the next day. Jones shouted down the telephone, emphasizing the first word: '*Drive* him back to work. And then, when he has recovered somewhat, let him come and see me.' This shock treatment was extraordinarily successful. Strachey was amazed to hear Jones's powerful voice on the telephone, he did return to work and he did visit Jones. The latter recommended a full analysis, and suggested that Celia should also undertake this therapy. They agreed and for the next three years both went to analysis separately, three times a week: Strachey to Denis Carroll, a bluff English practitioner, and Celia to Melitta Schmideberg, the daughter of Melanie Klein. Sometimes they would stay in London, sometimes they would go up and down from Essex in the day. Carroll was a suitable analyst for Strachey, since his rough-and-ready, rather naval, manner was exactly the type to give Strachey confidence.

The long-term consequences of this experience for Strachey are difficult to estimate: some of his later associates wondered whether the apparent coldness or rationality of his conversation derived from his analysis. Old friends, however, believe that he never changed in manner from Oxford days. But this analysis was one of the most critical periods of Strachey's life: the subject was often brought by him into his conversation, and he persistently analysed his own motives.

It is, perhaps, now time to speak of Celia, with whom in fact Strachey remained for the rest of his life. She was, as has already been seen, lively, high-spirited, energetic and devoted to Strachey. She was perfectly equipped to share Strachey's intellectual life, and he always talked matters over with her before he put pen to paper, or before he committed himself to a particular line of political action. Their life was indeed a perpetual dialogue on political matters. She had read some economics and knew something of Marx, and her background, *sehrmusikalish* and artistic, had many points in common with Strachey's. Her degree at Oxford had been in English, afterwards in Economics. She was an intense woman: Osbert Lancaster recalls her in 1932 or 1933 explaining that Strachey's service at tennis had improved since his analysis had begun. But she was intelligent, witty and quick and, while some men look to their wives for a complete contrast from their professional lives, Celia was able to appreciate that Strachey required a companion in the political struggle, and a woman capable of making up her own mind on political questions or on matters where character plays a certain part. She explained Strachey's marriage to Esther as if it were the consequence of some unusual disease and her own part in breaking that association as a salutary therapy.

By this time, Strachey had also expressed the wish to join the communist party proper. This request was, however, not entirely welcome to the party authorities. Pollitt, the Secretary General, had apparently 'entreated' Strachey to join the party, but Dutt and the other leaders were uncertain whether Strachey's intellectual wanderings had really come to an end or whether his new attachment to them, though doubtless springing from conviction, was likely to be as shortlived as his friendship with Mosley. His political course then seemed unsteady, though there was, as has been seen, rather more logic to it than appeared at first sight. The communists could not have been enthusiastic, either, about Strachey's analysis with Denis Carroll, though they knew of it, and Dutt, Strachey and Celia talked a great deal about Freud and Marxism, particularly about Engels' book on the family. The consequence was that Dutt and his colleagues hesitated; they wondered whether Strachey was quite ready to join the party. After a while, too, they added the argument that, even if Strachey were to become a communist, he could do more for the party if he were not a paid-up member. Strachey himself saw the force of this argument and he never became a full member. He was always interested in the intricate question as to whether Marxism and Freud could be combined.

It seems also possible that the communists, when considering Strachey's request to join them, may have been concerned a little as to how disciplined this argumentative scion of the bourgeoisie might turn out. Dutt, for instance, wrote to Strachey in January 1932, after a long castigation of the Labour movement, and with an apology lest he was being overharsh: 'It is one thing to reach a certain intellectual agreement with the correctness of the communist analysis, as demonstrated by events. It is another thing to reach real revolutionary consciousness, so that the question of entering the revolutionary movement no longer appears as a question of making sacrifices, losing valuable opportunities of work etc., but, on the contrary, as the only possible basis of work and realization.'[1]

Celia, on the other hand, now became a party member. Communism suited her temperament more than it did Strachey's. One friend of theirs, Jurgen Kutchinski, a German communist, would joke that Celia was 'the better man of the two': and perhaps, so far as communism went, there was truth in this.

The communists also seemed uncertain as to how to judge Strachey's role in the New Party. Thus William Rust, editor of the *Daily Worker*, and one of the party's stalwarts, wrote, in respect of an article which Strachey had sent to him for use in the *Daily Worker* in mid June 1932, that 'when I asked you to write the article from the standpoint of criticizing your own mistakes, I did not mean that it should strike such a personal note as is done

[1] Dutt to Strachey, January 1932, from 82 Avenue des Armures, Brussels.

in the first part, where there is also a hint of patronage to the *Daily Worker* and the Party. It seems to me that the main body of the article still shows a misunderstanding of the real role of the New Party. . . . What chances do you think there were of the New Party developing into a working-class party? Surely there were none at all, under any circumstances. . . . Then you also speak of Mosley developing a "new line" after a "few months". Surely it is clear that there was no question of a new line being developed? Certainly Mosley may have come out more openly and you, who did not realize where you were going, then began to see what the result was. But it is quite false to suggest that Mosley tried to develop a new line and failed because his associates would not become fascists etc. . . . Whether you and Young were responsible for the splitting up of the New Party is by no means a vital question. The real question is whether you can now show to the workers that you fully understand that your activity in the Labour Party as well as the New Party was absolutely wrong and opposed to the interests of the working class.' After this rebuke, Rust went on, 'I am sure that you will appreciate the fact that I and the other comrades in the party are not trying to lay down strict conditions and to prevent you from serving the party. [But] Your past training and associations make it very difficult for you effectively to throw off wrong ideas and to become an effective worker in the revolutionary movement.'[1] The article, slightly revised, was published as Strachey's first signed contribution to the *Daily Worker* in late June.[2]

At this time, Strachey was soon to be busy on a specific task which he had selected for himself to carry out for the party's benefit. This was a pamphlet which he hoped would win over the left of the Independent Labour Party to the communists. Perhaps he may even have thought that it could be converted into a new political grouping around himself. Dutt urged him on this course in several letters from Brussels: 'either the mass of them come over in a bloc or they break up.' Could not Strachey begin a discussion with the I.L.P. 'in such a way that it becomes clear that the answer and prospect can only point to communism. . .'? This

[1] Rust to Strachey, 15 June 1932.
[2] 'Fascism in Britain', *Daily Worker*, 30 June 1932.

would be directed particularly towards the left of the I.L.P., adding in 'some natural honest scorn for Maxton-Brockwayism'.[1] The I.L.P. did soon disaffiliate from the Labour party and several of its members did ultimately join the communist party but not, in fact, as a bloc, and not effectively.

The argument continued while Strachey, with Celia, went off to the Amsterdam Anti-War congress, a big meeting organized by Willi Muenzenberg, the Comintern propaganda wizard. This was the first occasion that Strachey had appeared at a large communist gathering. It took place at a tense moment in European politics, for this was, of course, the last summer of the Weimar republic, and the apparent imminence of disaster gave Strachey even further proof, if he had needed it, that 'the communist analysis' was the correct one. Also, perhaps, he was influenced by propaganda and by the exhilarating sensation of being close to a great cause.

Afterwards, as if to make the point even firmer, Strachey and Celia went off to stay in Austria with old friends of the former's, the Zeppelins, at Wernberg on the Drau, near Villach. Countess von Zeppelin had been as a girl a frequent visitor to Newlands Corner. Strachey was there busy correcting proofs of *The Coming Struggle for Power*. But, since Count von Zeppelin was drawn towards the Nazis, the arguments were too fierce for comfort and, after parting, the four never met again. (The Count later died, or was murdered, in the course of the Second World War.)

It may seem surprising that Strachey was so apparently unaffected in his motives by what was actually going on in 1932 in Russia. He did, years later, answer this criticism. In 1931, he said, the ideal or temporary state of things in Russia seemed a matter of secondary importance. 'In front of everybody's eyes, the Marxist prognosis of the development of a latter day capitalism was apparently fulfilling itself. Outside Russia, it was becoming more and more impossible to use anything like the whole of the productive apparatus; unemployment was consequently becoming endemic; the misery of the wage earners and peasants was ever-increasing . . . social democratic methods had failed: and, finally, Fascism was being established . . . and, decisively, in Germany,

[1] Dutt to Strachey, 2 August 1932.

one of the major advanced capitalisms . . . this apparition of evil incarnate, in the form of Fascism . . . gave the communist argument power. . . . Nazi Germany . . . was seen as the exemplar which each and every capitalist society must soon imitate. . . . How much did even the ugliest features of the new socialist society matter if it gave even the possibility of the rebuilding of civilization upon a viable basis?'[1] Strachey had, of course, been to Russia, unlike most of the new communists of the 1930s, and, if he had been critical of some aspects of what he had seen, this seemed less and less relevant.

During all these changes and political hesitations by Strachey, between 1929 and 1932, he was followed by his sister, Amabel Williams-Ellis. She, also, had 'a look at Mosley' before jumping off into the astringent waters of communism, *Anti-Dühring*, by Engels, apparently being decisive in her political education. But she saw less of Strachey than she had in the past. Celia and Amabel were not sympathetic to each other, and Celia knew that Amabel disapproved of her marrying Strachey. Amabel was thus influenced by her brother in a general sense, at this time, but they were not in close touch. (In 1934, Amabel joined the communist literary journal the *Left Review*, and was an assistant editor with Tom Wintringham and Montagu Slater, two prominent English middle-class communists.)

As for Esther, by the time *The Coming Struggle for Power* was published in the autumn, she had resigned herself to the finality of her separation from Strachey; she never became a communist, nor even a socialist; and it is difficult not to think that this factor, as well as the concurrent analysis, must have played its part in Strachey's decision to break finally with her. Boothby saw Esther a few months later in New York, and wrote that she seemed hurt that Strachey had left the day of her father's funeral. 'She said (without bitterness) that, after all, you had benefited by his money, and might have stayed. . . . To this, I could only reply that it was unlike you, as you were, without exception, the most sympathetic person in the world. Which she didn't deny.' By this time, Esther had made, in fact, something of a recovery. 'Her life,' Boothby reported her to have said, 'was here and in

[1] Strachey, *The Strangled Cry*, p. 18.

Paris. And so, by God, it is. You should have seen her at a cock-tail party last night. Right at the top of her form. I find her, as always, exhausting. But I like her. . . . I told her that your life must be based on the English countryside for some time to come, at any rate, and that she would cut her throat there. I told her that Celia was the girl for you, and that the sooner you got married, the better. . . . She has, I think, lonely moments. But only moments. She can, and will, recapture the only sort of life which could ever have made her happy. . . .'[1] Soon after this, Strachey did make the deci-sion to divorce Esther, and to marry Celia when that was complete.

Strachey, meantime, was indeed living in the country, with, as Nancy Cunard put it in a letter to him from the South of France, 'the pot of tea and the English gas fire. I envy you! I wish I had both *now*, instead of being once more on this lousy playground . . . and the bottle of Vichy and heatless radiator.'[2] She also soon followed Strachey into the communist world, to which she had always been attracted since the 1920s.

But the tension of the summer of 1932 did communicate itself even to the English countryside, despite the belief of Boothby and Nancy Cunard in its therapeutic qualities. While Strachey wrote and sawed wood, and Celia grew vegetables, both imagined that Mosley might attempt to have his own back on him. There was no shadow of proof that this might really happen, but the noise of a motorbicycle at night often seemed, at Bury Farm, to betoken a possible assassin. One day Strachey, Celia, Desmond Bernal, John Pilley, a physicist from Bristol University, and Harry Thomson, solicitor to the *Daily Worker*, were sitting under the apple tree discussing, in the beautiful summer evening, the best way to 'get rid' of Mosley. They heard a sinister noise, as of a gun going off by accident. All the party then methodically searched the hedgerows round the house for the enemy assault party. At last, Harry Thomson left and Strachey, Celia and the others retired. Just when going to sleep, Celia heard the sinister noise again. This time she recognized it. It was an apple falling from a tree. Nevertheless, the next week Strachey bought a revolver and kept it in his underclothes drawer.

[1] Boothby to Strachey, 11 November 1932.
[2] Nancy Cunard to Strachey, 29 November 1932.

Note – The Future of Esther

Esther eventually married again to Chester Arthur, an American, and grandson of the President. This marriage was also unsuccessful. After the Second World War, she lived in Paris, holding court among the intellectual world of Parisian Americans. She died in 1962. The Stracheys remained on excellent terms with her in later years and saw her whenever they went through France.

Chapter 9 / THE COMING STRUGGLE FOR POWER

Between 1932 and 1935, Strachey published three political books which established him as the most articulate spokesman for Marxism in Britain, indeed probably the most respectable English Marxist. *The Coming Struggle for Power* appeared in November 1931, *The Menace of Fascism* about the same time the following year, and *The Nature of the Capitalist Crisis* in February 1935. The first was a sophisticated interpretation of Marxism – sophisticated, in that it was not only free of jargon but dealt with such matters as literature and art. The second was a disturbing polemical tract on the theme of what was apparently ahead after the Nazi capture of power in Germany. The third was a more specifically economic text and contains more original thinking. These books were immensely influential. They could be read by people unable to cope with Marx himself. Well-intentioned, middle-class women could read them – as one of them said later 'under the hair dryer' – and appreciate their good writing. Probably these three books converted more people to communism, or to the communist way of thought, than anything else. Their author remained theoretically outside the party. In this respect, he resembled Malraux, who played the same role in France, for different reasons.

Strachey personally considered these books to have immense

educational importance. As he put it in a letter in 1934 to Gollancz: 'I do believe that I happen to be the only person who is putting over this particular information which people desperately need today, in a form which they can comprehend.'[1]

Strachey in consequence became in some respects an international figure, a familiar figure at communist-sponsored international conferences, and in international communist journals. Everywhere, even in Latin America and the U.S., his ideas excited interest. Romulo Betancourt, among hundreds of others, recalled that Strachey had persuaded him to become a communist, and Strachey was plainly delighted to receive a letter from Gide, in November 1934, saying that he had read Strachey's 'The Education of a Communist', in *Littérature Internationale* (a communist journal edited in Moscow) with 'the most lively interest and great joy', and had even read it aloud at a gathering.[2]

Considering the actual influence of these books, their first sales scarcely seem substantial: thus *The Coming Struggle for Power* sold, in its original 9/- edition, 1,664 copies; but it afterwards sold 7,486 and 2,503 copies in a 1934 cheap edition in cloth, at 5/- and paper, at 3/6; while *The Menace of Fascism* sold 4,871 in all.[3] *The Coming Struggle for Power* was later put out in yet another cheap edition, and sold another 3,125 copies over six years until 1943. Some other books by Strachey did even better, as will be seen, and his pamphlet, *Why You Should Be a Socialist*, the '2d Strachey' published in 1938, and, in effect, a *précis* of all his ideas, sold over 300,000 copies in a few weeks.[4]

The first of these books, *The Coming Struggle for Power*, published on 7 November 1932, was the most successful. It was widely reviewed, and usually favourably. The Beaverbrook Press even hailed it with enthusiasm. Kingsley Martin in his life of Harold Laski spoke of it as the 'most influential single Marxist publication. . . .'[5] It reads well over forty years on. First, it is full of sharp remarks: 'What after all is Protestantism but the free

[1] Letter from Strachey to Gollancz, 12 October 1934.
[2] Letter of Gide, 1 November 1934. This also appeared in the *Left Review*.
[3] Analysis of Strachey sales made by Messrs Gollancz, 1971.
[4] *See* below, p. 173.
[5] Kingsley Martin, *Harold Laski*, p. 104.

market in God?'[1] or 'we often fail to realize the essential fact about feudalism, the fact that you did not in the Middle Ages . . . live by buying and selling'.[2] There are also jokes: considering the importance of woollen goods in England not only the Lord Chancellor but the whole House of Lords should sit on the woolsack. It dealt with subjects other than economics. The chapters on literature – Wells, Huxley, Faulkner, Lawrence and Waugh – are all put in their place in the tide of declining capitalism. Waugh, Strachey tells us, had only three alternatives open to him after writing *Decline and Fall*: 'to commit suicide, become a communist, or immerse himself within the Catholic Church. He chose the last (and easiest) alternative.'[3]

Strachey began the book with an entertaining and short exposition of the general Marxist theory of history. Twentieth-century conditions had altered the circumstances of Marxism as they had seemed to be in the nineteenth century: these conditions had brought with them monopoly, nationalism and, after 1919, unstable money. None of these things was the cause of the capitalist crisis, whose real nature derived from the essential features of capitalism, of the fact, that is, that capitalist production was carried on without plan, that its only regulating mechanism was the mechanism of the market, and that the wealth of the community was concentrated in the small number of persons who owned the means of production. Capitalist crises were due to the anarchy of production which must always characterize any system dependent upon the mechanism of the market. Keynes might think that by controlling the rates of interest, he (or the government) could contain the volume of investment, but he was deluding himself. The religion, science and art of capitalism were also defunct or, in the case of some modern authors, dedicated to describing its weaknesses, though 'an appallingly large number of even the best intelligences are not today engaged in the task of burying the vast and slowly expiring boom of capitalist culture. They are taking no part in the essential work of clearing the ground for the new order.'[4]

All this was put in rather grandiose terms – 'although the

[1] Strachey, *The Coming Struggle For Power*, p. 18.
[2] *Loc. cit.*   [3] *Ibid.*, p. 223.   [4] *Ibid.*, p. 157.

activities by which men keep alive must be the foundation of any society, they are only the foundation. And men do not live on foundations alone. There is no need to deny the importance of the social edifice simply because we have at length discovered what its foundations are made of. And if a dry rot, starting quite explicably in those foundations spreads, as it must, to the whole great structure of civilization, if it lends the odour of decay even to the highest pinnacles of thought, to the philosophical religious, aesthetic and scientific concepts which crown the whole building, then certainly the decay of these higher parts will be scarcely less fatal to the building than was the original decay of the foundations.'[1] The chapter on religion is an admirable piece of writing in the grand old style. Freud ('one of the last great theorists of the European capitalist class') was invoked to assist the argument.

The only way, Strachey continued, whereby modern capitalism in its last stages could reassert itself was by dropping democratic forms, liberal ideas and democratic methods: 'Direct, open terror against the workers, violent aggression against its rivals, can alone enable a modern empire to maintain itself. A name for such a policy has been found: it is fascism.'[2] On the other hand, '160 million men and women have already... leapt out of the kingdom of necessity towards the kingdom of freedom – in Russia.'

Towards the end of the book, Strachey included a long analysis of the situation in England in 1931, written by Aneurin Bevan, though published simply as by 'the most gifted' of the younger supporters of the leadership of the Labour party.[3] (Bevan's contribution to other sections of the book is in dispute: Jennie Lee, who shortly married Bevan, recalls him stimulating Strachey to new fantasies and inventions, Celia denies this altogether. The genesis of ideas is, however, always a matter of controversy and this argument is now difficult to resolve. Jennie Lee said she recalled Bevan walking up and down in Strachey's drawing room, very excited, and Strachey 'milking him'; Celia has no recollection of this and hotly denies it.)

[1] *Loc. cit.*   [2] *Ibid.*, p. 245.
[3] *Ibid.*, p. 318–21. *See* Foot, *op. cit.*, p. 149n.

The last three chapters of the book consist of a measured, but passionate, appeal for the establishment of communism in Britain. Striking among the visions in this description of Utopia is the assertion that 'there cannot ever be (unless very temporarily) two communist nations in the world at the same time. . . .' Communism provided a basis by which the world could be united at last. As to methods, Strachey argued that the 'assumption of power by the workers can occur by means of revolution alone'. The argument is powerfully concluded. The reader of the 1930s was left to think, *'yes, that is how it will happen'*; there is no avoiding it; the revolution is inevitable, the disintegration of the ruling class almost complete, the collapse of capitalism unavoidable. 'There is no force on earth,' Strachey concluded 'which can long prevent the workers of the world from building a new and stable civilization for themselves on the basis of the common ownership of the means of production.' So the book was an appeal to the gloomy opportunist as much as to the idealist: to the latter it might depict a Utopia, but to the former it said 'look, here is the bandwagon: jump on it now or you'll be too late'.

Old friends wrote with enthusiasm. Typical was Boothby, staying in Long Island with a millionaire, Harrison Williams, who wrote: 'I've read the book with the greatest interest and congratulate you on your achievement. It is the first time the materialistic theory has ever been presented to the British public in readable form . . . in addition, it is a superb intellectual performance. . . . Needless to say, I disagreed with most of it.' Boothby denied vigorously that materialism was the main force in life and argued that chance always plays a large part. He added, 'the motive that has possessed you for the last ten years and which I have watched with such lively interest, has been the urge towards Faith. Without it, you have felt life would be intolerable. So the struggle has gone on and on, now waxing, now waning, with many doubts and hesitations, moments of valour and moments of timidity, until one day – plop – you got it. And now there you are. Full of Faith! And happier than you've ever been. [Though] I don't call your particular urge a material one. . . .' As for Boothby, 'The proletariat, the red flag, the Host, the Virgin and Child, unadulterated materialism, unadulterated spiritualism, I'll have nothing to do with any of it. I've always thought the Holy Roman Church with its fanaticism, its inquisition and its fundamental falsity, the most sinister organization in the history of mankind. Now it may be that we are in for a similar racket at the hands of the Third International and the G.P.U. Equally fanatical, equally cruel, equally false. . . .'[1]

He then went on: '[But] I envy you your present position. You've got your faith, your life, your girl, and your medium of expression. You are a brilliant writer (I do not exaggerate). And whatever happens, you are home. Whether you are destined to influence the course of events by ideas or by actions, or first one, and then the other, is uncertain and almost irrelevant. The point is that the obvious path spreads out before you to self-fulfilment. . . .'

The critical success of *The Coming Struggle for Power* caused Strachey to begin to feel that his influence, within the communist movement, might be exerted a little more. In November 1932, he wrote to Dutt suggesting that the membership of the communist party of 5,000 was far too small. That meant that 'every single party worker is grossly overworked'. That, Strachey believed, was simply because 'the average party worker does not want new recruits into his or her *local*'. 'Naturally,' he added, 'I am in the worst possible position for raising this matter with anyone. Everyone will simply think that I am making a fuss about my own case. Actually, *my* only complaint – and that doesn't matter a pin – is not against you for keeping me out of the party, which I think was very logical of you – but against Harry Pollitt for entreating me to join it – without, apparently, having got his authority for doing so. Ever since I have been working with the party . . . I've had nothing but the greatest kindness and helpfulness.' Dutt and other communist party leaders continued to find Strachey's ideas helpful and stimulating. Furthermore, Strachey and Celia helped Dutt with money when, in early 1933, Mrs Dutt became seriously ill, at a time when their own finances were far from fixed and when, indeed, both Strachey and Celia were themselves ill, the former from concussion by hitting his

[1] Boothby to Strachey, 7 November 1932.

head in the dark, and the latter from eye-strain in reading to him afterwards. They also afterwards helped Pollitt, when his baby son Brian was ill.[1]

Strachey's position was thus unique and perhaps, after a time, he began to see some of its advantages. It is difficult, after all, imagining an ordinary party member writing as he did, in April 1934, to Dutt suggesting that the party was narrow-minded in its failure to recognize favourably a declaration by a number of prominent Labour party intellectuals in favour of a united front with the communists.[2] 'The whole thing,' Strachey wrote, 'seems to me a question of tone and manners. I sometimes feel that communists who have a grasp of Marxian theory find it almost impossible to believe the importance which tone of voice has in dealing with non-Marxians; if the C.P. handles the matter in this sort of way, success is utterly impossible and the only prospect in front of the British workers is massacre. . . . [But] in any case I shall, of course, continue to do what I am instructed to do whatever the party decides is the right way. . . .'[3]

This problem came up acutely during 1933 over the continuing temptations offered to the communists by the disintegration of the I.L.P. At this time, the I.L.P. was in considerable difficulties, with many members indeed drifting over to the communists. Brockway, the chairman, and editor of the *New Leader*, had made an effort to prevent this, suggesting that some of the blame for the seizure of power by the Nazis had to be attributed to the communists, thus inviting a vigorous attack from Pollitt, under the headline: 'Brockway goes over to Counter-Revolution.' This seemed to Strachey far-fetched and ineffective. To Dutt he wrote, 'The I.L.P. leaders, however politically illiterate they may be, are quite experienced, subtle and unscrupulous controversialists. I am particularly worried about the effect of the German experience. It is so damnably easy for the enemies of the party to put over the Brockway case if the "C.P. of Germany

[1] Letters to Dutt.
[2] These were Frank Wise, Douglas Cole and Hamilton Fyfe. *See* letter in *Daily Worker*, 20 April 1932.
[3] Letter of Strachey to Dutt, 24 April 1932. Dutt actually agreed with Strachey on this point, as shown by his letter to Strachey of 2 June 1932.

was to blame too". Could the party have a really careful and exhaustive pamphlet written on the History of the German working class from 1918 onwards . . . ?'[1]

An entertaining glimpse of Strachey in 1933 is caught in a memoir by Patricia Cockburn, whose husband-to-be, Claud Cockburn, had founded his extraordinary newsheet, The Week, in March 1933. Strachey had tried to secure that The Week should have a conventional committee of management, treasurer, auditor and so on, and was distressed to find that Cockburn had begun the journal without following his advice. He did his best, at dinner at the Café Royal, to persuade Patricia Cockburn of the dangers of even associating with Claud, whom he described as a dangerous adventurer. He also hinted that the only explanation was that Cockburn, already more or less a communist, must have been in touch with Moscow before embarking on such a risky plan. He had not been so.[2]

Strachey had, meantime, been working on his next book, The Menace of Fascism, a long polemic against the swelling tide of Nazism and fascism in Europe generally. By this time, Hitler was in power, and imaginative people on the left – among them Gollancz – saw immediately what this meant. The book was deliberately provocative. 'I am frightfully keen on it,' Strachey wrote to Gollancz, who was going to publish it. 'It is highly polemical and sensational in parts. . . . I am doing my damnedest to make an overwhelming emotional appeal, backed by solid reasoning.'[3] To Dutt he wrote apologetically, 'It makes no attempt to take the reader the whole way to the full communist position.'[4] Even so, as with his previous book, Strachey took into account virtually all the points suggested by Dutt, Pollitt and Emile Burns, another member of the communist central committee, concerned with literary and intellectual activities.[5]

Soon after this publication (on 7 July 1933), with his divorce from Esther complete, Strachey regularized his friendship with

[1] Strachey to Pollitt, 23 June 1933, and Strachey to Dutt, same date.
[2] Patricia Cockburn, The Years Of The Week, pp. 17–18.
[3] Strachey to Gollancz, 23 April 1933.
[4] Strachey to Dutt, 23 June 1933.
[5] Strachey to Pollitt, 23 June.

Celia. They were married in Saint Pancras Registry Office on 13 October 1933. Present were Boothby, Amabel Williams-Ellis, Strachey's sister and Celia's mother. Mrs Amy Strachey was studiously absent. In the afternoon, both Celia and Strachey went to their analysts. That night, Strachey went to the U.S. on his first lecture tour. Celia remained behind, in a flat in Regent Square. While in the U.S., on this first visit there since the end of his marriage to Esther, Strachey conscientiously put into practice his admiration for the Soviet Union by purchasing $3,600-worth of 7% Soviet bonds of the Second Five Year Plan, through Miles Sherover, of the Soviet American securities corporation.

Strachey was so busy with writing that he was not very active in politics as such. He did, however, take part in a famous communist demonstration in Hyde Park against Mosley on 9 September 1934. Large detachments of police were necessary to keep the two meetings apart. Here Strachey appeared what his old friend of his own Mosley days, Allan Young, described in a letter as 'the most finished, calm, and distinguished of mob orators'. At this meeting, Mosley attempted what Strachey later described as 'an attempt to overcome London with his fascist thugs'.[1] The anti-fascist demonstration had, on this occasion, been organized by a new 'coordinating committee for Anti Fascist activities', an offshoot of the British branch of 'the World Movement against Fascism and War', an organization set up under the aegis of the Third International by the imaginative Willi Muenzenburg, during the Amsterdam congress in 1932. The plan was that well-intentioned and liberal anti-fascists of all complexions should attach themselves to an organization which was basically communist-run. Strachey was an ideal chief of this body, and his name attracted many to the cause. The coordinating committee in 1934 was able to recruit Maxton, the chief Labour whip in the House of Lords, and other sound names. The World Movement against Fascism and War was run from Paris and carried on innumerable activities, some admirable, some questionable. Thus, when in February 1935 a socialist deputy, González Peña, was condemned to death in Spain after the Asturias rising, the committee in Paris (of which the novelist Henri Barbusse was

[1] Dundee election special, 18 June 1945.

the titular leader) in their telegram of protest to Madrid 'used several signatures without previous demand. We ask you, dear comrades, to excuse our not having asked your permission in advance . . . and to accept our fraternal anti-fascist greetings.'[1]

Meantime, Strachey was busy on the third of his political books, which he entitled *The Nature of Capitalist Crisis*. This was finished in the late summer of 1934 and published on 11 March 1935. Once again, Dutt helped him a good deal with some of the thinking. Thus Strachey wrote to Dutt, in November 1934, that he 'drastically reformulated the "crisis analysis" part of my book as a result of our discussions and thinking the whole thing over as carefully as I can'.[2] He was also, as in the past, anxious to recognize Dutt's help in a preface, but Dutt's reply was that he 'should definitely prefer not'.[3]

The book, for all its portentous title, is still probably the most readable expression of the communist case as it seemed in 1935. For, of course, it did then seem, as the first chapter of the book put it, that the capitalist world was going through 'the most severe economic crisis which it has hitherto encountered'.

Strachey criticized Keynes, and also Lionel Robbins,[4] as excessively concerned with monetary undertakings. All professional economists seemed to regard a restoration of the rate of profit as a prerequisite of economic recovery. They differed only as to method. Did we not need therefore a new set of economic categories and concepts?

Nassau Senior, Strachey's great-grandfather, had rejected the theory of value. Other capitalist economists had done the same. This rejection was the fatal turning-point. Marx had not made this mistake, and made the critical distinction between labour and labour power: an artisan or peasant sells his labour embodied in a commodity on the market; a worker sells his labour power to a capitalist employer who then sells this worker's labour. This apparently terminological distinction was critical. A long dis-

---

[1] Letter to Strachey, 5 February 1934. González Peña was, in fact, pardoned.
[2] Strachey to Dutt, 23 November 1934.
[3] Dutt to Strachey, 30 November 1934.
[4] Lionel Robbins, later Lord Robbins, born 1898. At this time Professor of Economics at L.S.E.

quisition followed, covering several chapters, all justifying Marx's theory of Value, and applying Marx to the existing crisis. He believed that the application, for instance, of Marxism to Germany proved that German industrialists had either to expand or to burst.[1] The last chapter, 'The Two Futures', was an eloquent description of a world hovering between communism and barbarism. *The Nature of Capitalist Crisis* sold 2,437 copies in its first edition. Two later cheap editions in cloth and paper sold 2,022 and 1,677 respectively.

However, long before this, Strachey had returned to his series of complaints at the management of the communist movement. In early November 1934, a meeting had been held to discuss a new anti-fascist newspaper. The plan was that, though this would be edited by a communist (Claud Cockburn, then already editor of *The Week* and just back from reporting the Aturias revolution for the *Daily Worker*), it should represent 'all anti-fascist opinion', and, in effect, would be inspired by the committee of which Strachey was chairman. For, by this time, the world communist movement was moving gradually and reluctantly towards a renewal of the United Front policies which had characterized it in the 1920s, in order, primarily, to avoid war. But nothing was done about the paper by the party. 'I have seen Cockburn several times, in the meanwhile, and have each time reminded him about the dummy and he has each time told me that he is getting on with it, but he is overworked . . . and, of course, this is absolutely true. It is not in the least his fault . . . this whole business seems to me extremely typical of a lot of our work in this country today. We take solemn decisions to do things, and then, because we don't face up to securing the necessary means to do them, nothing happens for a long time. . . . We rush round with our hair on end from committee to committee, deciding everything in a rush and therefore usually deciding it wrong. I believe we should be ten times more effective if we did half the things which we do now. . . . I do think that you and Harry ought to reconsider the matter very very carefully.'

Dutt answered: 'of course, you are in great part right. . . . But there is another side to it. . . . Much as we should like to have

[1] Strachey, *Nature of Capitalist Crisis*, p. 374.

everything neat and orderly (and there isn't a better organizer in
the movement than Harry), one man, one job, and the rest of it,
it simply can't be done; and we can't solve it by arbitrarily proposing to cut off some things; the needs of the movement don't
allow it. The conditions of work in the revolutionary movement
are like that, appalling to an orderly business outlook, and
eternal shortages of facilities, material and personnel; and yet,
things have to get done, and do get done, even though not always
satisfactorily and with some terrible incidental misses, by
enormous energy, enthusiasm, drive, daily miracle-working,
overcoming the difficulties . . . it is the way everything worthwhile has been done in the movement, from the smallest paper
we have ever made a success of, to the October Revolution,
always against impossibilities pointed out by every wise, practical
person . . . "wise" "practical" outlook constituting Menshevism.
. . . There was just a feeling both Harry and I get from your
letter – the danger of seeing all the difficulties too clearly, rather
than putting in the forefront the determination to get over them.
. . . It's no good telling us you aren't a leader, as you argued here;
you are, in every sense, both publicly and in fact; and, therefore,
an enormous lot depends on you.'[1]

Strachey was left to brood on this for some time. There were
some respects in which Dutt's argument was right. The October
Revolution had *not* been launched by a neat committee. Meantime, Strachey's first lecture tour to the U.S. had been a success.
In consequence, Strachey received a further invitation for the
winter of 1934–5 and, on this occasion, took his wife and a baby,
Charles, who had been born to Celia in June 1934.

Strachey and Celia left for the U.S. on 18 December 1934.
Their intention was to remain until April.

Strachey's books had been successful in the U.S., as well as in
England. His books sold well there and, to a new generation of
intellectual left-wing people of middle-class origins, he was
almost as much of a prophet as at home. The lecture tour of
1933–4 had helped to establish him in the public mind and that
of 1934–5 was consistently successful, making its conclusion even
more bizarre.

[1] Dutt to Strachey, 30 November 1934.

In January, Strachey went away to the west of the U.S. 'preaching communism'.[1] Celia stayed in New York in a flat in Riverside Drive with, she recalls, a Nazi maid, who had the irritating habit of referring to baby Charles as Max Schmelling – the German world heavyweight champion. She told the *New York World Telegram* of 14 March 1935, how, like Dot in Mary Macarthy's *The Group*, she and her son liked to sit on the sunny side of Broadway, and tell the mothers that they ought to nurse their own babies instead of feeding them from bottles.[2]

Strachey stayed with Charlie Chaplin and Paulette Goddard in Hollywood, and even planned a film with them about Napoleon for which he wrote a script, 'What do you think of the idea of seeing the battle of Lodi while still hearing Bonaparte's voice in the garden?'[3] he asked Chaplin. The high point, however, of Strachey's tour was his arrest in Chicago in March.

His tour had all the time received critical attention from the Hearst newspapers, which called often for his deportation as a communist. Strachey had even himself written an article on the subject 'Should I be deported?' A lecture by him at the San Francisco Centre of the League of Women Voters had caused a good deal of opposition, with some of the more patriotic club-women trying unsuccessfully to prevent the lecture being given. But, in Chicago, things finally went less well for Strachey, though by then he had given over fifty lectures. He had just finished an address at the synagogue of the 'North Shore congregation of Israel', in a suburb of Chicago, in which he had 'advocated the overthrow of the capitalistic system'. He was seized by inspectors of the department of immigration, reinforced by a squad of local policemen. Strachey was accused of entering the U.S. by means of false statements, and only released on his own promise to appear in the office of the director of the Chicago Immigration department the following day. Meantime, Colonel McCormack, the director of Immigration in Washington, announced that Strachey had been arrested since he had denied, on arrival in New York, that he 'advocated or believed in over-

[1] Celia to Gollancz, letter of January 1935.
[2] *N.Y. World Telegram*, 14 March 1935.
[3] Strachey to Chaplin, 14 July 1935.

throwing the Government of the U.S. by force or violence', and also since he denied belonging to any organization which had such aims. It had also been established that Strachey was not merely a philosophical communist, but an active advocate of communism. Strachey, in his own writings, had spoken of 'we communists' and had said that he was a 'communist drummer, peddling Marxism instead of drugs'.[1]

The following day Strachey was served with a deportation warrant, but released on bail, on receipt of $500 in Liberty bonds provided for Strachey by Robert Lovett, Professor of English at the University of Chicago and representative of the Civil Liberties Union. A hearing was then fixed for the following week either in Washington, Chicago or New York, wherever Strachey cared to be. In the meantime, Strachey was free to carry on and, indeed, to complete his lecture tour.

This event ensured the tumultuous success of the next week's lectures, and provided publicity for Strachey's books. Meantime, his friends in New York were raising protests against the Government's action. Strachey's journey to Cleveland, Ohio, in black leather coat (standard communist garb) and black hat, was followed with eager attention by the Press. His remarks to reporters were cool: 'apparently this unfortunate situation is the result of a belief that I am a member of the communist party,' he told the *New York World Telegram*, 'it's all in the day's work;' and went to debate at Cleveland about communism with Herbert Agar, the writer. The audience of 2,500 listened with much pleasure to hear Strachey repeat his usual speech that capitalism was doomed. Communism, he said, merely meant the cooperative use of the right instruments. 'It's the only way of realizing democracy in this modern world.'[2]

But the U.S. Government then thought again, and summoned Strachey back to Chicago. He went, accompanied by Celia and a strong group of friends from the Civil Liberties Union and others – including Allan Taub, of *New Masses*, and Thomas

[1] *New York Times*, 13 March 1935. The two allusions had occurred in articles written by Strachey in the *Rotarian* magazine of December 1934 and *New Masses* of 26 February 1935.
[2] *N.Y. Herald Tribune*, 14 March 1935.

McKenna, secretary of the American League against War and Fascism. The hearing was brief, and adjourned to the next day. Asked to name a relation, Strachey said 'my uncle is Lord Strachie, of Sutton Court, Chew Magna, Somerset, England'.

Strachey's Press in these days assumed astronomic proportions. The most enthusiastic was a profile by Lionel Pearson in the *New York Times* in which he described as 'launching himself dynamically into forensic action; he is wildly beautiful; such at least is the testimony of adoring women who have sat at his feet'.[1]

Strachey's hearing was finally set for 21 March. He continued giving lectures, at Detroit, Yale and even New Haven High School, while protests mounted and speculation continued. Most liberal voices were in support. One opponent, however, was Walter Lippmann who, in his column, 'Today and Tomorrow', of 16 March, wrote that Strachey had neglected to 'stand up boldly and say just what a communist believes are his rights in a bourgeois capitalist and democratic society when it comes to advocating a system of government which makes no bones about its intention to destroy those rights'. Strachey, Lippmann went on, fights deportation, 'for the rather uninspired reason that, though he is a revolutionist, he is not dangerous'. But he asked Strachey to say where he stood on the issue of civil liberties.[2] Strachey wrote a long letter in reply, appearing in the *Herald Tribune* of 18 March: 'Communists hoped that their ideas could be put into effect without violence, but the capitalists never let this occur. Who now profited from civil liberties – only those rich enough to run newspapers such as Hearst. But, if freedom of speech and of the press means the right of the mass of the population to have access to, and control over, the means of publicity, then I would certainly maintain that it is capitalism which in fact, though not in form, denies this right, and that it is communism alone which will establish this right. . . .'[3] He added that communism would naturally suppress men like Hearst: and he thereby gave Lippmann an opportunity for an effective reply: 'It is precisely because they intend to destroy the liberty of men

[1] *New York Times*, 14 March 1935.
[2] *Herald Tribune*, 16 March.
[3] *Ibid.*, 18 March 1935.

who oppose them that communism and fascism present a challenge to the democratic state which it has never before had to meet.' Lippman added that 'Strachey was evidently really what is known in Russia as a radish, red on the outside and white on the inside, a gentleman who would like to have the theoretical advantages he finds in communism without its practical disadvantages. . . .'[1]

The Strachey hearing began in Chicago on 21 March, and, for the first time in history, the rule of secret deportation hearings was modified. The hearing had a farce-like character, since Strachey was due to return to Europe on 29 March, and it was possible that the deportation charge might actually delay his sailing. The hearing was characterized by the reading by immigration officials of sections from Strachey's books, followed by little speeches by Strachey in reply. Strachey was assisted by lawyers from the Civil Liberties Union headed by the famous Arthur Garfield Hays. Strachey handled his questions skilfully. A series of quotations from the communist manifesto were parried by Strachey saying that he was not a member of the communist party. Between hearings, Strachey continued to lecture, to crowded halls. In the end, on 29 March, the day that Strachey was due to sail home on the *Berengeria*, he was told that the government would abandon the proceedings. He went that night to a great dinner in Fifth Avenue, organized by the American League against War and Fascism. The audience were mostly communists who paid $1.25 for the pleasure. The dinner was full, with five hundred guests, and demands for space for two hundred additional guests was sought. In a speech at the dinner, Strachey said he was a communist, but 'not connected with the communist party. The only difference,' he added, 'is that I do not pay dues.'[2]

Strachey explained to Dutt on his return, that, in the U.S. 'the whole thing was worthwhile in the sense that it did do something to "put over" our point of view on the question of force and violence. I took the line which I learnt from Harry, of denying strongly that we ever *advocate* force or violence . . . in the *Labour Monthly* in 1925 . . . you put the point superbly, if I may

[1] *Ibid.*, 21 March 1935.
[2] *New York Post*, 30 March 1935.

say so . . . you were writing about the Liverpool conference and satirized Macdonald's speech on the basis of "vote for me" and no earthquakes. Earthquakes are only for the small countries such as Japan.'[1]

Strachey became quite conventional in some respects while he was a communist: whereas before he had settled down with Celia he had lived in a Bohemian style, he was now a householder, the earner of money and royalties, and a father. He might have welcomed the hunger marchers as they passed through Essex, but he continued to be an owner of stocks and shares, while he was writing of the decadence of capitalism, and later put his son down for Eton; 'given our system it is the best education,' he commented.[2] His houses were regularly insured, he was a member of the R.A.C., he played for, and paid his subscription to, the Bishop's Stortford Cricket Club, and he remained a shareholder in the *Spectator* – receiving indeed £254 5s in consequence in the year 1934.[3] The estate at Newlands Corner still brought him annually £422. In Strachey, muscular Christianity was replaced by athletic communism: he and Celia walked twenty-five miles a day, he played hockey with Joad and his friends on Hampstead Heath and tennis whenever he could – always anxious to win a point on the tennis court as much as in argument. Yet, if much of Strachey's life was conventional, in some ways he surprised his friends: thus, at the farm at Shalford, he and Celia one day asked a neighbour, the son of a local landowner, to lunch. The guest was surprised to find that he was solemnly introduced to the cook, Betty Goodchild, whom he had known as a village girl for years, and even more surprised to find her sitting down at the end of the table eating with her employers. She sat silent throughout the meal, and, thought the guest, rather more embarrassed than he was by the novel encounter. Strachey had also been dispossessed, on political grounds, by his uncle, Lord Strachie, and so could no longer regard himself as the residual heir, in succession to Lord Strachie's much older son, to the Strachey estate at Sutton Court and its heirlooms. This action did

[1] Strachey to Dutt, 18 May 1935.
[2] Orwell, *Complete Works*, Vol. IV, p. 45. Actually, Charles went to Westminster.
[3] Letter of Strachey's secretary, Miss Edgely, of 4 March 1935.

not seem to trouble Strachey, though he always had some family sentimentality. He would, though, have liked the family pictures, and he did once go into the question as to whether Lord Strachie had the power to dispose of Sutton Court in this manner.[1]

Lord Strachie's action carried with it seeds of difficulty. His only son was childless, and, though he had recently married, it seemed improbable that he would have children. Lord Strachie, therefore, made over Sutton Court to trustees, first on trust for his son, and afterwards for his daughter's son, on the condition that he changed his name to Strachey. The estate would then go to this grandson's family. But in perpetuity each of the successive inheritors of Sutton Court were to take the surname of Strachey. If this condition were broken, or if there were to be no male heirs, the house and two farms would go to the National Trust: the rest of the estate would go back to John Strachey or his heirs.[2] Having done all this – the new and final will of Lord Strachie was dated 15 October 1931 – Lord Strachie died in 1936.

It is perhaps appropriate to conclude here this curious story: first, the daughter of Lord Strachie married a peer. This meant that the new heirs to Sutton Court would not be known as Strachey even if that were their surname, since the title of the peerage would obviously take first place. The daughter's son, a youth of great charm, experienced guilt at the thought of dispossessing John Strachey of his birth-right, and after many years died in 1955, without having ever entered upon his inheritance. John Strachey listened to his pleas for forgiveness with sympathy. His son, the present Lord O'Hagan, is the present heir also of the Stracheys, though the second Lord Strachie, childless and aged eighty-nine (born 1882), still lives on at Sutton Court, carefully tending the heirlooms, surrounded by the pictures, the mementoes and even the dresses of his beloved ancestors.

Meantime, Strachey in the 1930s lived on at his farmhouse in Essex, retaining a flat in Regent Square (this he afterwards gave up when his mother gave him the lease of a large house in Regent's Park Road). By this time, Mrs Strachey senior had reconciled herself to her son's divorce and new marriage, the prospect of a

---

[1] *See* correspondence with Slaughter and May, May 1948.

[2] *See* memorandum in Slaughter and May's letter of 7 May 1948, to John Strachey.

new male Strachey being an intoxicating one from the moment of Charles's birth in 1934. An heir to the family was more important to Amy Strachey than the views of the heir's parents. In later life, too, Amy Strachey, though remaining formidable, mellowed, enjoying a more intimate relation with her grandchildren than she had had with her children: even Celia became fond of her.

Chapter 10 / THE LEFT BOOK CLUB

Strachey arrived back in England in mid April 1935, and for the rest of the year lived quietly in Essex and in London, completing his analysis, and working, with minor articles, on a new book, *The Theory and Practice of Socialism*, a study of communist and socialist practice, with historical passages on the rise of trade unionism and some contemporary political analysis of the 'Russian experiment'. This book appeared, however, in quite new circumstances.

Strachey's public political life had not been active during 1935, though he went twice to Berlin to protest against the imprisonment of Dimitrov, the Bulgarian communist attached to the German communist party, once being accompanied by Celia, once by Ellen Wilkinson. Celia was apprehensive at the visit, since Strachey looked so Jewish. But on neither occasion was Strachey asked by the committee organising the campaign to help Dimitrov to do much.

One day in early January 1936, Strachey, Stafford Cripps and Gollancz met at a Soho restaurant to discuss the idea of a socialist or anti-fascist weekly. Afterwards, on this, as it turned out, inconclusive occasion, Gollancz said to Strachey: 'Do you know, I believe that the next thing is some sort of Left Book Club or something of that sort. Will you help to select the books?' Strachey agreed and, soon after, Gollancz approached Harold

Laski, the most influential non-parliamentary influence in the Labour movement. He was regularly elected to the National Executive of the Labour party during the 1930s, despite his championship of Cripps's Socialist League.[1] Professor of Politics at the London School of Economics since 1926, Laski agreed to collaborate too, with enthusiasm.[2]

The 'book club' was an import from the U.S. No one had thought of a 'left' book club before. The idea assumed that there was a large unsatisfied demand for books about left-wing political themes, and interpretations of history, art, as well as economics, in a 'left' manner. Gollancz envisaged a selection committee to be composed of himself, Strachey and Laski, who would decide on what books should be chosen each month. He also wanted a monthly leaflet to introduce the choices, and perhaps some other literature; and he took up, with alacrity, a suggestion from a subscriber that local discussion groups should be formed up and down England to talk over matters raised by the monthly selections.

From the first, Strachey was at the centre of this project. On 10 January 1936, he wrote to Gollancz:

> I have been thinking over your proposition very carefully indeed. What I feel is this: it is no use pretending that such a job will not take a proportion of one's available time and creative energy. . . . Hence, if I take it on, I think it will mean that I shall not attempt to start a new book at all soon, after ending work on this one, which I hope to do about the middle of the summer.[3] In many ways, I think this would be quite a good thing. One cannot go on turning out books continuously without a risk of the quality dropping seriously, so I shall be quite glad of – say – a year's break before starting another one. . . . Again your job attracts me enormously. I think it might become something really influential if one made it a principal charge on one's interest. . . . There remains the

---

[1] The Socialist League, which grew out of Cole's S.S.I.P., was a Labour party ginger group.
[2] *Left News*, March 1937; *see* Strachey on Laski in *The Strangled Cry*, pp. 196–200.
[3] *The Theory and Practice of Socialism*, *see* below, p. 157.

question of money. It will mean a pretty serious loss of income for me if I do not start a new book for, say, a year after finishing this one. My book earnings have now become the main basis of my income and can, I think, be kept up to their present level if I go on writing a book every 18 months, as I have done for the past four years. Naturally, I do not expect you to pay me enough to fill this gap entirely, and, for the reasons I have already mentioned, I should be quite ready to have a reduction of income . . . we could do all right if your job could bring me in £200 a year as a substitute for the book earnings.[1]

After further exchanges, Gollancz wrote to Strachey at the end of February 1936:

In general, my idea is that I should only come in in cases of disagreement between you and Laski, in which case I would give my casting vote . . . my own view is that the work involved will be very small. We shall undoubtedly be able to agree to exclude quite a number of books simply on the titles etc., without reading them: others (such as Palme Dutt's[2]), although, no doubt, as a matter of form we must read them, will be such obvious choices that they will want hardly more than a cursory examination. . . . I must say, for all that, that this is emphatically not a commercial enterprise. I have not been able to look into figures, but I shall be extremely surprised if I find that our 'left' publishing of last year, taken as a whole, did not result in a heavy loss. This scheme is an attempt to get the thing together on an altogether sounder basis, to enlarge the whole market for 'left' books, and, above all, to have knowledge of a really keen body of 'left' readers. Nothing would please me better if it went beyond that and turned out to be profitable. . . .

The urgency of the situation seemed to be attested by Hitler's reoccupation of the Rhineland. Strachey seems to have seen eye

1 Strachey to Gollancz, 10 January 1936.
2 *World Politics* 1918–1936, eventually the Left Book Club's choice for July in 1936.

to eye with Boothby about this: 'Walking down St James's Street . . . when the startling news appeared . . . we both agreed that it was the opening move of World War Number Two; and ought, as such, to be challenged – if necessary by force of arms.'[1] Later that day Claud Cockburn called on Strachey. 'Isn't it catastrophic?' the latter said, with gloom. 'Oh, I don't know, surely not *catastrophic*,' said Cockburn. Strachey went into the kitchen, and Cockburn heard him saying loudly 'Celia! Celia! Claud says it isn't catastrophic after all!'

There were several differences here between Gollancz and Strachey, apart from those of temperament: Gollancz was a pacifist, and the Left Book Club was launched basically under pacifist auspices. In a later memoir, Gollancz himself contrasted Strachey with Laski on this very question: 'Laski was a citizen of the world; Strachey, for all his loyalty, over a period of many years, to the Soviet Union, was essentially a patriot. Laski was a pacifist by instinct, whatever (I really do not know) he may have practised or professed: Strachey had not the slightest objection to war as such – but it must be the right kind of war.'[2] Gollancz also believed that Strachey did not at 'this time think capitalism wrong . . . he thought it inefficient and historically doomed. The crux of the matter, of course, is the profit motive. Strachey favoured it; to me it was and is . . . greed.'[3]

Gollancz, however, was a capitalist, even if an unusual one, while Strachey was never to be engaged in the direction of any commercial enterprise. Even over the Left Book Club, Gollancz was concerned to cut his costs. Thus he offered Strachey two guineas per book read for the club – 'our ordinary fee for a special opinion by an expert on a manuscript' – and offered Laski only one guinea, 'as he has his regular job'. In fact, Laski did his side of the work for nothing.[4]

Gollancz's attitude to the communists was complicated. He never had any intention of joining the party but he had such strong feelings about Hitler, Mussolini and the fascist menace

[1] Boothby, *op. cit.*, p. 136.
[2] Gollancz, *Reminiscences of Affection*, p. 131.
[3] *Ibid.*, p. 132.
[4] Gollancz to Strachey, 28 February 1936.

that he was quite prepared to cooperate with anyone in the furtherance of the Popular Front and the fight against fascism. The communist party, though small in numbers, was well organized, and had people associated with it who were enthusiastic, hardworking and skilled in propaganda. Gollancz, therefore, at the beginning of the Left Book Club, was quite prepared to encourage the party to play a part in the Club's activities. This presented various difficulties in the long run, as Gollancz himself could have imagined if he had been in a calm mood. But he was not.

While the Club was being organized, the movements guided by the two old friends of the 1920s, Mosley and Strachey, clashed against one another, both being physically implicated. On 22 March, Mosley was to address a meeting of the British Union of Fascists in the Albert Hall. Strachey, chairman of the Co-ordinating Committee for Anti-Fascist Activities, had called on his own friends to demonstrate outside the hall; but the police had prohibited demonstrations within half a mile of the hall. Therefore, those who demonstrated outside the Albert Hall itself were pressed back by the police. Strachey and some followers repaired then to Thurloe Square nearby, and he and others (R. Maclennan of the National Unemployed Workers' Movement, Ted Willis[1] of the Labour League of Youth, and Mr Leonard Schiff) made speeches. While the Rev. Schiff was speaking, the police made their way into the crowd, and began to break up the meeting by using their truncheons.

Arguments as to what really happened continued for months. A commission of enquiry was organized by the National Council of Civil Liberties. Had the police asked the crowd to disperse first? How far exactly was Thurloe Square from the Albert Hall – by thoroughfares, or as the crow flew?[2] How extraordinary that, as the tides of ideological warfare seemed to threaten all over Europe, two such close one-time associates should have been on two different sides.

The Left Book Club had begun to be advertised, meantime,

[1] Later Lord Willis of Chiselhurst.
[2] There is a good discussion of this incident in Robert Benewick's *Political Violence and Public Order*, p. 203.

and the first book was published in May. This was *France Today and the People's Front*, by Maurice Thorez, the dogged French communist leader. A companion volume for that month was H. J. Muller's *Out of the Night*, an eccentric Marxist study of the genetic future of man by a professor of Zoology at the University of Texas. There followed *Hitler the Pawn*, a 'liberal' study by Rudolf Olden, a German exile journalist who had been editor of the *Berliner Tageblatt*, Palme Dutt's *World Politics 1918–1936*, a new, inferior, novel by Malraux (*Days of Contempt*) and Hillel Bernstein's *Choose a Bright Morning*. Out of these first six books, two were by acknowledged communist leaders and another three by people so close to the party as to make no difference. Only Rudolf Olden was in no way a communist. This selection was made by Strachey and Laski, with Gollancz's help, as planned, but, of course, the former obviously consulted Pollitt and the communist party.

By the early summer, the Club was fully organized; members guaranteed to buy the choices as they appeared and bought their books for 2/6 each volume from the booksellers with which they were registered, some being supplied by post. Bound first in limp orange cloth and then in pink paperboards, they were unmistakeable to the eye and, soon, most of those on the left in England had a long row of these volumes on their shelves.

Then, as Strachey and Gollancz had hoped, there was the *Left Book News* which in December 1936 was re-christened as simply *Left News*. This consisted first of a personal editorial by Gollancz; a major review, usually by Strachey or Laski, of the choice of the month; and a general article expanding on some other topical matter (the Spanish War, the Popular Front etc.). Another section gave general information about subsidiary activities, or volumes, of the Left Book Club. John Lewis, who became national organizer of the discussion groups, also later wrote a regular article: he was a presbyterian minister, then of near-communist views, though long ago, in 1924, he had been chairman of the I.L.P. in Mosley's old constituency at Ladywood. He and his wife were the main administrators of the Club, with an office in Gollancz's publishing house.

The swift success of this venture meant that, in addition to the regular books of the Club, 'extra volumes' (chosen by Gollancz alone) could be circulated for members of the Club to receive at lower than customary prices. The appearance of *Left Book News*, in May 1936, was a great event in the lives of Strachey, Gollancz and, indeed, of all on the left, at the time. With its foundation, Strachey returned to the regular journalistic work that he had had in the 1920s. There were, for five years now, few numbers of this monthly which did not include at least one article or review by Strachey. His life in the late 1930s was thus characterized by his visits to Pollitt in the communist headquarters on the corner of King Street and Bedford Street, Covent Garden; these were followed by visits, just round the corner, to Gollancz's office in Henrietta Street to discuss the next choice with him. Laski, though interested when asked his opinion, did not play such a critical part, though the London School of Economics, of course, was also within walking distance of Covent Garden.

Strachey, at this time, had, it seems, no doubts about the general validity of the communist position, nor of the Russian government's virtue. Doubtless he was protected from a cold appraisal of the purge trials by his continued close association with Dutt, whose intelligence he so much admired. On 26 May 1936, for example, Strachey made one of those reports on progress, and requests for help, to Dutt which were such a frequent feature of his life in the 1930s. 'What,' he asked, 'do you think of the Left Book Club venture? I am profoundly interested in, and encouraged by it. As you have probably heard, it has been a far greater success than we dared hope. We reckoned that we might have to start with no more than 3,000 members but we already have 11,500. This will mean that, by July, when your book [*World Politics 1918–1936*] appears, it should have a sale on the day of publication of anything up to 15,000. I do feel that to have secured an initial audience of that size is a really important piece of work. The *Left Book News* too can, I think, be made into something valuable . . . what both Gollancz and I are hoping for it is that, if and when the membership of the Club grows to really big figures, such as 20,000 or 30,000, we can turn the *Left Book News* into the long planned weekly paper. . . .

'As you may have heard, there were all sorts of rows and

intrigues about the starting of the Club. Consequently, it has many imperfections, the chief of which is, of course, its restriction to Gollancz books. But my feeling, with which Harry [i.e. Pollitt] concurred, was that the great thing was to get something going. Gollancz has his defects, but he is a man of intense energy and drive, and he has put this thing over in a way which, I am sure, nobody else could have. . . . Do look after your health to the maximum extent possible. It is essential that your pen should be more active than ever from now on. . . .'[1]

Dutt replied approvingly: 'The Left Book Club is a brilliant piece of organizing work all through; and its success and scope, so far from being injured, is probably the greater because it is recognized by the general public as an independent commercial enterprise on its own feet, and not the propaganda of a particular political organization'.[2]

But troubles soon began. Robert Graves and Alan Hodge, in their excellent study *The Long Week-end*, argue that the Left Book Club 'embittered the controversy between Labour and the extreme left'.[3] The trouble was that Labour, after being invited to participate, refused to do so unless its point of view was represented on the Selection Committee. Gollancz did not wish this, feeling that that view was well enough represented by Laski. But the consequence was that, from the summer of 1936, controversy grew within the British left, almost as fast as did the membership of the Left Book Club. Thus, on 16 July, Gollancz wrote to Strachey: 'There are one or two danger signs. In the immense correspondence which has descended on me since Monday, there is a letter from a man who enquires whether the whole thing is really a piece of C. Propaganda (but he does not resign); about five resignations, of which I think about a couple are to be attributed to this cause; a further letter somewhat on the same lines. . . . Moreover, I have the feeling that there is a good deal of 'official' disapproval. . . . You will recollect that our last big circularising scheme had, as its core, a letter to the Secretary of every Trades Council and local Labour party, asking them

[1] Strachey to Dutt, 26 May 1936.
[2] Dutt to Strachey, 1 June 1936.
[3] Robert Graves and Alan Hodge, *The Long Week-end*, p. 334.

to supply brochures to send to their committee people etc. There
has been *some* response but really very poor. The great growth of
the Club is coming from (a) advertisement, (b) personal recommendation – we are receiving a great number of applications
from members who are handing on to their friends the enrolment
cards contained in each Club choice. This sort of thing was, of
course, inevitable and must not be over-emphasized. But it does
mean that we must be wary and Leninist. . . .'[1] He added in
consequence that he was 'rather alarmed to discover how many
of the writers are on the extreme left. Taking the list up to July
[1937] and going back to the beginning of the Club, the only
choices that are not by members of the C.P. (more or less) are . . .
three out of fifteen[2] . . . . I think we certainly ought to remedy
this. . . .'[3]

Strachey replied: 'I do not feel that there is any way of avoiding
Transport House opposition to the Club. Indeed, I do not think
that there is any way of avoiding that opposition becoming as
vicious as Citrine, Morrison and Co., know how to make it as
and when the Club becomes dangerous to them, as it inevitably
must. I think that if we deviated from the United Front position,
which we have taken up from the start, in the very slightest
degree, we should fail to conciliate Transport House in the least
and disappoint terribly the maximum majority of the Club
membership.'[4] Then Strachey went on: 'I must say that I think
that the line of the books and of the *Left Book News* has been,
with the single exception of Laski's deplorable review of Dutt,
pretty well as good as it could be, as yet. [Laski had criticised Dutt
in *Left Book News* in July.] Obviously, there is no vigorous, clear-
cut political line which will not antagonize some people in the
Movement. . . .' Strachey was also unenthusiastic about a proposal
by Gollancz for a book on 'the condition of England' by Cole.
(Strachey never liked Cole very much, though Cole had become,
like the Webbs, something of a Marxist, in a general way, in the
1930s.) What if he 'produced a weary, dreary sort of thing?

---

1 Gollancz to Strachey, 16 July 1936.
2 The three were Olden, Brailsford and Salvemini.
3 Second letter of Gollancz to Strachey, 16 July 1936.
4 Strachey to Gollancz, 20 July 1936.

Would it be possible for you, before definitely commissioning the book, to have lunch with him and see whether there is any spark of vigour in him on this subject?'

Gollancz wrote back that he had no intention whatever of wishing to 'alter the line. On the contrary, I want to strengthen it. The matter is a purely tactical one: our whole aim must be to win the maximum number of members and frighten the minimum. . . . In this connection, Laski has suggested that we might get Attlee to do a general book on Labour policy. I am inclined to think that as a tactical move (accompanied by a suitable review in the *News*) might be very useful.'[1] Gollancz, in the event, eventually commissioned Cole to write the book proposed, not as a Left Book Club choice – to Cole's annoyance.

The Theory and Practice of Socialism, which Strachey had been working on during 1935, was the Left Book Club choice for November 1936. Dutt, Harry Pollitt and Emile Burns all made extensive suggestions, and the last chapter, which came under 'heavy fire from Harry and Emile Burns', was re-written.[2]

The book made extensive use of the Webbs' *Soviet Communism: a New Civilization?* published in 1935, and Strachey returned to contact with them for the first time since his break with Mosley in July 1931. Strachey was staying with them in Liphook when the Spanish Civil War broke out. His first article on the significance of this appeared in October 1936, in *Left Book News:* he argued that the 'position taken up by Great Britain will probably prove the decisive factor,' and, somewhat modestly, demanded that the Non-Intervention agreement should be extended to Portugal. Strachey never seems to have regarded Spain as quite the burning issue which many on the left considered it. He knew nothing of Spanish conditions before 1936, and was reluctant to pronounce. Not all his friends agreed with this caution. Nancy Cunard, for example, had written to him in August: 'SPAIN. . . . beyond words. But not to be beyond words indeed when I get there. The people of France will, oh surely, they will, and must, force this ghastly "neutrality" into helping.'[3]

[1] Gollancz to Strachey, 12 July 1936.
[2] Strachey to Dutt, 16 June 1936.
[3] Nancy Cunard to Strachey, 9 August 1936.

Since 1931, meantime, the Webbs had followed as left a course
as Strachey had. Arch-reformists though they had hitherto been,
they believed, in the 1930s, that the decay of capitalism was
inevitable and that the Soviet Union held the key to the future.[1]
They were not communists: they despaired of reformism. In
The Theory and Practice of Socialism, Strachey used the Webbs'
work extensively, though in the 1950s he described it as 'pre-
posterous', saying that, in 1936, 'even I was staggered by the
book's utter lack of any critical analysis of Russian society. . . .
They described it as if it were, in reality, what it was on paper.'[2]
Perhaps, here, Strachey was less than just to his old friends, since
his own ideas were much the same as those of the authors of
Soviet Communism. Indeed, his attitude to *Soviet Communism*
was in 1936 enthusiastic; he spoke of it as 'the culminating
achievement of the two greatest social investigators of the English-
speaking world'.

Strachey's *The Theory and Practice of Socialism* is an exceptionally well-written book but also starry eyed, in respect both of
Soviet achievements and of likely British developments. One
argument for a classless society has since escaped prophets of
Strachey's sort: that 'the far wider area of sexual choice to every
citizen of a homogeneous, classless society, will, over a few
generations, have a marked eugenic effect and so increase the
mental and physical powers of the race'. The interest of the book
now lies in the fact that Strachey, unlike Marx, talked a good
deal of what communism would actually be like. It would be
characterized, he believed (as Kropotkin had believed), by super-
abundance, with the 'means of production . . . developed to a
much higher point than they have yet reached, even in Britain
and America. We must have equipped ourselves with machines
and productive plants of every kind by means of which we can
satisfy all our wants with a minimum of labour.' There was a

[1] This weekend at Liphook was probably the occasion when the Webbs told him
that Keynes had been present the weekend before and that he had been heart-
broken because *The General Theory* had apparently fallen flat. Beatrice Webb
had evidently thought that the book's apparent failure was inevitable; that it was
a last despairing attempt to find a non-existent reformist way. (Strachey, *The
Strangled Cry*, p. 187.)
[2] *Ibid.*, pp. 187–8. This was a Third Programme talk given in 1960.

word of warning: It might be that we should waste and spoil 'the social store of wealth. . . .' But we had no right 'to suppose that our descendants would be as churlish or as childish as we are'. Strachey was confident that Russia, although still merely socialist, was approaching Utopia, and that the Soviet system produced a 'far wider measure of democracy than do parliaments or congresses', enabling large numbers of the population actually 'to participate in the making of the day-to-day decision'. As for the allegation that Stalin, and Lenin before him, had made themselves dictators, 'we can find no meaning in the allegation'. It was false to suppose that Stalin could rule according to whim. The book ends with the stirring exhortation that it is only through 'the action of those that know (know, that is, the new laws of political science) that the world can be remade by wisdom and courage, by patience and audacity!'

The reviews in England of *The Theory and Practice of Socialism* were often critical, though the book received one good one from an official Labour party spokesman, A. V. Alexander, in *Reynolds News*. Aneurin Bevan reviewed it interestingly in the *Daily Worker*; he talked disparagingly of the times in the 1920s when 'many were seduced into the paths of gradualist socialism'. Thus a 'generation has grown up almost entirely ignorant of what scientific socialism has to say on the living issues of our time. They can do no better than read this book.' Bevan makes clear that, at that stage at least, he shared Strachey's view that 'it is because of the refusal to attain to this attitude of scientific humility that the British Labour movement has gone astray'. What attitude? The attitude that 'society is a domain of law [i.e. a scientific law] and the possibilities of the future can be understood only by learning these laws and submitting oneself to their guidance'.[1] The book also sold well and all the reviews were prominent. In the Left Book Club, it was regarded as a prescribed text. A training school was even held to train group leaders who would be ready to go out all over England and organize study courses on the book. Left Book Club sales totalled 41,104, and the ordinary edition at 10/6 sold 2,385. A 1938 cheap edition at 5/- sold another

[1] *Daily Worker*, 18 November 1936.

5,801, and Left Book Club sales of this cheap edition numbered 2,745.

The Theory and Practice of Socialism became the Book Union selection for November 1936 in the U.S. Max Lerner's review in the bulletin of that club was euphoric: 'The young will read the book because it talks of life's opportunities and shows a way of realizing them. Others will read it who want to unlearn what they have learned. Above all, it will be read by workers everywhere, who must find their own way in the realms of knowledge . . . on a San Francisco wharf, in a Chicago stockyard, on a truck in Minneapolis. . . .'[1] Bennet Cerf, Strachey's New York publisher, at Random House, wrote that it was 'as important a Random House book as ever we published, I don't mind adding'.[2] The U.S. communist party made a special arrangement with Random House for their own distribution of 5,000 copies of the book, and the first printing reached 12,500.

By this time, the Left Book Club was well established as was Strachey's place within it. His successive articles, 'A People's Front in Britain', the 'Road to Victory', the 'Fascist World Offensive' and so on, had provided countless people with the basis for arguments with their parents, colleagues, children, and friends: they did for the socialist left what St Loe's *Spectator* leaders had done for the upper class before 1925: they gave ammunition. These articles were always explicitly communist, but, as usual, lucid and well written: their basic theme was that the world was, as the 'Fascist World Offensive' put it, now dominated by a counter-revolutionary attack: 'Such a world situation would not have come into existence if it had not been for the blindness and poltroonery of the leaders of the European working-class movements in the preceding decade. But out of men's very horror and loathing of the fascist assault arises our opportunity to unite forces, which are amply sufficient to destroy fascism. . . . We have only to grasp our opportunity to make certain of victory.'[3]

The psychological approach was exciting; on the one hand, the

[1] Max Lerner review in *Book Union Bulletin*, November 1936.
[2] Bennet Cerf to Strachey, 12 April 1937.
[3] *Left News*, December 1936.

awful spectre of doom; but, out of the dark, the winged figure of revolutionary victory still glimmered.

Contrasting demands were also made of Strachey of a different sort. Thus Strachey was approached by a branch of the Rushcliffe (Nottingham) Labour party to become their candidate in the next election.[1] Strachey replied that he would prefer to do nothing until the question of communist party affiliation to the Labour party had been settled at the party conference in October. Early in 1936, he had similarly been approached, through a rich central European bookseller of his acquaintance, by Louis Mountbatten; the new King Edward VIII, it seemed, desired a potted autobiography of Claud Cockburn, for *The Week* had begun to be read in Fort Belvedere. At the end of the year, Strachey was again the go-between between Mountbatten and Cockburn; the former desired, it was said, to publish some explosive material, which would help the King's cause, but which no respectable journal would print. Strachey conspiratorially passed on the message to Cockburn as they walked round St James's Park. Cockburn agreed. Cockburn recalls that Strachey 'rushed to and fro with mysterious messages'. But, in the end, a despatch rider brought Cockburn the message late one night: 'The situation has developed too fast.'[2] Few crises passed in the 1930s without Strachey being implicated at some stage.

Early in March 1937, Gollancz and Strachey had a meeting with Emile Burns, the chief propagandist of the communist party, at which Gollancz's ideas for the further development of the Left Book Club were even more closely linked with the communist party. At this meeting, it was agreed that ideally (in Gollancz's words) 'there should be one or two good Party members in all those groups in which there was none at present', and 'not only these but also existing Party conveners and prominent members of groups should be given the right line'. They all 'decided that it was best to do this from the centre – Harry first starting the thing in the C.C., and then working the thing through district committees'. Emile Burns was also to be 'quite privately co-opted on to the selection committee – in the sense that he would read

---

[1] W. Foulgar to Strachey, 13 August 1936.
[2] Claud Cockburn, *In Time of Trouble*, pp. 249–52.

and give his opinion on manuscripts, from time to time, before we have our formal meetings'.[1]

This did not, however, have any particularly disturbing effect on the character of the choices. Burns and Pollitt were as anxious as was Gollancz to have a few liberal faces in the list; and the choices made for July 1937 to July 1938, based on decisions in 1937 by Strachey, Burns, Laski and Gollancz, had much the same political complexion as those of the previous year. But a Left Book Club reader would have got the Labour party view only from Attlee's book in August 1937 (a dull month for publishing) until the following summer. The Webbs' *Soviet Communism* was a reprint volume for October 1937, though its subtitle, *A New Civilisation?*, with which it had appeared in 1935, now was written without a question mark.

Strachey was now busy in a large number of ways in addition to his work for the Club. Thus he debated on 17 February 1937, in the Central Hall Westminster with Father MacNab OP, under the auspices of the Distributist League.[2] (Father MacNab knelt before Strachey to ask his permission for planning to disagree with him.) He spoke on 10 February in Manchester, opening the Left Book Club's discussion of Stephen Spender's book *Forward from Liberalism*. On 1 March he talked to the Central London Left Book Club group about Frank Jellinek's *Paris Commune*, the choice for February 1937. On 8 February he was a speaker at a huge first Albert Hall rally, organized by the Left Book Club. It is most unlikely, at this time, if indeed Strachey ever refused an invitation to speak – for the Albert Hall rally was followed by similar occasions at Manchester, Glasgow, Cardiff, Birmingham, and many other places. Gollancz by this time seemed to have found a new dimension for himself: more than publisher, he seemed a prophet. An unkind observer, Malcolm Muggeridge, said that the acclamation which greeted his oratory suggested a Führer, of this anti-Hitlerian cause. But his achievement was striking. This in itself created troubles with the Labour party which might not have occurred if the Club had remained simply a Book Club rather than a movement. The

[1] Note from Gollancz to Strachey and Laski, 8 March 1937.
[2] *See* pamphlet *Communism or Distribution*, the Distributist League, 1937.

situation became more tense still when Gollancz proudly announced a scheme whereby there would be a special Left Book Club edition of *every* book published by Lawrence & Wishart, the communist publishers. A special 'News from Lawrence & Wishart' soon appeared on the last page of *Left News*.

Difficulties with the Labour party became more acute still when Left Book Club rallies began to attract larger audiences than did the Labour party in their membership drive. Gollancz wrote to Strachey euphorically in September: 'Nottingham was good, Leicester excellent, Chester and Warrington (in spite of unfavourable times and circumstances) the best political meetings known in the town for many years. At Liverpool, we turned away about 700 from the Picton Hall . . . three or four times the audience secured during the same week or just previously by the special Labour party campaign.'[1]

Soon, however, a few doubts and perplexities seem to have begun to beset the 'complete Muscovite' as R. C. K. Ensor had called Strachey in a hostile review in the *Spectator*. These were more explicitly political than psychological. During the course of 1937–8, Strachey was receiving disturbing letters on a variety of themes from people with whom he had been friendly for years. For example, Sir Richard Acland wrote, in September 1937, that Strachey's whole argument in a new book *What Are We to Do?*, then in manuscript, collapsed, if it turned out, as Acland believed, that since 1900 the standard of living had gone up by 30–40 per cent.[2] Strachey's initial reaction was to scribble on this letter the contemptuous comment 'emotional reaction'. But some of Acland's views seem to have sunk in. Then, early in 1937, Strachey had received a telegram from Esther in New York 'CAN YOU ASSEMBLE RADICAL LIBERAL OPINIONS IN ENGLAND AGAINST PLIGHT OF SOKOLNIKOV STOP THIS CASE WILL NOT HELP RUSSIA HERE ESTHER AND LORNA'. Grigori Sokolnikov, an old Bolshevik of the Zinoviev group, had been the ambassador to London between 1929 and 1932, and was an acquaintance and confidant of Strachey. In 1936, he was tried for treason and condemned

[1] Gollancz to Strachey, September 1937.
[2] Acland to Strachey, 18 September 1937.

to ten years hard labour. (He was probably shot in Orel Prison in 1941.) This must have affected Strachey since, after all, they had been quite close friends and Strachey had consulted the ambassador when he first became a communist. Nevertheless, in *Left News* in March 1937, he talks of the trials and says 'I believe that the psychological student of the future will look back on the long-drawn-out incredulity of British public opinion over the Moscow trials as one of the strangest . . . phenomena.' He then went on to dismiss as the height of implausibility the suggestions that the defendants in these trials confessed because their lives, or the lives of their wives and children, were spared; though these were, indeed, the main reasons for the confessions. The article suggested that Strachey had some doubts about his own arguments, by protesting too much.

One revealing article was also written by Strachey in the *Left News* in early 1937, reviewing a book by Reuben Osborn, which attempted to combine Marx and Freud, and which Strachey had himself selected. He criticized Marxists who dismissed psychoanalytical theory as unworthy of attention, and contrasted their attitude with that which he believed Marx and Engels would themselves have taken up. Were Marx and Engels really opposites?' Osborn, he believed, had proved that the 'purely empirical findings of the analysts both confirm the main generalizations of Marxism and, at the same time, supplement and make specific these generalizations in some important respects'.[1]

Another problem arose from an article by Strachey in *New Masses* of July 1937, in New York, entitled 'Radicals in Rompers'. Jo Freeman, the editor, wrote him a letter which gave warning that perhaps his style, the very thing which had endeared Strachey to large audiences, was causing a fluttering in certain left-wing hearts: there were

> several passages which created considerable misunderstanding in some quarters, and in others, where they were understood, considerable disturbance. This disturbance was created by those paragraphs which tend to confuse childish leftism that is sincere

[1] *Left News*, January 1937.

in intent, with such counter-revolutionary forces as Trotsky-ism, which have long ago ceased to be a political trend in the labor movement. Attention was centered, for example, on the point where you say that Lenin 'UNKINDLY' called Trotsky a windbag. You may have done this as a matter of style, nevertheless it fails to convey to the reader that what characterized Lenin's polemics was not unkindness, but precision – a precision which, in this case, expressed Lenin's foresight as to Trotsky's counter-revolutionary role. This misexpression, it was properly pointed out, then leads in a more serious misstatement along the same lines. In endeavouring to illustrate the terrible consequences of leftism and sectarianism, you point to the Barcelona uprising led by the P.O.U.M. and a section of the Anarchists influenced by them. But you describe this only as 'a profound tragedy', attributing to the P.O.U.M., a Trotskyite organization, 'a typical leftist' purpose in the rebellion. That action is described as an attempt to 'snatch in one handful at everything which the Spanish workers desire....'[1]

The P.O.U.M., of course, were regarded by the communists as spies and traitors, not merely misguided revolutionaries.

Strachey had finally a little trouble over an article which he wrote in the *Daily Worker* about the Soviet 'election' of December 1937. Pat Sloan, of *Russia Today*, wrote to the *Daily Worker* saying that Strachey had left the impression 'that the *Soviet Government* decided that there should be only one candidate in each constituency and that each candidate was a government candidate. . . . THESE ASSUMPTIONS ARE ABSOLUTELY FALSE . . . we must compare the Soviet elections with a Trade Union ballot for an executive at a time when the existing Executive is overwhelmingly popular. . . .'[2]

As yet, these points gave nobody any cause for anxiety. Had Strachey remained an orthodox communist, they could have been overlooked or forgotten, though if he had been a communist living in Russia, they might have figured in his charge sheet. Further, however, Strachey's and Gollancz's colleague in

[1] Joseph Freeman to Strachey, 24 July 1937.
[2] Pat Sloan to Strachey, 17 December 1937.

the Left Book Club triumvirate, Laski, though radical, had also been interested in, and influenced by, Roosevelt and the New Deal from the beginning. He passed on some of his enthusiasm for the President and his policies to Strachey, so that Strachey never attacked him in his articles in *Left News*. It was an omission which had considerable significance in the later development of Strachey's life and thought.

Chapter 11 / THE YEAR OF MUNICH

The second great Albert Hall rally of the Left Book Club was held on 16 January 1938. It was a double event, since the same speakers spoke at both the Albert Hall and Queen's Hall. They were Strachey (on the 'tasks facing the Labour movement in the new year'), Pollitt, and Gollancz, as the previous year, but also Acland, Sir Charles Trevelyan and Lord Addison, while Isobel Brown, a most eloquent speaker, collected money for Spain and China. In addition, at the Albert Hall, Paul Robeson sang, and, at the Queen's Hall, the 'Red' Dean of Canterbury, a passionate convert to socialism, talked about a recent visit to Russia. Gollancz read out messages from Mao and Nehru. These meetings were followed by further tremendous rallies – in Oxford, Sheffield, Manchester, Stoke-on-Trent and so on. Strachey spoke at the big meetings incessantly, as did his colleagues. The 50,000 Left Book Club members met in over seven hundred organized and well-directed groups. Members bought the Left Book Club song book, they adopted Spanish refugee children, they went to Left Book Club inspired theatres or cinema shows, they followed, with increasing anxiety, the progress of the war in Spain, as reported in *Left News*, and they collected money for the Republic, and later for China. They adopted temporary new heroes – such as Edgar Snow, fresh from seeing Mao, and Arthur Koestler (who went on a lecture tour prior to the appearance of his own *Spanish*

Testament). Many wrote letters, too, to appear in *Left News*, treating their outraged resignation or enthusiastic rejoicing as if they were initiates into a sacred cult. Associated activities blossomed – the Christian Book Club, under the Dean of Canterbury's inspiration; political Educational Classes; China Week; and so on: a level of political activity and participation rarely achieved outside the doings of the regular parties, and a great tribute to the energy and imagination of Gollancz.

All political events seemed to be occasions upon which to pronounce. The resignation of Eden brought a big meeting at Queen's Hall, the Battle of Teruel in Aragon led Strachey to go to Spain, accompanied by a Labour party delegation (including a member of the National Executive). The article which he wrote in consequence, 'A visit to Teruel', appeared in *Left News* for March 1938. Discussions with Colonel Galán and General Sarabia were described, as was a meeting of the rump Spanish Cortes at Montserrat. He also visited the British battalion in the International Brigades. He seems to have been chiefly impressed by his discussion with Portela Valladares, the Prime Minister of Spain at the time of the elections of 1936: he, though on the right, had handed over power to the left since they had won the election. This simple constitutional act was much at variance with what in theory was anxious to do himself, and much affected Strachey. The conversation was used by him in a book some years later.[1]

By this time Strachey had completed *What Are We to Do?*, the Left Book Club choice for March 1938. This, based on lectures at a summer school at Digswell Park in 1937, treated first the familiar theme of what had gone wrong with existing Labour movements. The second section dealt with the existing situation and argued for a Popular Front. 'Towards a United Left' was the title of the third section of the book; these chapters reflected the extraordinary attraction which the idea of a Popular Front then had for intellectuals. But there also was a long section dealing explicitly with the role of communist parties, which he described as 'new model parties', the disciplined and centralized instruments of revolution. With such reliable weapons, the workers and

[1] *See* below, p. 211.

enlightened bourgeoisie should not shrink from violence against capitalism.

Reaction was varied. Thus R. H. S. Crossman, then a don, though already associated with the *New Statesman*, on the right of the party and a rearmer, wrote from Oxford:

> May I just say that, having finished *What Are We to Do?*, this morning, I find it difficult to see where a right-winger and a communist differ, *if they are both under 40* and realize the fact of declining capitalism. The general tone and policy of your book seems to be completely correct. [After a consideration of one or two minor matters, Crossman wrote] Of course, you are right about the need of a new model, but you miss the point when you accuse people like me of objecting to the 3rd International as *super*national; our feeling . . . of resistance is due to a fear that its policy is a *Russian* policy dictated by Russian interests. If we did not feel this, lots of people would not only cooperate with, but join, the C.P. Most of us long for its discipline and demands and its Marxism, but we feel that it does not give orders to Russia . . . but is rigged by the Russians. . . . What strikes me in reading your book is that more difference exists between pre-war and post-war thinking than between left and right in our movement. Pre-war left and right believed in progress, we don't think that Progress can occur without our effort. On the contrary, we know that disaster will occur unless we act.[1]

Strachey was pleased enough with this reaction and with the fact that the Left Book Club ensured for him sales of almost 50,000 (47,968 in the Left Book Club edition, 1,313 in the ordinary edition).

What Are We to Do? appeared in the U.S. in August 1938. 'The incorrigible and pleasant-voiced John Strachey, he who is probably the most subversive influence still in possession of a British passport, is with us again . . .' wrote Leland Stowe, in the *New York Herald Tribune*. This version of the book was lengthened to take into account the situation in the U.S. The striking aspect

[1] Crossman to Strachey, 18 March 1938.

of the U.S. reviews was the extent to which reviewers who differed from Strachey in most respects went out of their way to suggest that even 'for those outside the ideological faith . . . this book contains much of value'.

But, long before this straightforward Marxist work had appeared in the U.S., and even before it was published in Britain (though it had been finished), Strachey had already begun to experience new uncertainties: in January 1938, he had again seen Denis Carroll, his analyst, and told him that he 'felt a pressure towards further analysis, more especially in order to avoid political follies'.[1] A few months later, he wrote to Carroll that further events 'had brought that feeling to a head'. The letter continued:

> . . . the prospect [is] opened up of an unending series of world wars between rival Empires of the fascist type. Moreover, this prospect of tacit cooperation between Britain and the fascist powers in the period during which they are being enabled to crush all popular resistance (as in Spain at the moment) involves a more and more anti-democratic type of regime here. (I find that my Conservative friends increasingly realize this.) [This must have been an allusion to Boothby.]

> Now, the point for me is that, in view of this prospect, I do not quite know how to go on living. (I don't mean that I feel suicidal; I mean that I feel that I must react to the situation in some way, but do not know what way). . . .

> I could, of course, simply continue, and intensify, my routine work of a communist, or generally left-wing, propagandist – striving harder than ever to make people see the world from my point of view and so to avert, by, for instance, changing the government of this country, the above prospect, which is unbearable to me. That work is, at a certain level, really rather successful. But my view is that, if I and my friends go on on present lines, we shall just about raise enough opposition to make it necessary for the British governing class to resort to repressive measures of the characteristic fascist type, without there being any real prospect of shaking their position. . . . Now

[1] Strachey to Carroll, April 1938.

the first issue on which I, very earnestly, ask you to give your opinion is this: Is the prospect of a world of war, fascism, or both, which, though you may feel it to be very much more remote than I do, surely faces us both, a result of neurotically motivated, hate-compelled, impulses from the left, producing their inevitable reaction of the right? . . . Our view is that such a degree of maldistribution [as exists now] is not merely inequitable, but is making the system worse and worse – it is becoming too lopsided to be workable. (I remember you saying in the analysis that my economic reasoning led to the conclusion that we could never be prosperous again. I said that that was so. I should have added 'except when making armaments'.)

We think that by a long, elaborate, but fully traceable chain of cause and effect this degree of unevenness of distribution of purchasing power . . . is the cause of the trouble: that you've got somehow to put that right before people can have any chance to behave decently.

One of my troubles is that, just as I have come to despair of the left's ability to do the job, I have become more perfectly convinced that this is the job which has to be done. . . . As I see it, if we of the left cannot do the job, then the extreme right must do it, in the fascist way. But this way involves not merely the destruction of my sort of person – and, to some extent, of your sort – but doing the job of altering the economic base only in the sense that they will give everybody employment on armament building, and the consumption of the armaments in periodic wars. . . . I believe that the predominant reason for the failure of the left is a grotesque underestimate of the subjective factor. I talked enough about that in the course of the analysis for you to know what I mean. . . .

I remember saying at one session that psycho-analysis is the theoretically minded man's way back to reality. In the same way, the psycho-analytic *attitude* may be the only way back to political reality for theoretically minded politicians – that is, Marxists.

You know that I have felt this for a long time, and have made a feeble attempt to introduce psycho-analytic theory to the left by sponsoring Osborn's little book, *Freud and Marx*....[1]

These are the problems which so agitate me. Do you, or do you not, think that I could get somewhere in some sessions starting out in this frame of mind? ...

So much for myself. But I feel a need to attack you as well as consult you. I attack you as a representative analyst. You have got, in your knowledge of psycho-analytic theory, and in your wide clinical experience, a unique safeguard against forming compulsive opinions on economics and politics. Now I don't believe that political and economic theory is really a very difficult subject: it is far less complex than psychology, for instance. But little progress is made with it – leaving the world to go to ruin for lack of guidance. ... Now, insofar as a trained analyst has freed himself from these inhibitions, could he not come to economic and political science with unique objectivity and see relatively easily into the nature of its problems? ...

Now why don't you feel it your duty to undertake this work? After all, it's your world which is turning into a pigsty as well as mine. You've got married and are going to have (or have?) children. It matters to you.

You'll tell me, I suppose, that you are doing a full-time job and incidentally earning your living. You do, however, an immense amount of unpaid social work, both on lunatics and on child guidance. Have you the right to give that time and energy to such work, however valuable, in the present political situation? To get at anything worth having you would have to read a dozen or so fairly formidable books; and to master them. Oughtn't you to do it? Your duty seems to me to be to the sane rather than to the already mad; to the sane who may be driven mad by war, civil violence, and economic dislocation, if we do not learn in time to solve our political and economic problems.

I am aware, to some extent, of the nature of the motives behind this combined appeal and attack. No doubt I want a father figure to come down and settle the whole thing. But still isn't there something in the idea? If you can't or won't do it, is there not some other first-rate analyst who will?

[1] *See* above, p. 164.

Carroll did not, however, act as suggested. Strachey remained suspended in these matters all through 1938. But it seems certain that the communists' neglect of the 'subjective factor' grated on him more and more from that time onwards.

In the spring, Gollancz persuaded Strachey to produce yet another new type of publication – a 2d pamphlet entitled *Why You Should be a Socialist*. This consisted of about ninety pages of reasoned argument on behalf of what Strachey called socialism, but was still undoubtedly communism. It represents the culmination of ten years of radical thinking and popularization. It was originally written as an educational pamphlet, but Gollancz rightly believed that it could be more widely distributed. The first edition of 100,000 published in May 1938 was sold out immediately. Three impressions of 100,000 each were printed by the end of June. 'On to the million – the Club's greatest achievement' were headlines in Gollancz's editorial in June: 'Ten million readers of a booklet that *converts* – this might well be the decisive factor in our political life.' Cripps, in a review, wrote that it was the best material for conversion ever brought out. Sales totalled 304,042, and there seems no doubt at all that it really did have the critical effect in many people's political lives that was claimed for it.

In the middle of 1938, Gollancz was beginning to have problems with the communists. He was outraged that the communist-run Unity Theatre group were trying to absorb the Left Book Club Theatre Guild, on the ground that the communists, in their efforts to woo the Labour party, thought that the disciplinable Unity Theatre group were more appealing to Labour than the more adventurous Left Book Club people. Gollancz also noticed that, at the Left Book Club summer school in August 1938 at Digswell Park, the communists simply regarded 'their duty as party members mainly to use the club to get people into the C.P., rather than to make the Left Book Club grow for its own sake'.[1] He for a time wondered whether he might lose control of the situation.

But still the greater difficulties were on the right: the Labour party had been attempting to carry their animosity into real

[1] Gollancz to Emile Burns, 13 August 1938, copy to Strachey.

effect by setting up a rival social democrat book club, whose board was to include leading Labour party supporters such as R. H. Tawney, Walter Citrine, Dalton and even Cole. When this idea collapsed, a Labour party book club was canvassed. Kingsley Martin, editor of the *New Statesman*, was asked to join the selection committee and promptly told Gollancz about it, in a letter which the latter sent on to Strachey: 'the details show that the whole thing is a slavish imitation of the Left Book Club, including study circles and a monthly periodical – flattery could scarcely go further!'[1] Gollancz, in a pencilled note to Strachey, wrote: 'The whole manoeuvre is on classical lines – particularly the selection of some of the "cover" names: it interests me particularly, as I've just finished the official *History of the Civil War in the U.S.S.R.* The Coles, Tawneys and Attlees can be paralleled again and again among the S.R.s and Mensheviks between February and October... all this makes it *very* clear that, without anything like a disastrous public statement, the party [i.e. the communist party] really should unobtrusively mobilize itself behind the Club.... I think you should show Kingsley's letter to Harry at once: he should be advised of every development immediately. Moreover, he may see some way of mobilizing the party behind the Club's autumn campaign at the B'ham congress, without, however, doing anything which can give them a handle for saying "you see it *is* the C.P.". Do you think there's anything to be said for having Acland on the Selection Committee? We could then say Laski (L.P. executive) VG Labour Party (!); Strachey, working closely with C.P.; Acland, Liberal. . . . See what Harry says.'[2]

The situation was further complicated by the capture by Gollancz and the Left Book Club in the summer of 1938 of *Tribune*, the left-wing Labour paper, founded by Sir Stafford Cripps, to agitate for the idea of the Popular Front. Gollancz became a member of the board of *Tribune*, as did Laski (for a time), with Bevan and George Strauss. Strachey wrote for it, Cripps became associated with the Left Book Club, while *Tribune* devoted two of its pages to the Left Book Club every

[1] Kingsley Martin to Gollancz, 22 August 1938.
[2] Gollancz to Strachey, undated but clearly August 1938.

week. In practice, this arrangement meant the subservience of *Tribune* to the communist line for two years or so. The paper never criticized the Moscow trials, though Brailsford, who had been associated with *Tribune* from the beginning, did so in articles for *Reynolds News* and elsewhere.

By this time, Strachey was at work on a book consisting basically of a critique of the views of Keynes. As always, he despatched a typescript to friends, among them, in this case, the communist economics don at Trinity, Maurice Dobb, an old acquaintance, and, of course, to Dutt. He excused his preoccupation with Keynes by saying that 'if, for good or evil, we have adopted People's Front Politics, we must have a People's Front economics also. If we do not, the result will be not that we avoid being involved in a Reformist economic policy, but that we get involved in a thoroughly bad Reformist economic policy.'[1] He quite consciously dealt with 'the whole new school of "Reformism" which is undoubtedly growing up on the basis of Keynes's work ([Douglas] Jay, Meade, [Roy] Harrod, Mrs [Joan] Robinson etc., etc.).' Indeed, Strachey was in touch with Joan Robinson over the book, and she looked at his two last chapters for him.

Strachey sent a copy of his ideas in typescript to Jay, then City Editor of the *Daily Herald*, whose book, *The Socialist Case*, Strachey had recently read with pleasure, despite its anti-Marxist tinge (and despite certain strictures about the title: was it, or was it not, *the* socialist case? Was it even socialist?). Jay sent back his own comments in a letter which, significantly, began with the words: 'I think I agree with most of your general conclusions.'[2] Not surprisingly, communist critics such as Dobb found, contrariwise, much to quarrel with about the book: 'I felt you had swallowed so much of the Keynes–Meade [line] as to give an almost Douglassite twist to the whole thing. . . . This is particularly clear in some of your formulations about the crisis being "a problem of purchasing power".'[3]

It seems thus obvious that in 1938 Strachey was beginning,

1 Strachey to Dutt, 19 May 1938.
2 Jay to Strachey, 20 August 1938.
3 Dobb to Strachey, undated MSS. This may have been later.

quietly but explicitly, to move away from communist orthodoxy. It would be difficult to say whether Marx's neglect of 'the subjective factor', or Keynes and his followers, or Roosevelt, or patriotism, or perhaps even a feeling that the depression was after all not the prelude to the final collapse, was decisive: indeed, all these points were interconnected. At all events, there are no more complaints in Strachey's letters that he could not be permitted to join the party proper. The idea was beginning to cross Strachey's mind that capitalist crises might be resolved without changing the system: as several letters to Sir Richard Acland in particular suggest, he was also having doubts in 1938 of the inevitability of 'growing pauperization' along the lines of Marx's predictions.

These ideas were evident at the Fabian summer school at Digswell in July 1938: they were 'extremely fresh and stimulating', commented John Lewis in *Left News*, without, apparently, irony. But Strachey certainly hinted at 'reformism' in these lectures. In addition, his review, in September 1938, of *Sigmund Freud*, by Francis Bartlett, was free of any attempt to link Freud with Marx.[1]

As yet, however, no accusation of actual desertion could be levelled against Strachey, for he went far to justify, once again, in a long article, the Soviet Show Trials, in *Left News* of July 1938. He wrote: 'no one, who had not . . . fixed his mind in the contrary opinion, could read the verbatim account of the trials without being wholly convinced of the authenticity of the confessions'. Indeed, he went on, 'no man can advance his political education more than by studying this supreme historical document,' which tells of the 'terrible story of the terrorist plots against the Soviet leaders'. 'The last stage of the conspiracy,' he said, seemed to have been reached in 1936–7. Gollancz had still much the same outlook; thus he solemnly published, in 1938, an 'electoral speech' by Litvinov in Leningrad. This collective naivety on the part of the British left, shared indeed by all sections of opinion, seems strange today; it is explained, surely, by the general optimism of European nationalists which had survived the First World War and only really foundered in the

[1] *Left News*, September 1938.

carnage of the Second, together with the effect of Auschwitz and the Russian purges themselves.

Already, however, anxiety about the future, and sheer patriotism, caused a much more vigorous strain to characterize Gollancz's editorial articles in *Left News* from the time of Munich onwards. In his October editorial, Gollancz faced publicly the accusation that 'there were too many communist books' in the Left Book Club, and went on to admit that, in the struggle against the evil of fascism, anti-democratic imperialism would be fighting in the same ranks as anti-fascist democrats – 'I intend to say this, for all the sneers of the leftists.' This article, despite its egotism ('I believe it to be literal truth that, if the Club had been founded ten years ago, and if it now had a membership of 10 million, we should be happily at . . . an honourable peace'), was the beginning of a major change in Gollancz's outlook. In his November editorial, dated 20 October, Gollancz went further. After admitting one or two minor criticisms of Left Book Club activities, Gollancz demanded rearmament, and ignored Marxism and communism completely.[1]

Strachey, meantime, went again to the U.S. He had been invited there in late 1938 to carry out another lecture tour. This was to coincide with another publication of his, *Hope in America*, a Marxist study of the U.S. economic situation, to be published by Louis Birk, the enterprising publisher of Modern Age Books, with whom he was on good terms. His first engagement in the U.S. was planned to be at a mass meeting in Madison Square Gardens on 5 October, to raise money for Spanish medical aid. Before leaving for the U.S., Strachey wrote to Boothby, who had now come out as one of the leading Conservatives opposed to appeasement. Writing on the day of the Munich debate in the House of Commons, Strachey said,

Before going, I feel an impulse to get my thoughts down on to paper in the form of a letter to you. . . . The issue during the coming months, and years, if we have so long, is that of the independence of this country. It is not a question now of whether this country is to become socialist or remain capitalist

[1] *Left News*, October 1938.

– or any issue intermediate between these two. It is a question of whether or not we are to be free to choose what we are to become. If a mixture of liking for the German and Italian *regimes*, and terror of war, is to govern our rulers' world policy, we shall very soon cease to be a free and independent sovereign state in the full meaning of the word. Hence the issue must be presented to the British people in that form. . . . Strictly following from this, the British people must be made to feel that those who ask them to, at least, risk fighting and dying for their country are determined to preserve their country and to improve those features which make it worth living in, and therefore dying for, e.g. its democracy, in the widest sense of that term . . . [and] a determination just as great as that shown by the fascists to deal with unemployment, *no doubt on Keynesist lines*. In two words, a 'progressive patriotism' must be the positive note struck. Equally important is the negative note, and that must be hatred of Hitler and all he stands for. . . .

Two things seem to be indispensable to the formation of such a potentially irresistible combination, which would isolate the very small, but very powerful, pro-fascist group which rules us today:

(a) The initiative must come from the right; from within the Tory party;
(b) There must be participation by the centre, Libs and official Labour, and support, or at the very least no opposition from the extreme left, i.e., the Crippsite Labour, Left Book Club and communist party. . . .

If the Chamberlain group is to be defeated, it will be . . . desperately important to mobilize the maximum press resources; to struggle for control of existing papers, and, if necessary, to start now at once. . . .

I and my [communist] friends cannot, of course, be of much help in these directions. Where we can play a certain role is on the question of Labour's attitude. It is true that we are loathed by the official leaders of the Labour party. Some, though not, I think, a majority, of the Labour leaders at heart sympathize with Chamberlain and so will be looking for excuses not to co-operate – e.g. Attlee's ignoble performance in recent days. On the other hand, the T.U. leaders, who, in the long run, control everything, are, from Citrine downwards, considerably better, because, I suppose, they can see that they could not exist in a fascist-controlled Britain.

Hence your forces could in the long run count, I believe, on the five million organized Trade Unionists as one of their bases, however badly the Parliamentary L.P. behaved (which it would).

The part which my immediate political associates can play is this. We can prevent the extreme left giving the left and centre the excuse that participation in such a united movement against the pro-fascists is impossible because it would split the Labour movement. I can honestly claim that the Left Book Club is now the main agent in moulding opinion, both in the left of the Labour party, and everywhere to the left of that. (The communist party itself will be all right. It will not, and should not, openly support, but, of course, it will, in fact, do everything to help.)

We are at once moving to widen the basis of the Left Book Club in two ways. First we have asked two Liberals (Richard Acland and Wilfred Roberts[1]), plus Cripps, to join the Selection Committee. Second, we are changing the title to 'Left Book Club and Anti-Fascist Association', with a view to making it ultimately simply the 'Anti-Fascist Association'. Already, it is by no means merely or really a book club. . . . If we succeed in rapidly changing the whole character of the L.B.C.; making it a body of the left centre, instead of the extreme left, and not limiting it to people who will read books, I do not see why the Club should not become one of the mass bases (the Trade Unions being the other) for fighting the pro-fascists. It *could* be an enormous educational propagandist force, comprising men of all parties, bent simply on giving us a core of several hundred thousand politically educated people who *could* not be swayed by fascist-manufactured mob emotion into betraying

[1] Liberal M.P. for North Cumberland 1935–1950.

this country as the unfortunate people of Britain have been cajoled into doing in the last few days. . . . You may ask what all this side has to do with you. Only this. We have by no means got to the point where any overt, organized cooperation between us is possible. But I do feel that it is vital that we (*that is, all anti-fascists fighting for the independence of this country from Hitler*) should be in touch across the party lines. And there should be touch not only between the people near the middle, but between the two ends – that is, between conservatives, and us on the real left. At present, there is only the narrow line passing through you and me. What I feel is that you and your friends should have touch with us – for example, while I am away: Celia, as you know, has in many respects better political judgement than I have, though possibly less experience and knowledge. Anyhow, not only on political, but also on personal, grounds, I hope you will be in touch with her. It won't be easy for her, or anyone else, this autumn.[1]

Strachey did not, of course, take the communists into account when he wrote this letter to his old friend. Thus Boothby complemented for Strachey the part played by his analyst Carroll in providing an outlet for his perplexities, and, it must fairly be admitted, his patriotic plans.

Strachey had received a U.S. visa in September. A few hours before he was due to sail, he received a telephone message from the U.S. vice-consul, James Callahan, asking him to call. Strachey went to the consulate. Callahan asked him if he was a member of the communist party. Was he opposed to organized government? Did he advocate the overthrow of any government by force? To all these questions, Strachey, under oath, replied in the negative. Callahan advised him to postpone sailing until his 'case' had been further discussed. Strachey asked whether the consul had orders to cancel his visa and whether he had information that he would not be admitted to the U.S. To both these questions the consul in his turn answered in the negative. Strachey, therefore, went ahead and sailed. Strachey arrived on s.s. *Normandie* on 10 October and was refused permission to land.

[1] Strachey to Boothby, 2 October 1938.

He was held at Ellis Island for fifteen days, when he was released on bail, pending appeal.

Strachey was then accused before a special board of enquiry at Ellis Island of being a communist, and also of being a member of the central committee of the communist party of Great Britain. Evidence was produced that he had addressed communist party meetings, and that he had contributed to the *Daily Worker*. As in 1935, Strachey was, of course, able to deny that he was a member of the party, or of its central committee. He said that he had spoken for the communist party, 'but added that he had likewise spoken at meetings organized by branches of the Labour party, the Liberal party, the League of Nations Union and many other bodies. . . .'[1] The argument ranged round the question as to whether Strachey had obtained his visa by fraud – that is, by giving the consul-general in London false information. Strachey was allowed into the U.S. pending an appeal, providing that he did not lecture. This was irritating, since the ban lasted till January. In the end, he was allowed free of all limitations. Celia wrote to him, 'Everyone here is amazed that you have succeeded. . . . Come back just as soon as you've settled your affairs, but not till you are ready. God knows what's going to happen to the world. V.G. [Gollancz] and I have endless telephone conversations – both of us at the bottom of things. If it looks as if there will be war before you come home, shall we come to you? I don't think personally there will be, but one can't tell for certain. . . .'[2] Nothing indeed was certain in 1939, as Celia and Strachey soon found out.

[1] *See* Brief on behalf of the Relator-Appellant, New York 1938, prepared by Arthur Garfield Hays.
[2] Celia to Strachey, undated (Friday) but, by inference, early 1939.

Chapter 12 / DISENCHANTMENT

On his return from the U.S. in February 1939, Strachey started, like other Europeans, on one of the darkest times. In early 1939, Gollancz's Left Book Club editorials were increasingly gloomy. Spain, the main 'cause' of the Left Book Club, was turning into a defeat. Gollancz was moving towards a more liberal position, despite some indecision in respect of Russia: thus, the editorial in February's *Left News* read: 'It would be idle, for instance, to pretend that [in Russia] there were not certain barriers against full intellectual freedom at the present time. The ordinary Soviet public is not in a position to arrive at the whole truth. . . . (But is not *practically* the great mass of Englishmen, who are at the mercy, day by day, of lying propaganda?)' Strachey still echoed this attitude, despite his respect for Keynes – a respect expressed in print for the first time in a skilful article in *Left News* for May 1939.

Nevertheless, even in this crisis, in which war seemed so close, the far left and Left Book Club, on the one hand, and the Labour party on the other, remained at daggers drawn. Cripps was even expelled from the party in January 1939 for circulating to all Labour M.P.s and constituencies an argument for a Popular Front position, and Bevan and Strauss were expelled for supporting Cripps. In March, the national agent of the party wrote to borough, divisional and local Labour parties specifically about the Left Book Club, and stated that, 'if the Club or its groups indulge in political propaganda in opposition to the Labour party, or in activities embarrassing to constituency Labour parties, very serious notice must be taken by the National Executive Committee and the Annual Party Conference. . . . If [the National] Executive Committee continues to receive complaints of Left Book Club activities antagonistic to the Labour party or to constituency Labour parties, it will be unable to avoid a declaration as to the Club's position. . . .'

This menace provoked a counter-attack from Gollancz and Strachey (Laski being still away in the U.S.) in the next issue of *Left News*, claiming that the Club was a bastion of civilization, an organization which could work well for the Labour party, and constituted the most promising contribution to left-wing politics made for a generation; and, at this time, with nearly 60,000 members and 1,300 groups, there was ample substance for this claim.

The third Annual Rally of the Left Book Club was held in the Empress Hall, Earls Court, and was of special importance, since not only were Gollancz, the Dean of Canterbury, Pollitt and Strachey speaking, as on previous occasions, but Cripps, Lloyd George and Norman Angell as well. Robeson sang again, as in 1938. Lloyd George sounded almost as radical as Gollancz and his wonderful voice, presence and authority lent lustre to the occasion.

In July, Strachey was still in intimate touch with the communist leaders. Thus he was asked by Dutt for help in drafting part of the communist party programme for the congress in October – in the sphere of the economy, finance and taxation, and also agriculture.[1] He was similarly still busy with further work on his book about Keynes's economics: but, as he put it later to Bennet Cerf, 'What . . . happened is that endless discussion went on all the summer with the economist pundits here – both party ones and the other kind – and in the end they went on so long that the war came!'[2]

The book ultimately became *A Programme for Progress*. This was finished by Strachey before the Soviet Union's agreement

[1] Dutt to Strachey, 10 July 1939.
[2] Letter to Cerf, 17 October 1939.

with Germany, and had been begun before Munich. It reflects Strachey's respect, though grudging, for Roosevelt's 'middle way', and shows that there was the stuff of revisionism in Britain's most respectable Marxist, even before the diplomatic events of August 1939.

But the news in August of Stalin's pact with Hitler appalled Strachey, as it did most communists. Perhaps too there were some fascists who were shocked. Strachey wrote on 25 August to Boothby:

'You can imagine how staggered I am by the Soviet-German pact. My friends on the left say that it is not inconsistent with an Anglo-Soviet pact of mutual assistance. Their policy is to press the Government to sign such a pact. I agree with this and am, privately and publicly, urging it – as I see a number of speakers, such as Aneurin, did in the House yesterday. I pin all my hopes to this proving the correct interpretation of the Soviet-German Pact, and urge you to use all your influence to get an Anglo-Soviet pact of mutual assistance signed at this eleventh hour.

'As you can imagine, I must pin all my hope to this view, for if it were to prove ill-founded, and the Soviet Union were to go into benevolent neutrality to Germany, my whole political position would be shattered. I should have to reconsider everything.

'I feel the need of telling you this as a friend in this extraordinary situation.'[1]

A day or two later Strachey and Boothby dined together. They walked for a long time on Hampstead Heath, until one o'clock in the morning. It had by then become clear that there was no chance of an Anglo-Soviet pact. Boothby advised Strachey to resign from the communist party. Strachey agreed, fundamentally, that he would have to do so. But for a long time he dilly-dallied. Indeed, he even appeared to some people, a month later, to be adopting the new Soviet position. Louis Fischer, for example, recalled Strachey and Celia talking with him in August: 'Strachey,' wrote Fischer, 'accepted the new communist stand. He said if Russia were a socialist country, then everything it did was in the interest of socialism. We threw Marx and Lenin

[1] Strachey to Boothby, 25 August 1939.

quotations at one another, and engaged in verbal dog-fights. John was not to be dissuaded.'[1] But Strachey's mind was in a turmoil. Kingsley Martin, his host on the occasion when he met Louis Fischer, had heard him only a few weeks before on a platform in a big meeting, proclaiming in his 'confident, resonant voice' that 'nothing is so certain amid the shifting sands of politics today as the absolute knowledge that the Soviet Union will never yield an inch to Nazi Germany.'[2] It now was obvious how false a prediction that was. Claud Cockburn recalls Strachey weeping profusely, and begging him to support him in an act of protest or of defiance.

The two weeks after the Nazi-Soviet pact were as peculiar in international politics as they were tragic. Thus the journal of the Comintern, *World News and Views*, in its issue of 26 August, published several articles which had been written before the Nazi-Soviet pact, as well as a policy statement by Stalin made after the pact. Next, the British communist party and the *Daily Worker* greeted the war with an anti-German statement; Pollitt wrote and published, in September, an exceptionally strong pamphlet supporting the war as just: 'to stand aside,' he said, 'from this conflict, to contribute only revolutionary sounding phrases while the fascist beasts ride roughshod over Europe, would be a betrayal of everything our forefathers had fought for.' But, soon after, Bill Rust, the editor of the *Daily Worker*, came back from Moscow with instructions to the English comrades to change their line. They were to describe the Soviet-German pact, in the words of Molotov, the Soviet premier, as putting 'an end . . . to the abnormal relations that have existed between the Soviet Union and Germany for a number of years'.[3] Pollitt recanted. Strachey made no overt sign, but perhaps he remembered Crossman's remarks to him of a few months before about Russian methods.

The Second World War began on 3 September, a fine day which Strachey spent sailing on the Blackwater estuary with his

[1] Louis Fischer, *Men and Politics*, p. 584. By context this must have been 24 September, when Fischer was staying with Kingsley Martin, at whose Sussex house the conversation occurred.
[2] Kingsley Martin, *Editor*, p. 207.
[3] *Daily Worker*, 2 November 1939.

friend Arthur Parrish. Strachey's first reaction was to try to join up but, as he put it in a letter in March 1940, 'they did not want untrained men, and refused me'.[1] He was after all nearly forty. Afterwards, his attitude to the war underwent several curious changes.

The first issue of the *Left News* after the coming of the war was abbreviated. It included a leading article jointly signed by Strachey, Gollancz and Laski, repeating that the aims of the Left Book Club were to help the struggle against fascism, and to fight positively for peace and for 'a better social and economic order'. The critical remark was the reflection that 'For us, Hitler is a symptom of a deeper disease; he is not the disease itself. We cannot make his defeat, therefore, an end in itself. . . . Members should . . . never fail to emphasize that we are fighting for a new world.'[2]

The next months were a time of reconsideration for both Gollancz and Strachey, as for many others. Strachey began this process by selling £1,000-worth of Russian Five Year Plan bonds in September.[3] He wisely re-invested in General Motors, the North American company, and one or two other English companies.[4] *A Programme for Progress* was selected as the Left Book Club choice for January 1940. As many of his readers discovered with alarm, this read when finished as frankly a 'revisionist' work. It accepted that, in the long run, socialism was the only remedy for the breakdown of capitalism, but assumed that most people were not ready for this. Pending socialism, the masses had to be offered an interim programme which would modify their grievances: otherwise, Strachey suggested, they would turn away from democratic politics altogether, and support any reactionary movement that offered them employment. Strachey, therefore, put forward a programme of economic and social reform for a 'Labour or progressive government, which cannot expropriate the capitalists and organize a socialist economic

1 Strachey to Mrs Heath, 13 March 1940.
2 *Left News*, September 1939.
3 Letter of 21 September 1939.
4 Letter of Chase, Hendison and Tennant, Stockbrokers to Strachey, dated 8 November 1939.

system of production for use.' Strachey's programme included six main points: the extension of public enterprise, low interest rates on loan capital, increased social services, including monetary allowances to individuals, and redistributory taxation; there would also be a state-controlled banking system and strict public control over foreign exchanges.

The reformism, and the very nature of the practical pre-occupations, evident in this book – promised difficulties for its author within the communist movement. But it was one of Strachey's sanest and most influential books. *The Coming Struggle for Power* made people communists. *A Programme for Progress* made them Keynesians – and, therefore social democrats, even though, as Anthony Crosland, one of those who read the book particularly carefully, pointed out many years later, Strachey's programme was 'incomparably more modest' than the then programme of the Labour party, the 'short-term programme' adopted in 1937.[1]

The most unacceptable section of this book, from the communist point of view, was that about the New Deal. For the New Deal did, after all, resemble Strachey's own programme, and it did provide 'a rich store of experience to guide us as to the real consequences of applying the type of measure' which he had himself suggested. Strachey also considered the extent to which the measure which he was suggesting had been applied by the Nazis: a brave intellectual effort, in the circumstances. Trouble was obviously brewing for him. But his indecision about his attitude to Russia was losing for him the sympathy of many people. 'In this matter,' Allan Young wrote to Strachey in October, after a discussion at a dinner, '*your* difficulties are greater than mine, because of your association with the C.P. Quite frankly, I think that is an association which you should break. It is not a question whether C.P. policy is right or wrong (and it changes so often that it can hardly avoid sometimes being right), but because the discipline over the thought and action of its members is ridiculous. The difference between Bolshevism and Socialism is not necessarily one of either policy or strategy: it is one of morality. It might be said that Marx stood for the

[1] Crosland, *The Future of Socialism*, p. 58.

"expropriation of the expropriators", but Stalin does not stop there, he goes on to "the exploitation of the exploiters" . . . the language [of the communist] was born in revengeful minds – not philosophic minds. It will be terribly difficult for you to accept this, because I fear that your whole political life has been cast among men who regard cynicism as a virtue. . . . The real difference between me and members of the C.P. is that I always think of myself as a worker (the slave tradition perhaps), and they always think about themselves as commissars.'[1]

This admirable letter did not, however, bear immediate fruit. Thus, in *Left News* of November, Strachey wrote a hostile review of Leonard Woolf's excellent *Barbarians at the Gate*. This, he said, was 'the first occasion on which I have had basic disagreements with the whole point expressed in one of the Left Book Club choices'. For Woolf's book was liberal in tone and criticized Stalin and the communists almost as harshly as it did Hitler and the Nazis. In his review, Strachey took Woolf to task for not considering that the 'conspiracy which the [Soviet] trial broke was the expression of the last stand of the last, and in some ways the most formidable, exploiting class, namely the Kulaks'. He added, 'is there not a great deal of evidence to show that, if the Soviet government has erred, it is in being over-optimistic as to the point at which the resistance of hostile classes to the establishment of socialism has finally ended?' Strachey still felt able to say that 'in 1936, Stalin had been looking forward to a time when contested elections would be possible'.

The letters following Woolf's book and Strachey's review of it were numerous, and critical. The trouble was partly that Gollancz had given the impression of having deliberately hedged his bets over Woolf by publishing a pro-Russian book, as the December choice, by the Dean of Canterbury – *The Socialist Sixth of the World*. This was an unfortunate moment, since it was that month that Russia invaded Finland. The protests, therefore, came from both sides. Thus: 'We are asked by Mr XXXXXX to cancel his membership. We do not propose to repeat the terms in which he gave his resignation, but they were to the effect that, if he wanted any anti-Soviet filth, he would prefer to join the Right

[1] Letter of Allan Young to Strachey, 18 October 1939.

Book Club'; and, 'Strachey's *critique* read this morning in the same hour as the news from Helsingfors makes me decide that I cannot honestly belong to a Club that includes Strachey'; or 'With Laski writing his imperialist tripe, thank God for John Strachey, who is sticking to his principles'; and, 'May I ask you to publish a British worker's advice to John Strachey? He must know that majority left-wing opinion in this country is against him. Are we all so very foolish as he would seem to suggest?'; and 'I promise myself a rare treat when I read Strachey again as I get back from work tonight'; and yet again 'J. Strachey's piece was first-rate. That shows you how a firm grasp of Marxist theory can keep a man straight when all sorts of people are wavering or proving downright traitors, going over to the enemy.'

The publication of *A Programme for Progress* in January, as the Left Book Club's choice for that month, was reckoned by Strachey's old readers as the beginning of a major change in his and the Club's life. This was particularly the case with the communist party leaders, headed by Emile Burns, who reviewed the book in the *Daily Worker*. Burns wrote to Strachey in February expanding on his hostile review, saying: 'I thought you understood from the first that I did not like the general effect of this book, besides disagreeing with many of the economic arguments. When the *Daily Worker* asked me to review it, I felt that it was necessary to bring out the whole tendency which seemed to me to run through it.'[1] The book sold less well than Strachey's other Left Book Club books, reaching 31,742 in the Club edition: still a huge sale for wartime.

The continuing 'revolutionary defeatism' of the communists and the disastrous war events meant that further rows could not be avoided. Clough Williams-Ellis recalls a meeting in Hampstead organized by Bobby Carter, Librarian of the R.I.B.A., where a speech by Strachey was severely criticized by the communists. Probably the review of *A Programme for Progress* in the *New Statesman* by Kingsley Martin exacerbated matters, since, understandably in the circumstances, it sounded patronizing, suggesting, under the title 'A Social Democrat', that what

---

[1] Letter of Emile Burns to Strachey, 5 February 1940. The controversy continued.

Strachey was now proposing had been urged for years by the *New Statesman* and other organs denounced for a long time by the communists as social-fascist.[1] This review outraged many friends of Strachey, particularly Maurice Dobb, who wrote urging a reply (Dobb had written a very temperate review himself). 'After using his own madcap ideas to distort your book,' wrote Dobb, 'and then, your book thus distorted, to pillory his own concept of what communism is, he has the impudence to invite you to join hands with him (plus Philip Toynbee[2] and Dick Crossman, presumably) in founding a new party. Nauseating imbecility! The war has made the man madder than I thought it had. If you don't refute him, Burns will begin to have a case.'[3]

During the early spring of 1940 Strachey was laid low with pains which were diagnosed as sciatica. It may have been a psychosomatic illness, akin to that which had affected him during the indecision over Esther in 1932. On this occasion, doctors recommended the removal of tonsils and all his teeth.[4] These were unhappy, and probably unnecessary, operations and Strachey was extremely ill with them. Strachey was also occupied with various problems relating to his parents' old house at Newlands Corner, then a hotel. These may have exacerbated the crisis.

The invasion of Norway and Denmark, at the beginning of April, decided him at last to take action against the communists. That event meant that the war was rumbling much nearer, and that France, perhaps Britain, might be actually imperilled. Yet the communist party were still pressing, in the *Daily Worker*, the Russian line of 'revolutionary defeatism'. Strachey decided to make his break in the columns of the *New Statesman* and, indeed, wrote from the nursing home where he was recovering from his operations what was in effect his letter of resignation. Gollancz, who was experiencing the same drama, took the letter to Kingsley Martin in person. Kingsley Martin published Strachey's letter in

---

[1] *New Statesman*, 30 March 1940.
[2] Philip Toynbee abandoned the communist party at the time of the Nazi-Soviet pact. He was, at this time, temporarily editor of the *Birmingham Town Crier*, the Labour paper which had given such publicity to Mosley and Strachey in the 1920s.
[3] Dobb to Strachey, postcard posted 30 March.
[4] Strachey had also had a tonsils operation in 1923. *See* above, p. 35.

the *New Statesman* on 27 April 1940. Its apparently pedantic and tactical tone made a very clear break, doing in effect what Strachey had wished to do since September 1939.

It is necessary [he wrote] for those who do not accept the attitude expressed by the *Daily Worker* to the German invasion of Scandinavia to disassociate themselves from that attitude.

On Tuesday, 9 April, the day before the invasion, the *Daily Worker* expressed the view that the laying of mines by the British in Norwegian territorial waters 'does not directly harm Germany in a military sense – that, indeed, it is obviously directed rather towards the general domination of Scandinavian policy by the Western Powers, with the principal idea of directing it against Russia'. Hence, there were indications 'that the German Government may, after all, prefer to let the situation ride for the moment . . . and act diplomatically rather than militarily'.

But after the German invasion, in the issue of 13 April, Frank Pitcairn [i.e. Claud Cockburn] wrote: 'Everyone knew that if Britain invaded Norwegian territorial waters with minefields, the Germans would respond with counter-action. Nobody is fool enough to suppose that they would not.'

The contradiction, though extreme, is not in itself particularly important. But it is decisive, in the sense that it shows the nature of the argument, used by Pitcairn in the same article, and by the *Daily Worker* on every day since the German invasion of Scandinavia. The argument is that that invasion was inevitable, easy to foresee, and, in that sense, a justified reply to the British violation of Norwegian waters; that the whole responsibility for the spread of the war to Scandinavia, and the sufferings of the Norwegian people, rested on Britain and France exclusively, and not upon Germany. The passages quoted show that this argument was resorted to only after the German invasion had taken place.

Examples of the apologetics for the German Imperialists into which the *Daily Worker* has fallen could be multiplied. But no one who reads, especially, the first half-dozen issues after the invasion of Norway, can possibly doubt what is the real attitude to the war of those who write and direct the newspaper. . . . If, for example, the *Daily Worker*, while consenting to report the German invasion of Norway, and even perhaps permitting itself a word of sympathy with the Norwegian people, as one latest victim of fascist aggression, had pointed out that the Germans, though by far the most obvious aggressors, were not the only people who took aggressive action; that all Imperialists, including the British and French, were aggressive; that the Norwegian people had been dragged into the war by the encroachment of their neutrality, first of one side and then of the other, I should be comprehended. But, in fact, the *Daily Worker's* attitude was one of apology, the more complete, in some ways, because tacit, for the German Imperialists; it was an attitude of apology carried, on the day after the German invasion, to the fantastic lengths of refusing to report that invasion at all. . . .

It is this identification of the interest of the Soviet Union with the success of the German imperialists which has, in the main, driven those responsible for the conduct of the *Daily Worker* to take their present line. It has driven them to an interpretation of Lenin's policy of revolutionary defeatism which makes it clear, in almost every line they write, that they now care nothing for the consequence of a total defeat of Britain, France, and now Norway, in this war at the hands of the Nazi Imperialists. That is what anyone who is not wilfully deceiving themselves must feel when he reads any of their pronouncements. . . . But every line written in the *Daily Worker* drives me to the conviction that those controlling the *Daily Worker* are prepared, for the sake of what they consider to be the interest of the Soviet Union, to give way to Hitler to any extent, and that they are utterly irresponsible as to the consequences to the British people of such unlimited giving way. So long as that remains the case I, and, it seems, almost everybody else in the country, can have nothing to do with them, however much we, like all sane people, 'do not want the war', and however much we may agree with them as to the general character of the war.[1]

[1] *New Statesman and Nation*, 27 April 1940.

Strachey could have been under no illusions as to the consequences of this breach of discipline. On the other hand, since he was not a member of the communist party, he could scarcely be expelled. The Scandinavian question was, to some extent, a pretext: Strachey had been suspicious for months of orthodox communism because of Freud and the 'subjective view', because of Keynes, and because of Roosevelt. He used this issue as a reason for his break with communism primarily out of patriotism. In the issue of the German invasion of Scandinavia, there was something in the *Daily Worker*'s view; the British and French had planned to mine the Norwegian waters, and to land at several points in Norway without the prior approval of the Norwegian government: the German action was, therefore, pre-emptive; and Liddell Hart pointed out in his excellent *History* that the inclusion of planning an aggressive war against Norway in the Nuremburg Trial charge sheet was 'a palpable act of hypocrisy'.[1] Still, the communists, though they reached the same conclusion, started from a different base.

The communists could not allow Strachey's letter to stay unanswered. Rust wrote to the *New Statesman* in reply, as did the Oxford communist historian, Christopher Hill.[2] But their main spokesman was Ivor Montagu, the journalist, writer and film director who had been a friend of Strachey's throughout the 1930s. He wrote to the *New Statesman*, sending a copy to Strachey. In his covering note to Strachey, he wrote: 'Tried to ring you for lunch the other day, but found your phone not working. Pity. It turns out we might have had a dialectical whatnot which would have saved your somersaults.'[3] Montagu's letter to the *New Statesman* began with a general statement anticipating the repression of the communist party, and went on:

Lastly, Mr Strachey. I do not understand the relevance of his quotations from the *Daily Worker*. The responsibility, or otherwise, of the Allies for the extension of the war to Scandinavia depends not even remotely on the time-table of landings

[1] Liddell Hart, *History of the Second World War* (1970), p. 59.
[2] *New Statesman*, 4 May 1940 and 18 May 1940.
[3] Ivor Montagu to Strachey, 27 April 1940.

or laying minefields – or on the accuracy of day-to-day estimates of their implications. It depends on general considerations. The Allies alone *cannot* fight Germany, the U.S.S.R. remaining neutral. The contestants are too well matched. Victory could come to either side only following a mutual destruction and exhaustion that would leave U.S.S.R. the predominant power in Europe. . . . But Strachey, blind to this simple proposition, can only explain matters by discovering what he is so anxious to discover, a tortuous underground motive to gain a victory for Hitler in the interests of the U.S.S.R. What vulgarianism! As if Stalin could wave a paper with Hitler's signature on it, and regard the safety of the U.S.S.R. as thereby secure, irrespective of the power of Hitler! . . . When will these ever-subtle ones start saving themselves absurdity by assuming, for a change, that, when the Soviet Union and the Communist International (including the affiliated parties comprising the latter) urge peace and the realization of the aims of neither contesting group in that way, that is precisely what they want and what they consider in the general interest?[1]

After this, Strachey began to receive many private comments of disapproval. But he maintained his position. He wrote to the *New Statesman* again, in terms which were in a way still rather ambiguous:

I have been challenged, however, by several private correspondents to say what line of policy to meet the present situation can be adopted if that advocated by the *Daily Worker* is rejected. To that challenge I wish to respond. . . . A new government, with popular support, must seek, by every means in its power, to secure what may be called, in brief, an anti-Imperialist, democratic peace: a peace involving such features as the freedom of India and all other appropriate parts of the Colonial Empire. . . . The main task of any People's Government in Britain must be, either in peace or in war, to strike off those horrible fetters with which monopoly capital binds our

[1] Montagu to the *New Statesman*, 27 April 1940.

limbs today; those fetters which prevent us developing any-thing approaching our full power, whether in the economic, military or diplomatic field; those fetters which produce that intolerable sense of national impotence and frustration which oppresses every one of us today. . . . Every ounce of effort which we possess should be concentrated on the struggle against the National Government. The forces which can rid us of the National Government exist – in the great Trade Unions, in the Labour movement and in the ever growing revulsion of the people as a whole against the disaster into which they are being led. But we shall utterly fail to mobilize these forces so long as we give the unmistakable impression that we are quite willing to risk the subjection of this country to Hitler.[1]

This suggests that, even if Strachey were disillusioned with the communist party, he was not disillusioned with communism – less so than Gollancz, for example. The suggestion, too, of peace negotiations presumably meant abandoning most of Poland, and all of Czechoslovakia and Austria to Germany, permitting Hitler to keep hold of all that he had gained during 1938 and 1939. The rallying of Strachey to the patriotic cause had still some way to go.

Strachey had, however, written privately to his mentor, Dutt:

I wrote my letter to the *New Statesman*, because I simply could not stomach, even for another day, the line of the *Daily Worker*. . . . I am a different kind of man, with different basic reactions, to yourself, and to those who determine the policy of the C.P. During the Seventh Congress, People's Front, period, this basic difference was obscured. But it cannot be obscured any longer. If I had not made any public protest now, over the Norwegian affair, I should have had to do so later, in circumstances, very likely, in which my action would have seemed to you still more base. . . .

I believe that I understand the revolutionary defeatist line. I have re-read the relevant passages in Vol. 5 of Lenin's *Collected Works*. None of us can know what Lenin's estimate of the present situation would have been. But I repeat that I cannot apply that line to the present situation in the way which you do, since I still attach great importance to the differences between fascism and capitalist democracy. This does not mean that I support the war; I wrote, and spoke repeatedly, in favour of accepting the German offer of negotiations, made with Soviet support . . . but always with the essential proviso that, if Hitler now refused such a peace, he must be resisted. . . .

No doubt this is partly a question of class origins as well as national origins. But the majority of the peoples of the Western Capitalisms have so enormously much to lose from being conquered by the Nazis that I cannot follow a policy which involves enormously increasing the risk, to put it no higher, of this happening.

No doubt the party's reaction to my last book has also influenced me. Not, I hope, by way of personal pique, but because I see that the whole conception of an interlocking economic and political struggle, which, as a matter of fact, I have always held, and which again seemed not to be in conflict with the party's view during the People's Front period, is now regarded simply as 'reformism'.

Well, there it is. All it amounts to is that I believe that I see what the line is, and why it is what it is, but still simply cannot accept it. . . .

Perhaps a new phase will arrive in which we shall find ourselves speaking a common language again. That would be the thing which I should like best in the world. I realize to the full how utterly politically homeless this makes me: and, how easily complete personal and political degeneration occurs in such circumstances. Everything that you all will necessarily think and say of me will be hard indeed to bear. But I am what I am, and only worse deception and disaster could come from my pretending, to a still further degree, to be something which I am not.

p.s. I can't help feeling too what a poor return this is for all the extraordinary trouble which you took about my political education. I shall always be profoundly grateful.[1]

[1] Strachey to Dutt, 6 May 1940.

In the course of the next few weeks, Strachey and Ivor Montagu carried on a protracted correspondence. There was no hope, however, of compromise. In the end, Strachey sent Pollitt a copy of these letters. In reply, Pollitt was brief and to the point:

'I have read the correspondence you kindly sent me and consider it prolonged.

'About your not liking to come to the office – it is surely your conscience, and I find it impossible to go anywhere else.'[1]

Gollancz had basically made the same decision. His article in *Left News* for April, long and much contested, made his position quite clear on the question of the war. 'I have made earnest endeavours,' he wrote, and 'I have failed to convince myself that the "stop the war" agitation could, if at this stage successful, result in anything but a progressive enslavement of the peoples, and particularly the working classes.' The same issue contained long, thoughtful, and basically social democratic articles by not only Strachey, but also Crossman, on the subject of Keynes's plan for paying for the war. Emile Burns's 'answer' cut less ice.

Laski, whose quarrel with Russia had been earlier in time but who remained more optimistic, wrote soon that socialists 'must work and hope for a British victory,' which would also benefit Russia.[2] But this was too sophisticated an argument for the brutal circumstances of 1940. Strachey's pamphlet, *Banks for the People*, naturally made little impact, since it was published in May 1940.[3] By then, a new stage in his life was beginning. He was still, in 1940, two years under forty, and great prizes would come to him; but when he abandoned communism, a spark went out of him which was never really rekindled. For he had placed all his creative power and physical energy at the service of something which he had believed to be a general guide to rational politics. But now Reason had failed him.

[1] Pollitt to Strachey, 7 September 1940.
[2] Preface to *The Betrayal of the Left* (1941), p. xix.
[3] Its sales were 1,669 of an edition priced 1/6.

Part 2

THE FORSAKER

Old and forsaken houses
  Lie and rot,
And all the lived-in rooms
  Grow thin and bare.
Stopped with a sickened sense
  We venture not
On soundless floor or naked treadless stair,
  Dead things that move,
Blown paper and the trivial crumbling of plaster
  Mimic life's stir,
Mimic you, the forsaker; mimic you gone.

John Strachey, *Oxford Poetry*, 1922

Chapter 13 / THE WAR

Strachey was now again in the political wilderness, with few political friends save for Boothby, whose star was again in the ascendant with Churchill's accession to power. Strachey was typical, however, of many left-wing socialists who had not either been able to stomach what they knew of the purges or Russia's war policy. There were countless voters who had been won to the progressive cause in a general manner by Strachey. There were also enough ex-communists to make him a political focus.

All too much so, perhaps. Strachey and his wife were on Hitler's 'blacklist'. If the Germans were to land in Britain, they and their children would be arrested. After the fall of Paris, in June 1940, this eventually seemed possible. Celia received an invitation to go with the children to refuge in Canada. The Stracheys walked through the cow parsley in the Essex country-side discussing what to do. They decided that Celia, with the children, should go to Canada, if possible. To Celia's dismay, Strachey procured passages easily. She, Charles and Elizabeth sailed for Canada in July. It was a terrible decision for her, and one which she regretted from the moment that she had taken it. But she rightly supposed that, had the Germans landed, Strachey would have been able to escape more easily without the encumbrance of a family, which might have been used as hostages in the event of defeat.

This left Strachey himself still at a loose end. What should he do in the war?

There remained the Left Book Club. But war was transforming it. In *Left News* for September, for instance, Strachey asked whether 'we should welcome or deplore, the present tendency for American assistance'. Here Strachey entered, for the first time, upon polemics against some of his old Left Book Club associates: thus, referring to an article by John Lewis, he argued, 'we see that Dr Lewis, and those who think like him, do not feel that the main, and immediate, danger of the establishment of fascism in Britain consists in the possibility of the defeat and subjugation of Britain by the Nazis.' Strachey continued on the committee of selection of the Left Book Club. He was, however, too old, it seemed, to fight. For a time, Strachey stayed with Celia's mother (who had always liked him) and later, briefly, at the house of Lord Rothschild (5 Bentinck Street), with, among others, Guy Burgess and Anthony Blunt and, later still, in his mother's basement at St Leonard's Terrace. With Burgess, he had endless political discussions, though Burgess's espionage was concealed from him; nor did he join Burgess on his wild raids through the blackout of wartime London, in the company of Brian Howard, in search of delectable youth. Burgess did, however, leave Strachey one lasting benefit: a concern for music, of which previously he had been ignorant: Burgess lived in a perpetual atmosphere of Mozart and late Beethoven quartets and Strachey profited from that.

Strachey's career in the war began modestly, as an air raid warden in Chelsea, where he was living, at his mother's house in St Leonard's Terrace. This position at the bottom of the firing line was of immense personal interest, and of value to him. Perhaps for the first time, Strachey gained knowledge of ordinary people and observed them under duress. From this experience, he gained the knowledge which enabled him to write an admirable half novel, half true story, *Post D*. *Post D* is autobiographical;[1] flatly written and graphic, it deliberately avoided the discussion of any ideas at all except in its last sentence. It made a considerable impact when some of it appeared in the *New Statesman*. Names are

[1] *Post D: Some experiences of an Air Raid Warden* (Gollancz 1941).

changed but, otherwise, one must assume that the events occurred much as described. The conclusion of the book is a paean of praise to English patriotism, and to the powers of resistance of London. 'Ford' as a self-portrait is a good deal less emotional, and entertaining, than Strachey was himself, for he is presented as a lowest common factor to whom, however, everything which happens is extraordinary.

Strachey's time as an air raid warden attached to observation post No. 46, Tedworth Square, was not otherwise memorable, save for a brief clash with the local air raid warden authorities on the type of matter frequently discussed in *Post D*: Strachey, after about a month as a warden, was ready to lay down the law, and take up the matter with a local councillor, on the question of extra protection and strutting for air raid posts. (This incident appears in *Post D*, scarcely disguised.) In addition, he narrowly escaped being killed during the blitz – once, when dining with his old friend Plummer, then assistant general manager of the Beaverbrook papers, at Simpson's in the Strand; once when walking with Boothby in St James's Street.[1]

But these bare comments scarcely give an adequate impression of the extent to which Strachey, in this year of drama, was, as one of his friends, Patricia Llewellyn-Davies, at the time, put it, *en fleur*: he had shaken off the shackles of the communist party, he felt exhilarated by almost every experience or new person: he was entranced by Burgess's music, he revelled in the dangers affecting St James's Street or the Strand, he dined at Prunier's, or the Savoy, with others beleaguered in wartime London. The combination of gaiety, danger and the willing acceptance of imaginative leadership, made this a most brilliant time for all who worked, or lived, in the capital. Strachey was also living much as a bachelor again. Overshadowing all personal points of view was the knowledge that victory was uncertain. Celia believes that the war afforded an outlet to Strachey's suppressed aggression.

During the autumn of 1940, Strachey was busy on three further projects: the completion of a book attacking federalism, published as *Federalism or Socialism*, which became the curiously irrelevant

[1] *See* Strachey's article in the *New Republic*, 10 November 1941.

Left Book Club choice for September 1940, the climax of the Battle of Britain;[1] secondly, a long essay addressed to his children on the theme of patriotism, published, as the Left Book Club choice for January 1941, as *A Faith to Fight For* – a book which today reads sentimentally but, at the time, was believed in passionately by Strachey as his political testament;[2] and thirdly, a contribution to *The Betrayal of the Left*, a symposium edited by Gollancz and published as the alternative Left Book Club choice for February 1941. Strachey was thus as usual busy. He made a brief contribution to the arguments about the communist policy of revolutionary defeatism in the form of an article in *Left News* of January 1941 about the communist-sponsored People's Convention. Another contribution, entitled 'Totalitarianism', showed that Strachey's break was with Russia, not with Marxism: for he said that, 'it cannot be denied that the Soviet Union is a totalitarian society. . . . But the doctrine on the basis of which this mental uniformity is enforced is incomparably truer . . . than is fascist doctrine. For the doctrine . . . is socialist or Marxist.'[3] If Marxism were absolutely true, there would be no objection to totalitarianism. But if it turned out that communism ('Marxism – Leninism – Stalinism'), though the 'best interpretation of social phenomena which the human mind has yet achieved', is not a fully adequate interpretation, then 'a larger and larger apparatus of mental coercion will be necessary'. Still, he had admitted, in *A Faith to Fight For*, in a chapter entitled 'Need We Bother About Truth?', that 'the facts about Soviet political development . . . are so violently in dispute, and I, for one, have found it so prohibitively difficult to assess the evidence . . . that I must tell you at once that I cannot base any conclusions on this evidence.'[4]

In the course of the winter of 1940, Strachey saw, in *The Times*, an appeal for adjutants in the R.A.F. With some misgiving, he filled in the appropriate form, and went to the Air Ministry for an interview. Strachey believed that his left-wing past would prevent him from having any chance of such an appointment.

---

[1] This sold 15,893 in the Left Book Club edition, 773 in the ordinary one.
[2] This sold 10,499 in the Left Book Club edition, 2,359 in the ordinary one.
[3] *The Betrayal of the Left*, p. 195.
[4] Strachey, *A Faith to Fight For*, p. 68.

Two 'fatherly' officers interviewed him. One asked where he had been at school. 'Eton,' said Strachey. The other asked what games he played. 'Cricket' was the reply. That went down well. 'Any other games?' 'Tennis and squash,' said Strachey. Finally, they both put down their pencils, and one said: 'As a matter of fact, Mr Strachey, we know *all* about you.' Strachey thought of his friendship with Dutt, his association with David Springhall (now in gaol for spying) and his old commitment to Mosley. 'Yes, Mr Strachey,' said the officer, 'your father was the editor of the *Spectator*.' Strachey was saved, not for the last time, by the 'old boy net'.[1]

As he desired, Strachey was called up and, after three weeks at an R.A.F. O.C.T.U. at Loughborough, despatched as adjutant to an unimportant air base, Uxbridge. In this base, he was given nothing of importance to do, primarily because of his close association with the communists, which was well-known to the security authorities if not to the recruiting agency. This was M.I.5's way of treating anyone who had had 'anything to do with the reds'. Strachey's letters were also opened. He was not at all satisfied. At one point, he even contemplated trying to transfer into his brother-in-law Clough Williams-Ellis's old regiment, the Welsh Guards.

While Strachey was at Uxbridge, disaster overcame the political fortunes of Boothby, recently appointed Under-Secretary to Lord Woolton at the Ministry of Food. He had filled this post with verve. But Boothby had unwisely neglected, in a speech on the disposition of Czech assets, to mention the fact that a Czech businessman, Weininger, had promised him a loan if the assets were to be freed. Boothby thus had an interest in the matter which he had not declared. The matter came out in early 1941, when Weininger, with many other foreign citizens, was arrested. Scotland Yard then took over Weininger's files, and found evidence which seemed to incriminate Boothby. Churchill arranged for a select committee to consider the case. Boothby believed his career ruined. In despair, he rang up Strachey in the middle of a heavy air raid, and begged him to come across London to meet him. Fearing suicide, Strachey interrupted his

[1] Strachey interview in *New Yorker*, February 1947, when in New York.

own dinner and made his way through the blackout to the Mayfair Hotel to find Boothby in better spirits than could have been imagined, sitting over champagne with his secretary. A few days later, Boothby had to defend himself in the House of Commons; Strachey could not bring himself to accompany him. He sat nervously in Boothby's flat, waiting for the outcome, in front of a bottle of sherry which, however, he did not touch. Boothby had to give up his appointment at the Ministry of Food, but kept his seat.

Afterwards Strachey wrote (when Boothby had won the confidence of his own constituency): 'warmest congratulations in swinging your constituency. As you know, I've always considered that *vital*. I think that you may well find it a *turning* point. Stick to your guns *at all costs*. . . . You must remember that I now finally *know* that my world picture . . . fell to bits with the signing of the Nazi-Soviet pact – in spite of all efforts to deny to myself that it had. Socialism, in the sense in which I had conceived it, is out for the century. Finally. And 20 years of my life go with it. After all, I could presumably have got somewhere by now if I had stuck to the *Spectator* and not become a socialist?'

After these melancholy thoughts, Strachey went on,

> I believe in fighting this war, because I expect to be shot and/or tortured by the Nazis if we are conquered. . . . But I've not got the *slightest* idea what will come out of this war. And it is extremely doubtful if it will be anything in the least good. Why should it be? But whatever it be, it is a thousand times better than conquest and enslavement. Nor does it still seem to be certain that we can avoid conquest. Apart from this, I cannot deny that, except about my family (and it is a huge exception), I have been rather happy in the past few months. Why, I don't know. Chiefly, no doubt, because I have had a girl,[1] and enjoyed the A.R.P. work. But, you see, there are some pretty bleak aspects to my situation.
>
> About you. Be as bitter as hell. It is far your best and healthiest reaction. It means that you are still fighting. And as long

---

[1] Probably A.B., one of Elizabeth Ponsonby's friends whom Strachey had known off and on since the 1920s.

as that is so, you are not broken. Of course, it was a plot and a purge. The fact that you were vulnerable and, in that sense, technically guilty (though not, at that, of many of the things which the report accuses you of) was utterly irrelevant to the blow they struck at you; though it was by no means irrelevant to the result. Certainly, never forgive. Why should you? But, especially as you will now be able to go on with your political life, if you can, look at the man at H.Q. objectively [i.e. Churchill]. The fact that he attempted a cold-blooded political murder of you (from whatever motives) should not blind you to his startling historical appropriateness at this juncture; which makes him very strong. [Strachey, at this time, regarded Churchill, as so many others did, as the supreme war leader about whom criticism was scarcely conceivable.] As I wrote to you when this first happened, it has made me more wretched than anything else in public or private life. My dear Bob – it is idle, but yet it is necessary for me to say how fond I am of you. It increases my bitterness . . . that there seems to be little or nothing I can do for you. . . . You have done so much, so consistently and so long for me that whatever I did could never repay the debt. That debt began . . . long ago at Magdalen when you were the one person who saw that I might develop into something human after all. It has grown ever since. Will you be in London soon? I am in my hut from 9 a.m. to 5 p.m. but then escape and am at present allowed to sleep in London. So don't fail to let me know if and when you come down.[1]

Boothby soon afterwards was offered a commission in the R.A.F. by Sir Archibald Sinclair, the Secretary of State for Air: he became adjutant to a bomber squadron; and soon, too, Strachey profited through the same influence. Patrick Blackett, the physicist, a friend for some years, heard of Strachey's problems and made a special complaint to Air Marshal Victor Goddard, an old friend of his own from the First World War and, in 1941, Director of Military Co-operation at the Air Ministry. Goddard went to Sinclair, who perhaps recalled Strachey from the parliament of 1929–31. Sinclair asked Goddard what he thought should

[1] Strachey to Boothby, 16 March 1941.

be done with Strachey in the air force. Goddard said that, in his opinion, he should be sent to an aerodrome in the centre of 'where the action is'. Sinclair agreed and, without Strachey ever knowing the name of his benefactor, he was despatched to a key base in fighter command. A new period in his life then began. It was, in effect, Strachey's first experience of government, and the actual carrying into effect of policies, after such a long time of discussion about it. But it was also another introduction to ordinary people, such as he had not encountered in the communist party.

Strachey became adjutant to 87 Squadron, a fighter squadron based between Bath and Exeter. This task was to be a deputy to the squadron leader, organizing the base and dealing with the problems of several hundred aircraftsmen, thirty pilots and twenty aircraft. In this administrative assignment, Strachey was an outstanding success. He seemed capable, calm and reliable, and a great help to his successive squadron leaders, both years younger than himself, Squadron Leader Ian ('Widge') Gleed and Squadron Leader Denis Smallwood.[1] Both these men were remarkable: Gleed had been one of the great pilots of the legendary summer of 1940, and, despite an emaciated physique and immature manner, was a man of courage, strength, and versatility. Gleed was Strachey's first experience of a dedicated service man, just as Strachey was also Gleed's first experience of an intellectual politician. Their collaboration was a success. Strachey also became devoted to the pilots and they to him. At that time, a fighter squadron was an autonomous unit, and problems of maintaining morale were greater than they later became. Strachey was invaluable. He became 'almost apolitical', in Smallwood's words, and none of those with whom he served was aware of his political past. His superiors expressed surprise that he should have so quickly adjusted himself to referring to these young officers as 'Sir': but that was half the fascination of the task for Strachey, who was intoxicated by the myth of the service, its demands for obedience and its hierarchy. Sir Victor Goddard's gamble thus paid off.

This exhilarating period of Strachey's life had one special

[1] In 1972, Vice Chief of Air Staff.

pleasure: 87 Squadron maintained a detachment on St Mary's in the Scilly Islands. Here, a handful of Hurricanes, assisted only by the coastguard's lamps, were ready to pounce on attacking Heinkels sweeping in from Brittany. For months, the squadron carried on this audacious work of interception, and did so uninterrupted, since the Germans had no suspicion that an aerodrome could be maintained on St Mary's. Strachey went down there several times. On his occasional leaves to London he described these visits as having the character almost of an aesthetic experience.

The pilots' jokes, the camaraderie of combat, the spontaneous patriotism, the team spirit were a revelation to Strachey, whose life had been spent in such different circumstances. He wrote once about these men – in a brief introduction to *Arise to Conquer*, a book which he inspired Gleed to write, and which Gollancz published in 1942 – and he always recalled the courage of these pilots who, 'when the telephone bells rang in the dispersal huts – when "Ops" said, "One hundred plus; or a hundred and fifty plus; or two hundred plus – now crossing the coast", jumped into their cockpits, took off, and fought till the German aircraft turned back. In so doing, they settled the kind of lives which all of us and our children, and probably their children, will lead.'[1] Strachey himself, as adjutant, did not have to fly, but he insisted on learning to fly himself, wrecking three aircraft while doing so.

When at Bath, Strachey ran into several old friends, among them Richard ('Diccon') Hughes, who had been at Oxford with him and was by then the successful author of *High Wind in Jamaica* and other works; Hughes, who was working in the Admiralty, urged strongly to his superiors that Strachey should not be left to waste his talents at a fighter station, and soon Strachey was removed.

Also at this time and before he left Bath, Strachey read Arthur Koestler's *Darkness at Noon*. 'In the ample leisure which is such a feature of life in the armed services in war time,' Strachey wrote later, 'during the long hours sitting in the adjutant's office at the airfield from which 87 Squadron operated, I nerved myself

[1] Introduction by Flight Lieutenant John Strachey to *Arise to Conquer*, by Wing Commander Ian Gleed, D.F.C. (Gollancz 1942).

to read the book. Though I had not liked it, it had made a stunning impression.'[1] This book, combined with the continued anti-war policy of the communist party, and with the positive exhilaration of patriotism in the R.A.F., completed Strachey's political re-education.

Work at Bath surprisingly did not mean that Strachey's pen was inactive. Thus, in 1941, he wrote a novel about an air force officer escaping in France, then entitled *James*, which he tried unsuccessfully to have published. The censor turned down the application on the ground that any discussion of any escape was prohibited. This book was not published till 1952.

The novel describes how James, a young, innocent, and almost callow R.A.F. fighter pilot has to bale out over Normandy. He finds his way to a farmhouse, where a girl some years older than him (Madeleine, based upon Yvette) befriends him and bicycles with him to the border of unoccupied France. There, James and Madeleine escape by taking part in a funeral party which has permission to cross the frontier to the local cemetery on the other side of the line – a strategem based on a real occurrence which had recently been discovered, and publicised in *Time* magazine. Once in Vichy France, James and Madeleine hide in a monastery, whose Abbé represents the spirit of survival. They meet 'Jean Castille', the leading communist writer of France, based on Louis Aragon (whom Strachey had met when Aragon had been friendly with Nancy Cunard) and overhear a conversation between Laval (who appears under the name of 'Nordenac') and the Abbé: Laval offers the Abbé the rectorship of the University of Paris, the latter toys with the idea, and turns the offer down when he hears British bombers flying overhead.

James, meantime, has, improbably, insisted on marrying Madeleine[2] (who even more improbably agrees), and he sets off for the frontier, with the Abbé and Jean Castille. After a long and interesting talk in a brothel in a southern French town, James and the Abbé escape from France by swimming to a fishing boat across what sounds like the lake of Geneva; they leave behind

[1] Strachey, *The Strangled Cry*, p. 13.
[2] An early draft of this section of the book avoided this formalisation of the friendship.

'Jean Castille', who has his communist party friends to help him, and Madeleine begins the long bicycle ride back to Normandy.

As a novel, *James* (or, as it was later named, *The Frontiers*) has its shortcomings. James is scarcely a successful character. His friendship with Madeleine is badly described. Madeleine seems real. The book is really an excuse for the Abbé, whose wordly character, and whose disillusion with all creeds, is successfully caught in a series of clever speeches. The critical point of the book is a story told by the Abbé to Nordenac–Laval: the former had, as Strachey had, visited Republican Spain during the civil war, and attended a famous meeting of the rump Spanish Cortes at Montserrat in Catalonia in 1938. There, the Abbé met (as Strachey did) Portela Valladares, the caretaker Prime Minister of Spain in the months before the election of February 1936. Portela recalls those days, and describes how, when the results of the elections were known, and it seemed that the left had won, Franco and a monarchist politician had visited him, and proposed that they should declare a state of war, and so nullify the elections. Portela wanted to agree with Franco's idea, but desisted on the ground that it was unconstitutional. Portela acted with what the Abbé described as 'blind integrity'.[1]

This incident is the crux of the book – whether or not Portela told Strachey that he had acted in this manner. The Abbé, and the author, see that individuals, however minor, can take decisions on moral grounds, against 'the tide of history'. Further, if political beings 'can still form only the most uncertain estimates of the consequences of their actions, then they are not justified in using all means to achieve their ends. For, however desirable those ends may be, however undesirable it is that their attainment would far outweigh the evils of the necessary means, there will be no assurance that the evil means will, in fact, attain the desirable ends. In that case, the old rule-of-thumb moral laws, the old values, the old capacities for disgust and enthusiasm, retain a validity.'[2]

One can well imagine that these must have been Strachey's thoughts in the spring of 1941, for the future then certainly

[1] Strachey, *The Frontiers*, p. 132.
[2] *Ibid.*, pp. 142, 145–6.

seemed uncertain. This renewed interest in tradition, and in conventional morality, was also expressed in a passage where the pilot suddenly grasps that the French funeral, which 'he had thought of simply as a way of escape for him, was, on the contrary, a real funeral . . . the hot, gritty clothes of the mourners, the hearse horses with their plumes, the whole of the *pompes funèbres*, now struck him quite differently. He no longer saw them as grotesque, out-of-date, maddening *petit bourgeois* conventionalities. He saw them as the valued, slowly evolved, civilized ways by which the people of France had learnt to deal with the basic occasions of their lives.' He compared this funeral to the German soldiers also present, in open-necked shirts and shorts; 'Now he saw what was wrong with them. They looked empty, bereft of something . . . de-rooted. He felt overwhelming solidarity with the French. Their complex, musty conventions, made them real, rich human beings still – and not the blank cyphers of a bad novel about the future.'[1] Thus so must Strachey himself have looked at London in 1940 to 1941.

This novel has considerable psychological interest. Strachey was never as unsympathetic, as dull or as gauche as the pilot officer James, even on his visit to France to stay with Yvette at Le Mans. But, like Ford in *Post D*, this Englishman's conduct had something of Strachey: the pilot insists on marrying Madeleine, but does not think that she might have, therefore, wished to accompany him out of France; and his relationship with the wise and dominating Abbé is comparable to Strachey's relationship with many strong men. James drinks in his ideas, and is fascinated by them, but, in the moment of action, 'he is appalled to find that the Abbé wishes to swim away into freedom alongside him – it spoilt the whole prospect of the swim alone, in the night. James realized that he'd been passionately looking forward to swimming off by himself.'[2] In the end, he does leave the Abbé to drown: as in their day, for him, Mosley, Dutt, Joad, and even old St Loe had been drowned also, in the end.[3] *The Frontiers* was eventually published in 1952, when it received a far less enthusiastic and interesting press than it would have received in the 1940s had it been published then.

[1] *Ibid.*, pp. 68–9.　　[2] *Ibid.*, p. 201.　　[3] *Ibid.*, p. 215.

From Bath, Strachey also continued, from time to time, to write for the *Left News*. Increasingly the 'New Deal experience' seemed to make, intellectually speaking, the offer of a new safe harbour: 'the virile, if chaotic, empiricism of the American mind ensured that almost every conceivable expedient should be tried during the course of those eight years. Some failed, some succeeded brilliantly.'[1] In a Political Letter in *Left News*, in May, he wrote that 'if you ask me, then, what I can feel that indispensable living enthusiasm for . . . I answer: for the revolt of everything that is healthy in the British people against the things of the men who made this war possible; who lost the first half of it.'[2] In June, he wrote that he still regarded Marxism as 'incomparably the sharpest tool of historical and, therefore, political theory,' but from this time onwards Strachey kept his writing for the Air Ministry, though a final article by him appeared in May 1942. By this time, the Club's membership had dropped to 15,000, and Gollancz had lost most of his interest, though he did not bring it formally to an end until 1946. Strachey left the Russian entry into the war uncommented upon. This event had a numbing effect on Strachey's political thinking: if Russia was as good as she was now depicted by even British propaganda, how had he broken with communism? If as bad as he had been arguing, why was she an ally?

In early 1942, Strachey was assigned as Public Relations Officer to the Fifth Bomber Group at Grantham, under Air Marshal Slessor. Strachey again made an immediate impression. Still older than most of the other officers, he made himself popular by insisting on going on operations when he could easily have stayed at the base. Slessor soon sent him on a mine-laying operation in the North Sea. Strachey was beginning to find in the R.A.F. a substitute for that institution which he had abandoned, the communist party, and, in some respects, to find in the senior officers whom he encountered, Slessor in particular, yet further examples of the hero figures, or the lost elder brothers whom he had previously met several times before and allowed, in the end, to escape. Here perhaps education and background counted

[1] *Left News*, April 1941, p. 1687.
[2] *Ibid.*, May 1941, p. 1724.

critically. Despite his long period with the communists, Strachey had never been a friend of the underdog, though he had been often his advocate. He found it, on the contrary, instinctively easy to associate, and to sympathize, with people in positions of command or leadership. St Loe's training, or Sir Herbert Warren's, told effectively. Strachey later wrote a profile of Slessor for the *Observer* which, published anonymously, expressed his real feelings for the air marshal, who at the time of publication was Commander-in-Chief of Coastal Command: 'I remember the nights when I first saw Slessor making his decisions. He would be informed, for example, that within the next ten minutes he must decide whether to recall or not. He would nod, say nothing and sit down on one of the kitchen chairs which furnished the Ops Room. For anything up to ten minutes he would literally do nothing at all. He simply sat there and thought. Everyone in the Ops Room instinctively fell silent. Then, very quietly, he told his duty officer what to do. . . .

'At the end of the day,' he added, 'we have looked for something else as well [as energy] in our leaders. What we have come to consider, first, is whether or not they really care; whether or not, that is to say, every minute of their working day has been inspired by an unswerving concern for the issue of the war. . . . Those of us who have worked or fought under Slessor have taken away with us a sense of this overmastering concern for the issue of the war, as our abiding impression of the man. . . . It will be profoundly interesting to follow the post-war career of this remarkable airman, who has interests a good deal wider, perhaps, than the average.' Perhaps Strachey thought that if the shadow of Bonaparte, or even merely of Wellington, were afterwards to fall over England, it might be Slessor who would cast it. Slessor's friendship also gave Strachey a good deal of personal confidence: it told him 'the Establishment was on his side', in Boothby's words. From now on, Strachey took care to be always on the 'inside' in political life.

At the end of 1942, Strachey left Grantham to become P.R.O. to the Assistant Chief of Air Staff, Air Marshal Sir Richard Peck[1]

[1] Air Marshal Sir Richard Peck (1893–1952) was A.C.A.S.(G), from 1940 to 1945.

at the Air Ministry. Strachey now received the rank of Squadron Leader. Working under the Labour politician Wedgwood Benn (later Lord Stansgate), his first task ironically enough was to approach the *Economist* 'on the subject of a particularly ill-informed anti-bombing article'.[1] Strachey made several successful broadcasts in 1942 explaining to the public certain R.A.F. activities. Air Marshal Peck quickly grew to regard Strachey with respect, and spoke of him as his 'one ewe-lamb' when he was finally transferred to other operations.

Strachey's political spirits had by now risen considerably and, for a time, he contemplated the creation, from out of the ranks of ex-communists such as himself, of a new political party which would have a generally communist programme without being attached to the apron strings of Russia. In early 1942, when still at Grantham, he tried to interest Stafford Cripps in this scheme and he frequently talked about it to Plummer. Philip Toynbee, an ex-communist of similar views to Strachey, went to lunch with Strachey once or twice at the R.A.C. in Pall Mall, but could not be persuaded that the plan was practical. Strachey's plans for 'a new association' began by asking: 'Since Hitler is not to rule the world, who is?' Democratic capitalism or Soviet Communism? . . . People had to discount the fact that, when at war, capitalism had a spurious vitality. But, so far as Russia was concerned, 'We have all come, for example, to doubt whether the impeccably democratic words of the Constitution reflect a reality of democratic practice. Finally, we do not pretend to know what all those leading and minor figures of the communist party who have been executed over the past five years were doing.'

The consequence was undoubtedly the failure of the idealistic appeal of communism in the Russian manner. 'A great case has turned into a great nation', but the creative side of the Revolution was spent. The communist parties of the world had refused to back the struggle against Hitler between 1939 and 1941, so risking not merely the West, but the Soviet Union itself: yet 'the Soviet Union, and all that it stands for, were saved by the refusal of the British working class to follow the line then given it by the British communist party.'

[1] Strachey to A.C.A.S.(G), 6 September 1942.

Allan Young, now in the civil service, to whom Strachey sent a copy of this manuscript, wrote tartly: 'Your pessimism [about the possibility of using democratic politics] springs from an appalling sectarian conception of politics and the dynamics of political life. There is not one line of confidence in the masses. They are merely cattle to be led, or driven, by superior people. Where we differ, fundamentally, is that I really trust the mass movement, and never more confidently than when they are making mistakes. . . . Don't let the destruction of your faith in the C.P. destroy also your faith in the much greater thing it sought to lead.'[1]

Strachey's solution seemed indeed deceptively simple: 'we have only to turn the gigantic productive resources which, as in the last war, we have . . . shown that we possess, on to the tasks of peace. . . . A future of unprecedented plenty is ours for the taking.' Still, to secure this our 'economic programme must be unequivocably socialist. . . . That is we must establish the common ownership of the main resources of production.'

To secure this a new party or, rather, 'an association-of-the-new-type' was necessary. This would 'necessarily start small . . . tightly organized' and would not compete with the existing political parties. Membership would entail 'obligations considerably more onerous than those to which men and women in public life are accustomed in this country', though Strachey looked forward to a day when all countries would have similar societies, at least all 'highly developed societies'.

All members, Strachey thought, would have to have clearly defined obligations: 'failure to do work for the society without good reason constitutes grounds for the termination of membership.' Subscriptions would vary according to income; perhaps those earning £200 a year should be able to join by paying 1 per cent of their income, those over £1,000 perhaps 7½ per cent.

None of Strachey's friends was enthusiastic about this idea and Gollancz was particularly critical. Strachey himself seems to have abandoned any further thought of it after he became more fully occupied at the Air Ministry.

In addition, by the middle of 1942, he was already once again

[1] Allan Young's annotation on p. 39 of Strachey's MSS.

in touch with the Labour party, and began therefore to embark on a new stage of his political life.

Strachey went to North Africa in November 1942. He travelled in s.s. *Scythia*. This vessel was torpedoed in Algiers Bay. The ship did not sink, but the forward hold was damaged.[1] Strachey stayed about six weeks with the Eighth Army, and spent Christmas Day 1942 in a caravan disguised as a haystack with John Hare, later a Conservative M.P. and Minister, at Medjez el Bab.[2]

In early 1943, after returning from North Africa in January, Strachey joined the Directorate of Bomber Operations, whose director at that time was Air Commodore Bufton.[3] This body lay at the very centre of allied war operations, and, it should be said, also of controversy at the time and since. Bomber Operations worked directly under Air Marshal Portal, the Chief of Air Staff, and devoted its attention to general policy as well as to precise questions of targetting and of the presentation of these matters to the public. The group was in perpetual argument with Bomber Command, led by Air Marshals Harris and Saundby, over many minor matters but also over the special question of area bombing. Bomber Operations believed, rightly, that Harris's policy of area bombing at night was a mistake: the bombing could not be accomplished with any accuracy.

'Bomber Ops' had an operational section and an economic section. A temporary Wing Commander, Arthur Morley, a Birmingham businessman, headed the economic section and, in the course of 1943, Strachey became his aide. In this job, Strachey worked hard, often sixteen hours a day for seven days a week, with little or no leave, primarily on the question of where to make the economically most effective raids. He became what his commander referred to as 'a fully integrated member of our bomber policy team . . . we all liked him and placed a high value on his views and judgements in the many problems which we

[1] A semi-fictional reconstruction of this incident exists on pages 135–50 of *The Strangled Cry*.
[2] Hare later referred to this while Strachey was Minister of Food and described his skill at public relations at explaining away to the public why Tunis had not been captured (Hansard, Vol. 462, Col. 846).
[3] Later, Air Vice Marshal S. O. Bufton (b. 1908). Afterwards became A.C.A.S. (Intelligence).

tackled.'[1] Strachey later became secretary of the Anglo-American Strategic Targetting Committee, responsible for deciding what should be bombed. Strachey had earlier, as an air raid warden, naturally had good reason to know the consequences of strategic bombing – the only man in Bomber Operations who had been an air raid warden. His earlier view had really been one of support of the idea that bombing can be effective – though he had put this negatively in his only piece of writing on this subject – namely, in the *New Republic* of New York, in which he had written that his experience 'did not lead me to the conclusion that it is an inherently impossible task to night-bomb even the largest city into destruction and capitulation'.[2]

The first brief included in Strachey's personal file in the R.A.F. Ministry deals with the question of the proposed bombing of Schweinfurt in 1943, and was to be given out to bomber crews for that purpose: it is a good example of his style. (Air Commodore Bufton had long urged this attack, though he was thwarted in the matter by his superiors.)

Once or twice, in the course of the war, aircrews are called on to undertake a decisive operation [wrote Strachey]. Tonight's operation will be one of the major battles of this war. . . . The object of the operation is to paralyze the German war effort by smashing one indispensable link in the chain of armament production. . . .

The town of Schweinfurt lies 50 miles east of Frankfurt. It has 50,000 inhabitants, is congested, old, and highly inflammable. In it, live more than 20,000 highly skilled workers, who manufacture ball bearings in four factories which lie within the town boundaries.

The intention of the operation is simple. It is to make the production of that 70 per cent of indispensable ball bearings which takes place at Schweinfurt impossible for an indefinite period. *The men detailed for this operation have the opportunity to do more in one night to end this war than any other body of men can do.*[3]

[1] Air Vice Marshal Bufton, letter to the author, November 1971.
[2] *New Republic*, 10 November 1941.
[3] *See* Sir C. Webster and Noble Frankland, *The Strategic Air Offensive against*

The U.S. Eighth Air Force did, in fact, soon bomb Schweinfurt, but the British did not do so until February 1944, after there
had been a considerable dispersal of the plants concerned.

But, by 1944, Strachey's most important activity, though not
that which took up the greatest part of his time, was his broadcast talks; 'air commentaries', that is, delivered after the B.B.C.
nine o'clock news. These, undertaken in the first instance under
the inspiration of the ubiquitous Guy Burgess, who was then
at the Ministry of Information, made Strachey's a familiar voice
all over Britain. Although the books which he had written in the
1930s had made him well known to politically minded people
on the left, it was, ironically, as 'Squadron Leader Strachey' that
he became a national figure. Strachey was told in early March
1944 that one of his talks had the highest ever recorded number of
listeners for a radio talk – 'a figure which even popular enter-
tainment might envy'. Crossman later commented, unfairly in
view of the attitude of Bomber Operations, that these talks were
'a vital factor in quelling public protest against Bomber Harris's
total destruction of German cities'.[1] The Observer a year or two
afterwards put it slightly differently, suggesting that Strachey's
broadcasts 'took the public mind off the receiving end of the
bombing attacks, and fixed it on the courage of the crews'[2] –
justifiably, in view of the casualties borne with stoicism by
Bomber Command.

A special characteristic of these broadcasts was their rationality,
their calm and their total freedom from rhetoric. The listener was
conscious of no sense of hatred, scarcely even one of violence.
He heard an understanding and educated voice speaking confidently, with discernment and even dispassion, of the great
Allied war machine which was, apparently according to plan,
gradually overwhelming the enemy. Strachey was certainly
among the three or four best wartime broadcasters, and thus
played a part in the victory.

In March 1943, meantime, Celia and the children succeeded in

_____

Germany 1939–1945, Vol. II (London 1961), p. 62, where this passage is quoted,
though not its authorship.
[1] R. H. S. Crossman, 'The Politician as a Writer', Guardian, 28 September 1962.
[2] Observer, 2 June 1946.

returning home from the U.S. She had had a dull, distressing and lonely war, on the whole, having left Canada for New York. She returned to England still an extreme socialist, though not a communist. She had found *Darkness at Noon* (sent to her by Strachey) unbearable, and nearly had a breakdown in the spring of 1941. She had, however, in consequence, 'slid out' of communism, though she never became anti-communist and never made a really sharp break. That meant a clash with some of Strachey's new friends. For example, Strachey had been in the habit of dropping in to see Arthur Koestler every night for a talk and a drink at his house in Tryon Street on his way back to St Leonard's Terrace from the Air Ministry. But one night he rang up Koestler and said, in his matter-of-fact voice: 'Arthur, I'm afraid that my nightly visits to you will have to stop. Celia cannot stand you, and you see that I'm really in a position of having to choose between you and her. I'm sure you will understand that I shall have to choose her.' Afterwards, however, Strachey and Koestler met surreptitiously. (Koestler was naturally distressed.)

Strachey, Celia and his family moved back to their old London house, in Regent's Park Road, until the so-called Little Blitz of 1944. Then the children were again sent out of harm's way, as it seemed – Charles to a preparatory school in Sussex, Elizabeth to her grandmother at Harrowhill Copse, Newlands Corner, the house built by Williams-Ellis on the old Strachey estate. Celia remained in London, and worked in a naval radar factory.

After D Day, Strachey went to France to collect material for war commentaries for the B.B.C., and for articles on the R.A.F.'s part in 'Overlord', for U.S. periodicals. He was able to observe on the ground the consequences of bombing in the course of battle.

During the summer of 1942, meantime, Strachey had been approached once more by the Labour party. This was done on the initiative of Laski, who, still a member of the Labour party executive, suggested, on a visit to Scotland, to the Dundee constituency Labour party that Strachey might be approached to become one of their two parliamentary candidates (Dundee at that time returned two members, and, though Labour had had two candidates for a time, both had withdrawn in the years since 1935). Strachey's chief supporter in the Dundee Labour party was a cultivated schoolmaster, John Torrance, a Left Book Club member and therefore a man obviously interested in, and impressed by, Strachey's left-wing past. After several visits to Dundee, Strachey was adopted Labour candidate for that city in the course of 1943. At that time there was no prospect of an election until the end of the war. But his adoption did give Strachey a firm political base.

The R.A.F. gave approval. William Teeling, an Oxford friend and now a would-be Conservative politician, recalls that 'when I was out of the room, Strachey would be ringing up Dundee; and when he was out of the room, I'd be on to Brighton'. Strachey's broadcasting fame helped him, as the sitting Conservative member Florence Horsburgh discovered to her annoyance. She complained to Sir Richard Peck, who, however, told her that he could do nothing to help her over this intricate problem.

Strachey tried to secure, as a trade unionist colleague in this double member seat, the young George Brown, but Brown went away from a meeting with Strachey in the R.A.C. – the first time Brown had entered a club – unconvinced that he was talking with a democratic socialist. This was not the last time this doubt was voiced, but it was no longer appropriate. The war had transformed Strachey as it had transformed others. The rebel of the 1930s was quite willing to be a ruler in the 1940s.

Chapter 14 / UNDER-SECRETARY OF STATE FOR AIR

In June 1945, Strachey returned to the conventional political scene which he had left fourteen years before in such different circumstances. The electoral campaign in Dundee was full of life. Dundee was the only double member constituency – two members, one geographical area – north of the border. Strachey and Tom Cook, a local electrician, aged thirty-six, were standing against Florence Horsburgh and Dingle Foot, Miss Horsburgh being Conservative, Foot being a Liberal who had been a junior minister in the wartime coalition, at the Ministry of Economic Warfare and who, at the time, using his middle name, referred to himself as Mr Mackintosh Foot in an attempt to please Scotland. There was also a Scottish Nationalist, A. Donaldson, the treasurer of that party. Dundee had had a Labour M.P. continuously from 1910 till 1931, among them Tom Johnston, Strachey's associate with Lansbury and Mosley in the 1929 parliament, and E. D. Morel. Dundee had had only two Conservatives in the previous hundred years, though Churchill has been Liberal M.P. there in the first part of the century.

Strachey's campaign emphasized his fight against fascism before 1939, avoiding undue reference to the fact that he had been far, as it seemed, to the left of the Labour party. That, anyway, made no difference to the voters of Dundee, who had themselves, in many cases, been left-wing dissidents, and advocates of 'working class unity'. Dundee then lived on its jute trade with India, and both Cook and Strachey played up the theme that 'our interests are the same as the Indian workers' '. (They were not, in fact, since Dundee's jute mills were artificially protected at the cost of the Indians.) Dundee had suffered tremendously during the depression: from 1930 to 1934 there had never been less than seventeen per cent unemployed, with a peak of fifty-three per cent in 1931, and misery had been widespread and savage. Strachey still spoke from the left of the party on many issues. Thus he criticized the Polish government-in-exile as having their 'only hope – to cause bad blood between Russia and us, and that they were a menace to the peoples of the world'.[1]

The campaign was very different to Strachey's three campaigns in Birmingham. He and his wife were shocked by the bitterness and the low level of political education of the half-starving Dundee working class. In addition, they found their fellow Labour candidate, Tom Cook, ignorant and 'absolutely mad', though he considered himself 'a coming man'. He would make non-sensical speeches with no verb and no meaning; even so, he was loved by the people of Dundee. Tom Cook drank like a fish, and so was often quite incomprehensible for that reason too. The Conservative candidate and previous member, Florence Horsburgh, had also inspired a passionate Labour campaign against her as a result of an injudicious remark some years before suggesting that, if food were short, people 'could boil up bones for soup and then hand them on to the next house'. The campaign was thus an exciting one. The election of 1945, with its still large meetings and tremendous spirit, was the last of the old-style political campaigns, though Dingle Foot regarded the relative absence of violence in 1945 in comparison with 1935 as ominous – as, indeed, it was, for him.

Strachey presented himself in the election as 'Wing Commander Strachey' and, in the election address photograph, appeared in uniform. The poster 'the Army, Navy and Air Force

---

[1] *Dundee Courier and Advertiser*, 21 June 1945. The *Dundee Advertiser* had been the subject of one of F. E. Smith's jokes while Churchill was member – 'According to the Dundee Advertiser – the newspaper not the politician'.

ask you to vote for Strachey and Cook' outraged the Conservatives. Strachey and Cook had a joint election address which
criticized the Conservatives and Churchill in a traditional manner,
and restated that Labour's programme was based on public
ownership. One link with the past in the Dundee election was
Dan Davies, Strachey's agent in Aston from 1927 to 1931, who
followed Strachey into the New Party, being one of those who
went to work on Allan Young's invitation at the New Party
headquarters. He had been Young's agent at Ashton-under-Lyne
and became Strachey's again in Dundee. But Davies's presence
was not a help, since he hated Dundee, and, though efficient, did
not get on well with the Dundee people. Strachey's sister, Amabel,
also electioneered for him. Strachey and Dingle Foot, an acquaintance, were staying with their wives at the same hotel, the Royal
British Hotel. After the day's electioneering they would dine
together in a private room screened from their supporters.

On 26 July, to tumultuous cheers from large crowds, Strachey
and Cook were elected members, with 48,804 votes and 48,393
votes respectively. Their majority was over 15,000, since Foot
only got 33,230, and Florence Horsburgh 32,209. The Scottish
Nationalist polled 7,776. Dingle Foot made a generous speech
conceding defeat, and Strachey and Celia then took the night
train to London, being seen off by cheering crowds. Once they
had left the station, they walked along the train to where Boothby,
safely returned for East Aberdeenshire, as he had been every election since that of 1924, was waiting for them in his sleeper with
a bottle of champagne.

Strachey had only just got back to London when, to his
'intense surprise' (as he put it later in an autobiographical note),
he was sent for by Attlee. When he arrived at Downing Street,
Edith Summerskill was coming out of Attlee's door. 'Good
Lord,' she said scornfully, 'What are *you* doing here?' It seemed
most improbable that Strachey would get a job in the new
government. (Edith Summerskill, an M.P. since 1938, had just
accepted the appointment of Parliamentary Secretary to the
Ministry of Food.) But Attlee had admired Strachey's wartime
broadcasts and offered him the post of Under-Secretary of State
for Air, a particularly testing appointment, since the Secretary

of State, Lord Stansgate (Wedgwood Benn), was in the House of Lords. It would, therefore, fall on Strachey to answer Air Ministry questions in the House of Commons, and they clearly would be many. (Attlee and Strachey had first met in the 1929 parliament; and, after 1931, not at all till 1945. Attlee considered Strachey's communist period as much an 'aberration of youth' as his Mosley days and overlooked both without difficulty.)

The consequence was, therefore, that Strachey returned to the Air Ministry on his return to London, though in quite a different guise to what he had expected. He appointed a young lawyer, Elwyn Jones, as his Parliamentary Private Secretary; Jones had begun to be drawn towards active left-wing politics directly because of Strachey's writings in the 1930s and later had himself been a Gollancz author. Indeed, his *The Battle for Peace*, a vigorous appeal for a United Front policy against fascism, had been the Left Book Club choice in August 1938. Elwyn Jones only remained Strachey's P.P.S. long enough to applaud his efforts to make ministerial answers more elegantly written. Then he went off to assist Sir Hartley Shawcross in the preparation for the Nuremburg Trials and was succeeded by 'Bill' Mallalieu (J. P. W. Mallalieu), an ex-journalist and also a Gollancz author, who became over the next few years devoted to Strachey and his interests. In the Ministry, Strachey dismissed one official private secretary, and another had a breakdown, before he found an admirable one in Michael Cary, an unconventional civil servant of real intellectual distinction.

It is difficult to recreate the mood of elation which characterized the Labour movement at the election of 1945. It seemed that the long years of preparation and struggle were over, and that the party, the greatest social democratic movement in the world, had captured a majority at last and was in a position to impose its ideas, with a consenting and enthusiastic electorate behind it. The leaders of the party were admittedly weary after the war, in which they had worked as hard as anyone. But the opportunity ahead of them, accompanied by the euphoria of victory, seemed to cleanse them from fatigue.

Strachey, who, with Gollancz, believed that he had done so much, through the political education of the Left Book Club, to make this victory possible, was very much a new boy in the new House of Commons, despite his experience there so long before. But still, with his new post he was able to look forward to a creative part in the great adventure. His first task, however, was to deal with the vast correspondence on the subject of demobilization that had accumulated in the Air Ministry during the time of the election. Five thousand unanswered letters from M.P.s were stacked in his office. Strachey's solution was practical: he hired four graduate secretaries, and set them to write all the replies and, on occasion, to imitate his signature. There were too the innumerable letters of thanks which the Government sent to all officers, temporary and professional, who had served in the wartime R.A.F. These letters mostly differed slightly in form. Their despatch was a highly successful piece of public relations, and it seemed quite appropriate that Strachey, known to millions as a Wing Commander on the wireless should be the signatory of these unusual documents.

His skill at these challenges and others gave Strachey an immediate success at the Air Ministry. He impressed senior officers, seeming more successful as a spokesman for the Air Ministry than his minister, Lord Stansgate, who had also been in the Air Ministry as Director of Public Relations in the war but who, as Strachey commented some years later, in an auto-biographical note, seemed 'essentially a parliamentarian, born for the House of Commons, not the Lords, and not for administration'.[1] Stansgate was, perhaps, past his best. Once, when asked why Strachey had allowed his Minister to abandon one point in an argument, Strachey tartly replied, 'Well I can take him to the door of the cabinet room but no further'. With many senior officers, such as the new Vice Chief of Air Staff, Slessor, he had already been on good terms. Slessor recalled him from this time as a man of 'absolute integrity', who 'got through the papers well' and 'stood up well for the service in department meetings'. Many problems occurred in the first few months; there was the case of a clever communist sergeant who threatened mutiny all over Asia unless demobilization was swift. Strachey coped with

[1] Strachey's comment was in an autobiographical passage in his unpublished book about the Blackwater river.

this quite satisfactorily, though there followed a dispute over various actual mutinies which, after the Second World War, as after the First, more severely, broke out, particularly among men serving abroad.

The second political point at issue in the early months concerned the right of serving men to consult their Members of Parliament in cases where they had a dispute with the Ministry. Strachey yielded in one particular case, and wished to put out a general statement in the Air Ministry orders that that, indeed, was the right of serving men: Slessor opposed this, on the ground that such an order would invite an avalanche of complaints. The order was not issued. A similar problem related to the question as to whether airmen could write direct to their Minister on these or other matters.

Attlee himself was evidently impressed by the skill with which Strachey mastered the vast amount of information relating to demobilization. Few ministers answered so many questions, so successfully, as Strachey did in the first session of the parliament of 1945. The questions often related to tedious matters, but Strachey was always courteous and unruffled in his replies, whether dealing with the closing down of the National Pigeon Service, or with the case of whether a certain individual, invalided out of the R.A.F., might receive his pension or his Burma Star. There were no great issues. But Strachey went to endless lengths, in conjunction with his secretaries, to anticipate all possible supplementary questions.

Strachey's most important task was the introduction to the House of Commons of the Air Ministry estimates, in March 1946. In the course of this debate, Strachey's predecessor as Under-Secretary of State for Air, Quintin Hogg, who had been briefly at the Air Ministry in Churchill's 'Caretaker' Government, made a specially glowing reference to Strachey's achievements: 'The Hon. gentleman's easy parliamentary manner, his complete masterly of his subject, and the art which he developed, during the war, in his radio talks, of making a difficult subject perhaps a little easier than it is . . . have endeared him to the House of Commons, and permit us to say that when a certain quantity of dead wood has been removed from the Treasury benches, these qualities will enable him to find rapid promotion.' Hogg added, however, that Strachey's parliamentary performances should not let them forget Strachey's 'murky' political past. He proceeded with an elaborate metaphor recalling how Strachey, having abandoned the 'Messerschmitt of Mosley', and 'the Stormovik of the communist party', had found himself in the celestial bandwagon of the Labour party; Hogg speculated how one day perhaps, if that machine should ever become airborne, and get into difficulties, the world might see a pale blue parachute detach itself and make its way to the 'slightly unexciting embrace of his Conservative Mother Earth'.[1]

On another occasion, Strachey wound up a 'supply day' debate on demobilization for the Government and, in the course of an effective speech, quoted back at Churchill one of his own comments on that subject taken from his book *The Aftermath*: thereby fulfilling a day-dream which, he later admitted, he had had in his bath at Shalford, during the war, of causing the war leader to give way and to admit being out-talked.

Thus Strachey passed the first nine months of the new Labour Government, establishing himself once more in political circles, living in Regent's Park Road during the week, and at Ewenbridge Farm at weekends, and developing into an accomplished parliamentary performer. His natural adaptability rendered easy his transition from official to political life, and the fact that he had known the Ministry in which he now exercised power was critical in making him one of the early successes of the government. Strachey's inclination to see political matters in terms of a perpetual tug of war between ideas and leaders also found some measure of receptivity in the personality of Attlee: Strachey admired Attlee's economy of style and his capacity to make a ruthless decision; and, while Celia remained on the left of the Labour party, Strachey was moving rightwards, partly at least under Attlee's inspiration, and partly because the fact of being a service minister was an activity calculated to make a man less inclined to radical ideas. Only on Palestine did Strachey have any serious dispute with the Government. One day, Crossman, now in the House of Commons, came to see Strachey. The former was

[1] Hansard, Vol. 420, Col. 1011.

devoting his efforts to the Zionist cause. He had heard from his friends in the Jewish Agency that they were contemplating an act of sabotage, not only for its own purpose but to demonstrate to the world their capacities. Should this be done, or should it not? Few would be killed. But would it help the Jews? Crossman asked Strachey his advice, and Strachey, a member of the Defence Committee of the Cabinet, undertook to find out. The next day in the smoking room of the House of Commons, Strachey gave his approval to Crossman. The Haganah went ahead and blew up all the bridges over the Jordan. No one was killed, but the British Army in Palestine were cut off from their lines of supply with Jordan. The Jewish Agency had demonstrated that they were much more powerful than anyone had supposed. A few days later, the Foreign Office broke the Jewish Agency code. Crossman was for several days alarmed lest he and Strachey might be discovered.

Strachey remained, between 1945 and 1946, on the left of the Labour party, and seemed still inclined to be optimistic about the possibilities of reaching agreements with Russia: a Foreign Office official recalled being summoned, most unusually, by Strachey to the Air Ministry and being asked why he was 'trying to sabotage British sales of Rolls Royce engines to Russia'. The official reported this incident and Bevin immediately cancelled all sales of such engines to Russia, not having known that such a trade existed at all.

Chapter 15 / THE MINISTRY OF FOOD

During the winter of 1945–6, the Stracheys went for a weekend with Attlee at Chequers. They had got on very well, walking through the beechwoods and 'jumping stiles'. A little later, Dalton was at Chequers: he and Attlee discussed the possibilities of making several 'promotions', and Attlee (probably after talking to Morrison) said that Strachey, who had been 'doing very well . . . and had good all-round ability' should be the first to be considered.[1] Attlee offered Strachey the Ministry of Food. Sir Ben Smith, the Minister, an ex-trade unionist, had been a failure in that, as Laski put it in a letter to Strachey, he 'never understood the urgency of taking ordinary people into your confidence and making them fully aware . . . of the realities of the position'.[2] Indeed, Ben Smith, doing an unpopular job badly, had been a godsend to the Conservative opposition. He was, however, really a courageous man, whose failure, such as it was, partly stemmed from an old trade union quarrel with the, by 1946, politically dominant figure of Ernest Bevin, and partly because he was economically illiterate: officials had to spend hours explaining the meaning of a paper.

Strachey agreed to take this appointment and, therefore, at

[1] Dalton, *High Tide and After*, p. 102.
[2] Laski to Strachey, 28 May 1946.

the age of forty-four, took over the direction of a large department of State.[1] Though, to his disgust, not in the Cabinet, the
appointment was one of 'Cabinet rank' – a ridiculous verbal
anomaly, characteristic of the country at that time, made to
apply to ministers who were called to the Cabinet, but who were
not regular members of it.

The Ministry of Food, with rationing continuing and with a
world food shortage, was evidently one of the most important
ministries. It was, too, a more important ministry than Attlee
and his colleagues had supposed, for they had imagined that, with
the coming of peace, the food problems of war would easily be
resolved. But that was a miscalculation: there were now enough
ships to bring food, but, with the liberation of Germany and the
large food-importing countries of Europe, there was a shortage of
food itself in the world. Attlee had not, at first, appreciated this,
and had hoped that the Ministry of Food might have been
'wound up' by the end of 1945.

The Ministry was, naturally, one of those most exposed to the
public, which was hoping for a return to the plenty which peace
was expected to revive. But some in the Government were
determined to use, by bulk purchase, the Ministry of Food as a
means of controlling the 'speculative evils' of the old commodity
markets, so ensuring cheap food. The 'Food Front' was connected
too with most major problems of government policy. The
Ministry of Food was at the centre of the government's main
economic problem: the question of dollar imports. The U.S.
loan of 1945 had smoothed over, for some time, the end of
Lend-Lease but, by 1946, it was evident that it could not last for
long. One of the Ministry's tasks, therefore, was to seek non-
dollar sources for Britain's food, while using wartime controls
to restrict consumption.

The Ministry was an unusual one, since it was staffed, in 1946,
by an agglomeration of regular civil servants, dons, and businessmen experienced in the food trade; it was also a department
with flexible, and, by the standards of the then civil service, unusual relations with the business world.

Thus Strachey was given a great opportunity, and one where

[1] He was succeeded at the Air Ministry by Geoffrey de Freitas.

success or failure would affect not only his career, but that of the Government. Doubtless Attlee, when making the appointment, considered Strachey's skill, at the Air Ministry, in public relations, his effectiveness at answering parliamentary questions and his generally agreeable manner, as well as his economic flair and clear brain.

The letters of congratulations to Strachey at this high point in his career (as it turned out to be) were many, from people with whom he had been in touch at all stages of his life. Most of them added a brief comment on their own hopes for, or complaints about, the Ministry. Boothby's mother wrote, old friends and secretaries in Bomber Ops wrote, the editor of the *Spectator* wrote, and contributors to *The Miner* wrote, as did old comrades from Aston, and followers of the Left Book Club days. Mosley's sister-in-law, Lady Ravensdale, sent a homily on how to behave as a statesman, and unknown people wrote 'Now the housewife will have a man with a background of knowledge, brains and ability to look beneath the surface to see the . . . facts. . . . I hope soon to leave the queues, but it has been an education in social conditions to stand in them.' An old friend from West Hoathly, the Sussex village where Strachey and Celia had stayed in 1931–3, sent a long letter, including a poem, and several complaints – no place to obtain extra mid-day meal in the country, as in towns, ration inadequate for men away all day at work, more cheese would be much appreciated, stop the Black Market, and, 'I hope you will give us more food for our big sons. [Signed] Mrs Baker . . . who worked for you.' Finally, the Bloomsbury Stracheys wrote letters of congratulation: and Marjorie Strachey saw in the appointment 'the seeds of a wonderful New World Order'. The Press also was almost universally encouraging.

But this was a difficult moment. When Strachey arrived, for the first time, at the Ministry of Food in Portman Square, accompanied by Mallalieu, whom he had brought with him as Parliamentary Private Secretary from the Air Ministry, the officials laid papers before him arguing that bread should be rationed. Indeed, Britain had already offered on 10 April at the (allied) Combined Food Board to ration bread. Bread had never been rationed in England during the war. But now, the European and world grain situation was such that the only alternative seemed to be a sharp increase in price.

Partly this was a consequence of a diversion of the Australian wheat ships in time of famine to India – a decision taken by Douglas Jay, then in the Prime Minister's office, with Sir Herbert Broadley, deputy secretary at the Ministry of Food. Partly it was because Sir Ben Smith had lost an argument with Bevin, who had declared that he could not bring peace to Europe unless there were food in Germany. The U.S. had promised to help India, and had caused Germany to be considered a combined Allied problem; but, in return, she had deducted 200,000 tons of wheat from the British quota. Partly the decision was the consequence of over-caution on the part of the second deputy secretary at the Food Ministry, Sir Edward Harwood, who always became alarmed when stocks of wheat seemed to be running low. As Max Nicholson, then in the Lord President's office, pointed out, the chances of famine were greatest in the months before the harvest.

Strachey was thus in a stormy position. He managed skilfully to win over the, at first, hostile commercial advisers at the Ministry of Food; Jaspar Knight of Unilever, Sir William Rook of Czarnikow, J. V. Rank, a leading operator in the commodity market, all came round to Strachey's plan, and to Strachey, though these were businessmen, opposed to the government and to the Minister of Food's apparently ideological commitment to bulk purchase (though they were notable in that none of them was ever accused of favouring his own firm). Strachey also persuaded the Cabinet comparatively easily, despite the political dangers of the scheme. But it was more difficult to convince the bakers and the national Press. The Housewives League, a manifestation of spontaneous conservatism led by a Kentish vicar's wife, sent petitions. All this overlooked the fact that the rationing was light, and that none suffered in consequence of the scheme.

From the beginning of his time at the Ministry of Food, Strachey had a hostile public. Gone were the days of Lord Woolton when food was not a matter of political controversy. For a time, it even seemed as though the bakers might refuse to put into effect the Ministry's rationing scheme. The small master bakers were appalled at the likely paper work. They begged the Minister to seek alternative ways of saving flour, though to no avail. Meetings with these bakers, and the regular Press conferences of the Ministry of Food, turned into political meetings, for Strachey antagonized the journalists by his intellectual voice and ironical manner, which were much less effective in these rough circumstances than in the House of Commons.

Strachey's first task in the Ministry of Food was to answer many awkward parliamentary questions at twenty-four hour's notice. On this occasion, he brought in Celia to help draft the replies – an experiment which was unpopular at the Ministry, and which was not repeated. Strachey's first speech as Minister of Food, on 18 June, was, however, an outstanding success, though he had had to speak in it of the probability of bread rationing. He justified this by speaking of the threat of famine in the rest of the world. He quoted, in conclusion, on Mallalieu's suggestion, Donne's lines, suggesting that 'the bell of hunger and famine' was tolling in many parts of the world.[1] Churchill was moved to tears, and congratulated Strachey on the eloquence of his reply. Strachey then flew to Ottawa to negotiate a new long-term wheat agreement, and to Washington, to attend the inaugural meeting of the International Emergency Food Council.[2] Flying back to Ottawa from Washington, he prevailed on the attendant Air Vice Marshal to allow him to take the controls, as befitted a wartime Wing Commander. While 7,500 feet up, the petrol supply gave out, but, with presence of mind, Strachey maintained equilibrium. On his return to England, on 27 June, Strachey introduced an order going ahead with bread rationing, as from 21 July. The ration covered bread and flour. The rations were based on Bread Units, each representing a given weight of bread. Manual workers were to get more than normal adults, children less. A normal adult's ration was nine Bread Units a week, for which he could obtain 3 lbs of flour, or two large loaves and ½ lb of cakes or buns.

Strachey explained in a debate on 3 July that the stock position

[1] Hansard, Vol. 423, Col. 1575.
[2] See R. J. Hammond, Food, III (off. History of War), 'Administration and Control', Appendix K.

had rendered rationing necessary. But, in the days after that, Strachey had second thoughts. He had received a 'slightly better estimate of Canadian crop prospects', and began to believe that bread rationing was unnecessary. He therefore tried to persuade the Cabinet to go back on its decision. The Cabinet was against this, on the ground that 'the Canadian crop prospect was only one detail, though a most important one in the world picture, and because it was also most important for us to get the Americans to provide some of the food for the British zone in Germany, rather than to load it all on to us'.[1] Wheat policy was admittedly a complicated matter: sometimes the crux of the question related to the difficulty of carrying wheat across Canada, sometimes to its general availability. Another debate went ahead on 18 July as planned. Strachey spoke, and well, despite interruptions, and the Opposition was generally discomforted, despite clever speeches by Churchill and Hogg.[2] Plans were made for the implementation of bread rationing for 21 July. Endless problems were raised and settled: was there anything in the sinister rumour that there would be 'a darker loaf'? Did hospital nurses qualify for manual workers' rations? Would people have to register with a single baker? In restaurants, should bread count as one of the three courses allowed? Was the Minister aware of the wastage of crusts of bread used in preparing snacks for cocktail parties? During these discussions, Strachey became more and more convinced that rationing was unnecessary.

Thus, on 19 July, a Friday, when all was ready for bread rationing to begin on the following Monday, Strachey circulated the Cabinet with a paper depicting Canadian wheat prospects in even brighter terms. At the time, Attlee happened to be in Durham for the annual miner's rally, with Dalton and Bevan. In London, Morrison proposed to call a Cabinet on the next day, 20 July, to discuss Strachey's paper, for most of the Ministers left in London wished to suspend rationing. Attlee agreed to hold a Cabinet, but arranged it for the Sunday. After discussion, it was decided to go ahead with rationing, as planned.

Strachey had given, during these days, an impression of indecision, irritating colleagues such as Dalton, Bevan and George

[1] Dalton, *op. cit.*, p. 142.   [2] Hansard, Vol. 425, Col. 1448.

Strauss.[1] But the pressure on him at this time was great. His answers in parliament had to cover a myriad of technical matters of minor importance, and he inherited, from Sir Ben Smith, other problems apart from bread rationing.

In fact, however, Strachey was almost certainly right: bread rationing was unnecessary: wheat stocks were probably higher than Sir Edmund Harwood supposed; the mere knowledge that bread might be rationed had greatly increased the pressure on stocks. Admittedly, it is always a matter of difficult calculation in politics or in war, as to when it is desirable to reverse a policy that is known to be wrong if the preparations for it are under way. But in recollection two things should be said: first, the stock position, current and prospective, was never such as to call for bread rationing, and second, the rationing scheme that was introduced would have been inadequate if it had been.

Strachey naturally now believed that he would not be able to manage his demanding ministry without being in the Cabinet, and having become a member of the Privy Council on 4 June he went to the length, within only a little over a month of being Minister of Food, of writing to Attlee on the subject: 'experience of this office in the past five weeks,' he wrote, 'has convinced me that what I put to you so strongly on my appointment was sound; namely, that at the present critical juncture, the Minister of Food cannot perform his duties successfully unless he is a member of the Cabinet. . . . To ask a Minister of Food to shoulder the terrific responsibility – which I feel acutely – of assuring an adequate food supply to the British people today, without allowing him to have a voice as a member of the Cabinet in these decisions of [general] policy, is asking too much of any man. I fully appreciate the difficulty which faces you in making so junior a member of your party as myself a member of the Cabinet. But in that case, someone else should have been made Minister of Food. I cannot believe that you can really doubt that the Minister of Food must be a member of the Cabinet at this time. If, therefore, you feel that you cannot include me, I cannot help feeling that you should find someone else who you do feel that you can put in the Cabinet, for the job.'[2] Strachey's idea had much to commend it.

[1] Dalton, *op. cit.*, pp. 142–4.   [2] Strachey to Attlee, 5 July 1946.

In addition, it seemed inappropriate that Sir Tom Williams should be in the Cabinet as Minister of Agriculture, while Strachey was not, as Minister of Food. But there were precedents for these arrangements from the end of the First World War.[1]

Attlee's reply to this letter is not preserved. But, doubtless, he settled the matter in his blunt way, and in person. Strachey was at all events not, for the time being, made a member of the Cabinet. That was a mistake on Attlee's part, for the Ministry of Food was a decisive department in the Administration – as was confirmed to Strachey when he found Dalton, Morrison and other ministers interfering in his undertakings.

Attlee in this matter probably bowed, and unwisely, to the views of Dalton, who disliked Strachey, whom he regarded as an amateur politician, of whom he was suspicious as an ex-communist, and whose concern with theoretical economics he distrusted.

The summer of 1946 brought release to Strachey from parliamentary interrogation, and bread rationing, in the end, was operated justly, with savings of flour claimed at ten per cent. But it never became clear whether that figure was accurate, because of hoarding, and it is most doubtful if the scheme could have worked if it had been made more astringent. Yet Strachey claimed that possibility as one of its advantages. The ration was ample for adults, so that it was difficult to get bakers' roundsmen to collect Bread Units; but coupons were usually demanded in shops. The lack of rigour in the operation of the scheme, in the words of R. J. Hammond, the official historian of the Ministry of Food, meant that it 'affords no sort of guide to the administrative possibility of making a really worthwhile reduction in flour consumption, for this would require coupon counting . . . on a scale not attempted'.[2] In some senses, bread rationing was an administrative bluff.

In the autumn, attacks in Parliament also revived. Fish meal, oat meal, tangerines, dried fruit and suet – the theorist of *The Coming Struggle for Power* gallantly ploughed through innumerable interrogations on these matters, learning exactly what Power

[1] See R. J. Hammond, *Food and Agriculture in Britain*, p. 218.
[2] R. J. Hammond, *op. cit. See also* his volume in the official history of the war in Food Administration.

is. The winter of 1946-7 was, also, phenomenally hard, and the Labour Government became hard-pressed. The shortage of fuel caused most households to suffer from cold, and the rationing of food, in this second winter of peace, seemed almost too much. Unemployment rose to over one million. The Conservatives used Shinwell, Minister of Fuel, and Strachey, as their chief butts: 'Shiver with Shinwell and Starve with Strachey', was an irresistible slogan. The *Daily Express* attacked both venomously. A cartoon by Low depicted Strachey and Shinwell at the wheel of a car, out for a picnic, with Strachey saying 'Run out of fuel I suppose', and Shinwell replying 'And who forgot the sandwiches?' Conservatives made the most violent speeches on such harmless subjects as British restaurants for which Strachey was reponsible, though Strachey coped with attacks, or even affronts, with moderation, intelligence and, sometimes, grace. But Woolton, Strachey's Conservative predecessor as Minister of Food, who had been a master of public relations, was now chairman of the Conservative party organization, and lent his support to ill-informed criticisms of the policies of bulk-buying and of food restrictions generally.

The consequences affected the whole Strachey family. Strachey's son Charles, at that time at the Hall, a private school in Hampstead, was teased: masters even would enquire 'O Strachey, have you brought the sweets?'

But, apart from his understandable indecision over bread rationing at the start of his time in the Ministry, Strachey continued to make an excellent impression in his department, the House of Commons, and in Cabinet, when he attended. He was respected and liked at the Ministry itself, except by his undersecretary, Dr Edith Summerskill, who was never friendly with him. With officials, he was successful. He had disliked, it is true, his first permanent secretary, Sir Frank Tribe, and, with difficulty, arranged for him to be removed. Nor did he see eye-to-eye with Tribe's successor, Sir Percivale Liesching, who was in a strong position, since no Minister could expect to dismiss two permanent secretaries – though Strachey tried. With Liesching's successor, Frank Lee, he was more happy: Lee once remarked to George Bishop, Strachey's loyal and indefatigable private secretary,

'What a pleasure it is to work for a Minister capable of writing economic papers of a calibre to withstand Dalton's criticisms.'

The Ministry of Food was also pleased, in its English way, by Strachey's continuing passion for cricket, and it joyfully sent down an annual 'Whitehall' team, with Sir Frank Lee as wicket-keeper, to play against Strachey's village side. Strachey also did his best to secure, for the post-war civil service, as many as possible of the more intelligent academics or businessmen who had joined the government service in the war. Though he failed to persuade the philosopher, Stuart Hampshire, to remain in the Supply Secretariat, the chief of that body, Eric Roll (who, before the war, had been an economics don), did remain in the Ministry, on Strachey's urging.

Roll recalls Strachey as being quickly aware of the limitations of a Minister in Whitehall and as accepting these limitations with understanding. Perhaps Strachey recalled Mosley's impatience with Whitehall, and his own part in feeding that impatience, as P.P.S. in 1929–31. At all events, Strachey settled down as a confident Minister. Since it was the Ministry of Food, however, there were always possibilities of eccentricity. Thus, Strachey was specially interested in the powers of decision of James Rank. Rank had made a spectacular reputation, during the war, as a man who was able to know exactly when to make bulk purchases at low cost. He was able to do the same in the late 1940s. Yet, to Strachey's amazement and fascination, Rank, who was taciturn and without formal education, was unable to explain how he arrived at these excellent decisions.

A full study of Strachey's tenure of the Ministry of Food must await the release of the papers of that department under the Thirty Year Rule. Any fair estimate, however, of his activities would give praise to his innovating zeal, and to his persistence and patience over a variety of socially and politically important tasks. It was Strachey, for example, who took an initiative in the 'battle for decontrol' of fruit and vegetables – to the initial alarm of producers used to the comfortable circumstances of war production. How ironical it was to hear Strachey, the Marxist Minister, explaining to jam manufacturers that the market itself would in future dictate to them how much jam they should produce. It was Strachey too who took the lead in persuading Sainsbury's to institute self-service shops, after a visit to the supermarkets in Washington. Strachey, too, should take some of the credit for the effective establishment of the F.A.O., as for the realization that food subsidies could be cut, with advantage to the ordinary consumer. Here he showed himself more open-minded and less dogmatic than some officials – particularly Treasury officials – argued him to be.

Of course, not all his Ministry's schemes were successful; for example, whalemeat, frozen cod and imported rabbit were delivered onto the market and, being unwanted, caused embarrassment. Frozen pineapples arrived without customers in Dundee – giving him the temporary nickname in Scotland of 'Pineapple John'. Still, it was undoubtedly Strachey, who, personally, largely freed Britain from dependence on dollar food imports – a specially important subject when, as became clear during these years, shortages of food began to disappear, only to reveal a shortage of hard currency with which to purchase such food that did exist.

Bulk-buying loomed large as a contentious political subject but, as Strachey pointed out in a Food Supplies debate in July 1947, its abandonment was scarcely conceivable, while rationing continued.[1] But the Ministry remained a politically exposed one, particularly when the worst potato crop since before the war persuaded Strachey to introduce a scheme for the controlled distribution of potatoes – another rationing system which went further than the wartime restriction. Further, the whole crisis of 'hard currency' led the Ministry of Food to attempt some most unpopular experiments. Lord Woolton had failed to persuade the English to eat salt-cod and the Lend-Lease bean: Strachey was equally unsuccessful with *snoek*, a tinned fish imported from South Africa, whose name – it was pronounced 'snook' – caused derision. There were other schemes, such as an attempt to discriminate between luxury and non-luxury restaurants. The former, defined as establishments where charges were over 2/3 for a main meal, were allocated smaller allowances of meat on the ground that these were able to obtain unrationed

[1] Hansard, Vol. 439, Col. 1161 (July 1947).

foods, such as poultry, more easily. Strachey was in fact running the Ministry of Food when the difficulties of supply were greater than at any time since 1941-2. But now no measures of austerity were popular. In addition, the 'spiv' was believed to be able to procure at an inflated price anything which was short.

The controversies over bulk-buying were counter-productive: Conservatives attacked 'bulk-buying' as the cause of food shortages, while the Ministry spoke of food subsidies, and the distribution of vitamins, in hushed tones more suitable for prayer.

By late 1947 Strachey, however, seemed in a strong position politically. Despite his failure to get into the Cabinet in 1946, he was now in the habit of staying on at Cabinet meetings, even when matters unrelated to food were being discussed. This practice irritated Dalton and some other Ministers, for Strachey had been using his frequent Cabinet attendances as an excuse for circularizing Ministers with papers on a variety of economic subjects, not always connected with food. Attlee told him that this was irregular. After some prompting by his energetic P.P.S., Mallalieu, Strachey let it be known that he would resign unless he were made a member of the Cabinet. After a meeting of the Cabinet on 20 October 1947, the day of Parliament's reassembly after the summer, Strachey told Dalton that he wished to go to Attlee immediately and make this clear. This was a bid for power in no uncertain terms. Dalton, however, was against this. He disliked Strachey. But neither he nor anyone wanted his resignation. Accordingly, Dalton asked Strachey into his room in No. 11 Downing Street, and opened a bottle of Australian rum. They talked. Dalton deliberately tried to intoxicate Strachey, and he succeeded. When Strachey came out of Dalton's room, he had been persuaded to settle for a status of 'constant attendance' at the Cabinet – that is, he would attend unless asked not to. Strachey thought this a victory, and seemed, to Mallalieu, triumphant. But it was no victory. After two months, and despite Dalton's own forced resignation in November over budget leaks, Strachey's old status outside the Cabinet was reaffirmed. The bid for Cabinet rank had failed. It was, perhaps, a tribute to Strachey that Attlee did not dismiss him. But Strachey's difficulty was that he was too much of a lonely man to have a strong political position. He was a follower of neither Bevin, Morrison nor Dalton – the old men of the Cabinet – if closer to Bevin (and to Cripps) than to the others; and, unlike his contemporary Bevan, he had no following of his own.

In the course of the winter of 1946–7, Strachey went again to the U.S. and Canada in order to negotiate new wheat allocations. He and his staff went in the Prime Minister's private aeroplane, which developed serious trouble at Ottawa and ultimately blew up after a crash landing in the snow. There was too a long stay in Iceland en route at a particularly difficult moment of Anglo-Icelandic relations over fishing, and the Icelanders, therefore, treated the Minister with care. On their way back, the delegation came on the *Queen Mary*, and their irregular departure – a strike had made it impossible to get easily to the dock – was the occasion of Strachey's first meeting with Kenneth Galbraith, who, with a Press card, negotiated their passage past the New York police.

Some other incidents at the Ministry of Food deserve recall. In the spring of 1947, Boothby was approached by a firm of German wine-merchants. They said that the German vineyards were being destroyed by French nationalism: French occupying authorities were preventing the vineyards from receiving nitrates for the soil, and stones to repair the walls of their terraces – the German vineyards are set often on high slopes. The French High Command was against these policies, but the orders came from Paris. They even had instructions to take away the entire produce of the vineyards over several years. Boothby arranged a lunch between himself, Strachey, and the Germans. Afterwards, Strachey got in touch with Duff Cooper, the ambassador in Paris. Duff Cooper hated Germans, but was brought to believe that German wines were part of Western civilization, rather than of Germany. He intervened too, and threatened a boycott on French wines in England unless this policy was reversed.

A special interest during the Labour Government were the dinners given by Stafford Cripps in the House of Commons (after he had become Chancellor, in November 1947) for 'Production' Ministers. Strachey attended. Here he showed how much he still enjoyed general discussion of economic policy. He admired Cripps too, more than he did Dalton. These occasions were often transformed by Bevan, with whom Strachey was again on terms of political friendship, and who 'used to orate', yet they were, to begin with anyway, useful meetings between men who, curiously enough, 'would not elsewhere have met often informally'. During 1949, as Strachey recalled much later, enmity broke out between Bevan and Gaitskell, who had become Minister of Fuel and Power when Shinwell was transferred in 1947 to the War Office. Bevan would persistently lash Gaitskell with his tongue, and Gaitskell would endure this silently. Strachey once asked Bevan, afterwards, why he was going out of his way to create a rift with one of the considerable men in the Government: 'Considerable?' Bevan replied, 'but he's nothing, nothing, nothing.'[1]

During the course of 1948 and the first half of 1949, Strachey's chief intellectual relaxation at weekends, apart from working fast through red boxes, was a reading of Toynbee's A study of History. It is clear that he did this in order to compare one new complete view of history with his own old picture as described in Marx's Kapital. When he had finished Toynbee's many volumes, he wrote appreciatively to the author, and sent detailed notes, thereby beginning a correspondence with the historian. Although these notes criticized Toynbee from what was evidently still in some ways a 'Marxist' position, Strachey included the admission that he himself was 'a Whig, by conviction, as well as by descent. My real heroes are the English leaders of 1688 and above all, 1832. . . . They adjusted their communities' institutions so wonderfully . . . and I don't think Mr Attlee's first administration is an unworthy successor to them.'[2] Strachey afterwards remained Toynbee's most devoted admirer; no criticism, refutation, or denunciation by other historians could shake Strachey's belief in Toynbee as a modern prophet, whether or not his prophecies were false or true.

When Minister of Food, Strachey, and Celia, had bought a new home, a beautiful old rectory at Lambourne, near Abridge, just in the country beyond Loughton in Essex, for £12,000. In this house, Strachey lived for sixteen years, riding, entertaining

[1] Strachey's article on Gaitskell, 'The Unreaped Harvest', Sunday Times, 20 January 1963.
[2] Strachey's notes on Toynbee, Typescript, c. 1949.

and busy in local activities: for example, he played cricket for Abridge, a good village eleven. Colleagues and friends would come for the weekend. Here he played endless and furious tennis with his unwilling children – Charles then at Westminster and Elizabeth at Loughton County High School for Girls. Westminster was more civilized than the Hall over Charles Strachey's parentage. This did not mean, however, that Strachey and his family were left alone by the public. Celia would receive odious letters, adjuring her to take 'that brolly nosed husband of yours' to 'the zoo and give him to the Lyons (sic); but wait until they are hungry. It seems a pity to poison them. . .' but that would 'oblige the country's Housewives'.[1] Strachey continued to receive much attention from the Press. Reporters accosted his servants to ask how large his butter ration was, whether he had received food parcels from abroad, or what was the weight of his Christmas turkey. A specially trivial incident, exultantly made much of, concerned a pig which the Stracheys fed and killed at Abridge: Strachey, on this occasion, wished to keep for himself the trotters and other trimmings which, by tradition, went to those who had killed it. Local papers, and then national ones, seized hold of this tale, making Strachey out to be mean. But Strachey became, in the end, a popular local figure in Essex, partly by dint of playing for the Abridge cricket team. Another relaxation was sailing, particularly in the Blackwater estuary, north of Chelmsford, whose mysterious light, and grey reaches, exercised on him, more and more, a special charm. Higher up the river, in the 1930s, at a point where the Blackwater is a mere stream (or 'drindle', as it is described in Essex), Strachey had used to dam the flow to give his children, when at Shalford, a paddling pool. The revolutionary and the Minister thus kept to the same district, and even the same water.

[1] Undated and unsigned letter to Celia, c. 1947.

Chapter 16 / GROUNDNUTS

By 1948, however, Strachey had become much concerned in the scheme for alleviating the world shortage of fats by growing groundnuts on a large scale in Tanganyika. This is a very curious story, since the Press and the Opposition skilfully manipulated public opinion to make it seem that the ultimate failure of the scheme was a national disaster of the first magnitude. This it never was, though it did become a personal and political disaster.

This project originated with Frank Samuel, Managing Director of the United Africa Company, a subsidiary of Unilever. He had thought of the idea, while R. W. R. Millar, director of Agriculture in Tanganyika, had suggested that success would depend on the project being both large in scale and mechanized.

Samuel next produced a plan for the mechanized clearing of $2\frac{1}{2}$ million acres over five years, at a cost of £8 million. This proposal was presented to Sir Ben Smith in March 1946. The chiefs of Unilever added that, with more home consumption of Indian groundnuts, a permanent shortage of fats would occur unless some scheme of this sort was adopted. They knew that East Africa was the best area to test the plan. They also believed that they were, as a company, not large enough to be responsible for the success of such a scheme. Sir Ben Smith thought Samuel's idea admirable, as did the Colonial Secretary, and both backed it in the Cabinet. The Cabinet called for a detailed analysis, and entrusted this to a commission led by John Wakefield, an ex-Director of Agriculture in Tanganyika. Wakefield and his colleagues (David Martin, plantation Manager of the United Africa Company, and John Rosa, a banker and wartime civil servant) presented their report to the Colonial Office in September 1946, by which time, of course, Strachey was Minister of Food.

Their recommendation not only endorsed Samuel's ideas, but proposed the clearing of about 3¼ million acres in East Africa, mainly Tanganyika, in six years, with a capital cost of £24 million. This huge area would be divided into 107 farms of 35,000 acres each. Costs were estimated as £14 5s. 6d. per ton of groundnuts at a time when the average world price was £32 a ton. If the plan were to be begun in 1947, 600,000 tons of groundnuts should be produced in 1951, saving then, and thereafter, £10 million from Britain's food bill. But this document was more than a mere solution as to how Britain (and the world) should try to resolve the problem of its shortage of fats: it suggested that the proposed development would, as the report of Sir Phillip Mitchell, Governor of Kenya, suggested, provide 'ocular demonstration' that rehabilitation of old land, in Africa, and settlement of new, was possible.

Strachey read this report in September 1946, and became excited by it. The idea of sending bulldozers to Africa for peaceful purposes was the fulfilment of an old vision which he had experienced when travelling with tanks to the western desert in 1942.[1] He supported its conclusions in the Cabinet in October, and, soon after, the Cabinet directed that a section of the Ministry of Food should be set up to make recommendations, in its turn, on the Wakefield Report. This section reported to Strachey in December, and encouragingly. By this time, most of those associated with the scheme, from Strachey downwards, had become exhilarated by it. Either because of technical ignorance or for some other reason, few noticed that the scheme had shortcomings: that, since no full study was made of rainfall records, 'the evidence concerning rainfall is perhaps not wholly satisfactory' – in the words of two scientists whose views were con-

[1] See Hansard, Vol. 443, Col. 2032 and his New Yorker article on the subject of his journey in 1942.

tained in the Special Report. Nor did the Wakefield Report itself make evident that, in the selection of one area proposed for development, Kongwa, the Commission had been influenced by a single farmer.[1] The soil was not, it seems, subjected to full analysis. There were also some doubts expressed about the efficiency of mechanization. George Bishop recalls Strachey taking note of this point; but he did not follow it up. After all, this was a report by a major company, with much experience in this field.

The Report also glossed over the importance of finding effective staff, who had to be flexible and imaginative, as well as resilient and informed. It under-estimated the cost, since it assumed that the undertaking would provide for roads, houses, workshops, railways, air-strips and hospitals, not to speak of shops and cinemas for the labourers. It was, in a sense, an ambitious effort at colonization. But no one accurately anticipated the difficulty with which the Gogo Africans of Tanganyika would adapt themselves to the opportunity.

The project was to be undertaken by the Ministry of Food, and not the Colonial Office. The former Ministry did not wish this, but Sir Stafford Cripps, Minister for Economic Affairs, insisted that the Colonial Office was not capable of running such a complicated and large business. Strachey meantime persuaded himself, and all associated with him, that the proposed scheme was a sketch for a promised land.

The question arises, whose fault was it that the groundnut scheme now was pushed ahead? Attlee, in an obituary of Strachey for the *Observer* in 1963 wrote: 'Looking back on it, I think his only mistake was to go in on a large scale, instead of starting with a pilot scheme.'[2] But though Lord Huntingdon, an old friend of Strachey's from Oxford and then the Labour Under-Secretary for Agriculture, suggested that, the United Africa Company had not proposed it, and their golden recommendations seemed generally acceptable. Wakefield was held to have known Tanganyika well; and 'time', as Strachey later explained, 'was of the essence': to delay two or three years with a plan designed to reduce the problem of fats seemed a terrible mistake.

[1] See Judith Listowel, *The Making of Tanganyika*, p. 145.
[2] *Observer*, 21 July 1963.

Since Strachey was in a hurry, he commissioned the United Africa Company to embark on the project. The U.A.C. formed a sub-company, which, in its turn, contracted Sir John Gibson, of Pauling & Co., known for his achievements during the war, to clear the area. Gibson chose, out of an immense number of volunteers, about 1,200 men who had worked on clearing railways, and airfields of craters, during the war. An advance party set off for Tanganyika in January 1947, and toured the regions in Tanganyika and Kenya proposed for development. A scientific adviser reported favourably on the soil in Tanganyika and, by March 1947, an elaborate organization had been set up for this undertaking. The clearing of thick, low scrub, of cactus and aloe, began in June in the Kongwa area, with the stirring cry from Strachey: 'On your success depends more than any other single factor whether the harassed housewives of Britain get more margarine, cooking fats and soap. . . .'

There were, however, delays. The necessary tractors were delayed by the harshness of the winter. The problem of soil erosion was great. The ground might be cleared, but many roots were left behind: the instrument to cope with this was unsatisfactory. There were strikes which, starting from the docks of Dar-es-Salaam, spread to Kongwa. Even more difficult, the tractors broke down, and there were inadequate repair shops in Tanganyika. Wakefield proposed the conversion to tanks, and nearly six hundred, converted for peace, were sent to Tanganyika. New areas of the country began to be opened up in the west and the south. But in all these activities, carried out by the United Africa Company, there was one general deficiency: no, or poor, accounts were kept of the stock of machinery.

At the end of 1947, many fewer acres of Tanganyika were ready than had been anticipated. Men who had joined the project in the hope of swiftly becoming managers of 30,000-acre farms became dispirited when they found themselves, a year later, still performing minor tasks. The Africans found it difficult to cope with the Massey Harris machines introduced to plant the nuts. These, too, met difficulties similar to those met by the tractors: dead jackals, stumps of beobah trees, and shortage of acid for batteries.

By now, the administration of the groundnut scheme had been

changed. Strachey had introduced into the House of Commons, in November 1947, an Overseas Resources Development Bill, which created a Colonial Development Corporation and an Overseas Food Corporation. The latter was to direct the groundnut scheme and to take over from the United Africa Company. At this point, though, there was no hint of controversy. The Conservative party, and even the Beaverbrook Press, endorsed the scheme with warmth. Alan Lennox Boyd, the Conservative spokesman on the Colonies, even claimed a Conservative paternity for it.[1]

Strachey had to choose a Board for the Overseas Food Corporation and the names of the Chairman and other members were announced in May 1947. Discounting several other recommendations made in the Ministry, Strachey chose, as the Chairman of the Board, his old friend Dick Plummer, at the time Assistant General Manager of the *Daily Express* group and, in the 1920s, manager of both the *New Leader* and *The Miner*. Plummer was a controversial choice. He had remained a socialist, but had made money with Beaverbrook, towards whom he had that relationship of love-hate which was characteristic of Beaverbrook employees who were also socialists. He was also a large-scale farmer on his own account. He was an energetic, bustling man, with a strong sense of humour which had, off and on, been an inspiration for Strachey, as for their mutual friend, Stephen Potter, in his 'Gamesmanship' jokes.[2]

It was at the Plummers' large house in Essex in fact and at Francis Meynell's, nearby, in Topplesfield that 'Gamesmanship' had its inspiration. 'J. Strachey' appears once or twice in that famous book of jokes as a guileful tennis player. Strachey chose Plummer, since he seemed one of the few men who was both a supporter of the Government and had the respect of the City. In retrospect, he was probably unwise to appoint an old friend, however well qualified, to such a post. The friendship exposed both to unnecessary attacks and limited their freedom of action.

Plummer's deputy was James McFadyen, prominent in the Co-operative movement. Other members of the Board were

[1] Hansard, Vol. 443, Col. 2104.
[2] *See* Stephen Potter, *Gamesmanship*, pp. 91, 118.

John Wakefield, author of the original report; John Rosa, the banker and wartime civil servant associated with the Wakefield Report, whom Strachey persuaded to join; and Sir Charles Lockhart, from the Colonial Office. There were three part-time members – Sir Frank Stockdale of the Colonial Office: Lord Rothschild, another old left-wing friend of Strachey's who became scientific adviser to the Corporation; and Frank Samuel. Major General Desmond Harrison became resident member of the board in Tanganyika and director of the scheme in the field. He had been Chief Engineer under Mountbatten in Burma. Harrison took command – and it was such, indeed, that it seemed – on 1 April 1948. The transition was not easy: the men of the United Africa Company who were staying on with the new management were unhappy about the changes, while the new men were resentful of the old directors. It also seems that Harrison's very excellence as a military engineer militated against his chances as an agricultural manager; for agriculture is a different science to the organization of war. In agriculture, the multiplication of a number of units may create different problems or opportunities to what might be expected; but, in war, an army is often no more than the sum of its parts.

In this atmosphere, the first harvest began in May 1948 and Strachey paid his first visit to Tanganyika to inspect progress. This journey was a success. Strachey visited the areas designated for development, drank with the European managers and opened a game of football with the Africans. He made optimistic speeches.

The harvest, however, was less successful. The mechanical diggers did not arrive until after the end of the rains – so that the ground had, in some places, set hard. Some nuts broke as they were dug up, having ripened earlier. Many nuts – from irregularly planted bushes – were left in the ground, to be gleaned unofficially. The total crop was half the original plan's prediction.

This harvest occurred in the Kongwa province. But the groundnut operation had, by now, encountered difficulties in the south as well. Sometime in late 1947 a decision was made to clear immediately one 30,000-acre farm unit, before the full establishment of a port, railway and oil pipelines. This was a mistaken decision taken, presumably, by Colonel Stirling, resident director on behalf of the United Africa Company, against the advice of Hugh Bunting, the scientific adviser, and of the chief mechanical engineer, both of whom pointed out that if 'too many tractors were sent to the south without adequate workshops the result would be disastrous'.[1] These views were ignored. With new enthusiasm, the managers of the groundnut scheme improvised port facilities. But progress was slow. Not only were the new tractors difficult to keep in repair, but the scheme seemed over-centralized, being still dependent on General Harrison, whose headquarters were in the central area. There was also friction within the African labour force: Kongwa had become a new Johannesburg, a golden city, where the labour force turned over at the rate of twenty per cent a month. These frictions grew, as it slowly became evident that, during 1948, even the targets for effective clearing for 1947 could not be met: but, unfortunately, Plummer and Harrison continued to speak as if it was certain that 140,000 or so acres would be cleared in 1948. As the year wore on, expectations sank while optimism continued to be voiced.

News of this defeat began to leak out, and Conservative members with African interests started to speak of Strachey's 'over-exaggerated optimism'.[2] It was also obvious in Tanganyika that the social implications of the groundnuts scheme had been underestimated. Africans had been told that the great undertaking had been for their benefit but they had seen few of the major social improvements which they had been promised: few schools, few houses, few hospitals. The Africans believed that the rain gods were supposed to live in some of the huge beobah trees which had to be cut down. Witchdoctors had to be found and propitiated, while Strachey was asked in the House of Commons, not wholly with jovial intent, as to the scale of their remuneration.

More technical problems arose: one problem of the first year in Kongwa derived from roots left in the soil. Mechanical root cutters on a large scale were, therefore, imported. Alas, it was only in August that they were tested. It turned out that, in Urambo, the cutters would not work: trees snapped off and the roots would not come up. The soil of the Kongwa region turned

[1] Alan Wood, *The Ground Nut Scheme*, p. 135.
[2] Hansard, Vol. 454, Col. 656 (22 July 1948).

out to be 'abrasive', in the sense that it was so gritty as to wear out, fast, all blades introduced into it. New steels were introduced; none was successful.

All these problems, and others, began to run into each other in late 1948. The Board in London grated on General Harrison, he on they, both of them on Strachey, who was obliged to defend the project in England, and to criticise it, constructively, in Tanganyika. In 1948, the rains were late; and Kongwa almost ran out of petrol and coal. Finally, it became obvious that nearly £20 million had been spent, that commitments had been made to spend much more, but that the profits were most uncertain.

General Harrison returned to London in September 1948 with recommendations for a new plan, based on ideas from his own departmental heads. He proposed a general simplification of the project, a reduction of the rate of clearing; three-and-a-quarter million acres were to be cleared in ten years, rather than in six. The plan was accepted. Unfortunately for its swift introduction, General Harrison had to retire as a result of ill-health – before, in fact, it became evident that the cost of the revised plan would be £120 million – of which only £50 million had been provided for. It became, therefore, necessary to ask the Treasury for new funds. Cripps refused. Strachey, in a debate on 14 March 1949, told the House of Commons that the plan would have to keep to its original budget. This was the first occasion when the groundnuts scheme was fully debated. Strachey made a long speech which, twenty-five years later, in the light of knowledge which certainly must have been available then to Strachey, reads over-optimistically.[1] Meantime Strachey had tried to secure, as Harrison's successor, Arthur Morley, his old chief in Bomber Operations; Morley refused.

The Harrison plan was not public knowledge. But Cripps's decision meant that the project as originally conceived would not be able to be put into effect even over ten years. There was no chance of clearing more than a few of the acres before there was no money left at all. These unpalatable facts were, unfortunately, not made public until the autumn. In the meantime, the morale of the men on the spot in Africa declined. Demands began to be

[1] Hansard, Vol. 462, Col. 1758 ff.

made that Plummer and the Board should resign. As early as January, the departmental heads in Africa complained of the frequent changes of policy; resignations followed thick and fast: and, in their wake, redundancies and 'reorganization'.

1949 saw new disappointments and further failures. Even the newest ideas, including the sunflower project, turned out badly. Rainfall in 1949 was lower than usual. At Urambo, the 'rosette' disease attacked the whole crop. The single encouraging development in 1949 was the discovery that forests could be cleared successfully by using tractors harnessed together in the most barbaric but simple fashion, by anchor chains.

During these months, a sense of public outrage, skilfully provoked and managed by the strong Conservative Press, was growing against the whole project and against its leaders, particularly Strachey. Strachey had been so enthusiastic about this undertaking, and made so many others enthusiastic, that he could not imagine that it might turn out a failure. He began to think that all who criticized it were part of some odious conspiracy. In July 1949, for the first time, Strachey sounded pessimistic, and he invoked the failure of the Manchester Ship Canal and of the Tennessee Valley Authority to pay dividends for many years, in order to justify the groundnuts scheme – an ominous comparison.[1] On 21 November he sounded most distressed. In that debate, he put forward a revised plan, providing for a limited reorganization of the Corporation. This included a dismissal of the banker, John Rosa, and of the agronomist, John Wakefield.[2] These dismissals made Strachey even more unpopular, since it seemed that he was seeking scapegoats. The membership of these men of the original commission seemed to be the only real reason for singling them out for blame. If Rosa and Wakefield went, why not Plummer? And, even, why not Strachey? Rosa, in mid 1949, had urged a delay before pressing ahead with the scheme to discover if it would work, and, if so, how: a sensible suggestion, which did not receive proper consideration. Strachey, when dismissing Rosa, made the unfortunate comment: 'generals are not sacked, it is the colonels who pay the penalty'.

The House of Commons exonerated Strachey in the sense that

[1] Hansard, Vol. 467, Col. 2549.   [2] Hansard, Vol. 470, Col. 36 ff.

they refused the demand for public enquiry. But the Conservatives now sensed a kill, and pursued their prey for all they were worth. Strachey became the main target, their enmity being exacerbated by the old slur that he was a 'traitor of his class' – a class interpretation of politics which has found special favour among anti-Marxists. Strachey had told the House that he had found that the managers in Africa supported Plummer. But several executives in Tanganyika demanded, on the contrary, a withdrawal of this statement. Strachey flew to Tanganyika. On his behalf, Lord Hall in the House of Lords (the Labour deputy leader there, and First Lord of the Admiralty) explained that Strachey had not put a direct question to the staff about its confidence in Plummer; he had merely sought to 'ascertain morale'.[1] But in Tanganyika, the agronomist, Hugh Bunting, told Strachey formally that Plummer was disliked. Strachey pointed out that the Government had only just affirmed its confidence in Plummer. A general election soon followed, and afterwards Strachey left the Ministry of Food for the War Office.

The groundnuts scheme, in retrospect, certainly seems to have been an object lesson as to how not to run a public undertaking. First, the speed with which the project was launched was mistaken: it would have been wiser to have had two years preliminary planning before starting, and, despite the pressure for early results, to have spent perhaps £1 million on a pilot scheme. It was rash to embark on so large a scheme with so much improvised machinery, and a more careful analysis of the soil and rainfall in Kongwa would have been desirable.

The loss of £37 million of public money on a scheme which attempted to alleviate the world food shortage is admittedly less of a catastrophe than the loss of many more millions on military projects or upon expensive aircraft such as has occurred since that time. Much of the superstructure also contributed to Tanganyika, such as the harbour at Mtwara, railways, roads and houses. But this investment was not in the places most needed for the development of Tanganyika. The railway which was built in the southern province to serve the scheme was not economic, and was ultimately closed. Even the port at Mtwara was afterwards operated

[1] Hansard, House of Lords, 14 December 1949.

very much under capacity, because of its placing. All in all, the investment in the colony was probably no more than £7 million, leaving nearly £30 million lost or wasted. Such anyway was the belief of the Tanganyika Chief, Lugusha, who took over as chairman of the Overseas Food Corporation's successor, the Tanganyikan Agricultural Corporation, in 1953.[1]

Strachey's own mistakes in this matter can be limited to two: his enthusiastic acceptance of the original report; and his insistence in 1949 on continuing to say publicly that the scheme would be successful. These mistakes were, perhaps, the consequences of Strachey's intellectual approach to political matters ever since he had left Oxford. It was ironical, too, that he, a leading advocate of socialist enterprise, should suffer damage to his reputation in consequence of too great reliance on the recommendations of a private company such as the United Africa Company, which had regarded the scheme as too big for it to run.

Strachey's last days before the general election of 1950 were less than happy. There had been a failure in respect of Gambian eggs as well as groundnuts – far less spectacular, it is true, and adopted against the advice of the Ministry. This had not been compensated for by some success in the Queensland sorghum project. Strachey's stock was low in consequence of the failure of an idea upon which he had pinned so much. He had made several verbal mistakes of a trivial nature which were seized on with delight by an enthusiastic Opposition. For example, in April he confused the relative sizes of the pound and a kilo in a debate on food supplies.[2] He was worn down by the trivial attacks on him in the *Daily Express* and other Tory papers. He had parted on bitter terms with his P.P.S., Mallalieu, to whom he had been close for four years: Mallalieu once ventured to wonder whether the groundnuts scheme would work in the end, to receive the reproof: 'Oh, so you've joined my enemies too!' When Mallalieu voted against a Three Line Whip (on Northern Ireland), Attlee wrote to Strachey requesting his dismissal:

[1] Judith Listowel, *op. cit.*, pp. 154–5. Tanganyika only received £6m on independence in 1961.
[2] Hansard, Vol. 463, Col. 1976. The debate ended in uproar when Sir M. Lindsay accused Strachey of having been a fascist.

Strachey did not defend him but merely said: 'Well, now what shall we do about a successor?' (This was to be, in fact, the Derbyshire trade unionist, Jo Champion.) Strachey also lost in 1949 his ebullient private secretary, George Bishop – replaced by a namesake, Freddie Bishop, who was, however, a no less able civil servant.

Some thought that Attlee should have dismissed Strachey during this affair. But the Cabinet had approved the idea in the first instance and Attlee refused: 'That wasn't my way,' he said. Attlee himself had been keen on the scheme. Strachey had handled Attlee cleverly and had prepared him in advance, so that Attlee's instinct was to defend Strachey, rather than 'join the enemy'. Even so, if it had not been for the groundnut scheme, and the tremendous and personal attacks launched by the Conservatives on Strachey in consequence, he would have been regarded as a successful Minister, one certain for promotion, and perhaps for one of the two or three senior posts in the Government.

Strachey's successor as Minister of Food, Maurice Webb, decided finally to dismiss Plummer. Webb, a journalist before being a politician, had once been given a job by Plummer on the *Daily Express* at a critical stage of his life when he wished to leave the *Daily Herald*. Strachey was distressed at Plummer's dismissal, and did his best to find Plummer appointments in agricultural development in the F.A.O., for example, and other undertakings. But, despite the fact that Plummer had come into the Overseas Food Corporation a year after the groundnut scheme had begun and had had nothing to do with the original Wakefield Report, he was inevitably associated with the failure and found it hard to find a satisfactory place. He eventually became a Labour M.P., and joined the Bevanites in the 1950s.

The end of the groundnuts scheme was melancholy. In late 1950, Maurice Webb, together with the Colonial Secretary, told the Cabinet that 'There seems no escape from the view that the original conception of the East African groundnut scheme must be abandoned. It has not proved possible to carry on "the large-scale production of groundnuts" on a commercial basis, and there is no hope of the U.K. receiving any significant supply of oil-seeds from this scheme.'

Chapter 17 / SECRETARY OF STATE FOR WAR

The General Election of 1950 was held on 23 February. Labour was defending its record in achieving what Strachey described in *Tribune* as '4½ years of Democratic Socialist performance. For the first time in history, a number of major industries in a medium-to-large country have been transferred to public ownership: a significant redistribution of income has been managed, consciously, in a large measure of independence from the world market, and managed in such a way as to provide enough (indeed slightly too much) total demand to keep all our available productive resources at work.'[1]

Strachey fought his own election campaign in Dundee in 1950 on the Labour party's local record – the seventeen new factories and three thousand new houses in the city, the Health Service, expanded social services and, very important in Dundee, full employment: 'If the Conservatives were returned, you would be extremely likely to lose your job,' wrote Strachey in his election address. But rations still affected bacon (5 oz a week); fats (10 oz); meat (1/6 worth a week); tea (2½ oz) and eggs (105 a year). Sugar and cheese were also rationed, at 8 oz and 2 oz respectively. The abolition of bread, milk and potato rationing could scarcely be regarded as a great victory five years after the war.

[1] *Tribune*, 23 February 1950.

In the event, Strachey was returned as member for Dundee West, polling 28,386 against 23,685 for an old Oxford acquaintance, Scrymgeour-Wedderburn,[1] and 986 for the Liberals – a very much reduced majority of 4,701. Tom Cook was also returned in the other constituency. (This was the first election campaign in which Dundee returned two separate constituencies, Dundee East and West.) The election as a whole was a serious reverse for Labour and an unexpected one, since they had not lost a by-election since 1945. Strachey never knew whether he would win in Dundee since the Dundonians began to vote Conservative when they moved to new housing estates.

With his reduced majority, now only eight, Attlee reshuffled the government. To his disappointment, Strachey was asked to leave the Ministry of Food to become Secretary of State for War. The move was a move sideways, if not downwards, in the government. He was still not in the Cabinet, and was subordinate to the new Minister of Defence, Shinwell, whom he had never much liked and who had, as a moderate member of the I.L.P., disliked Strachey's radical line on the *Socialist Review* between 1926 and 1929. Shinwell, with a Chief of Staff of his own, was also trying to achieve that unification of the services completed by Denis Healey in the 1960s. That made Strachey's job more difficult, and less independent, than his old activity at the Ministry of Food. Shinwell had himself been an outstandingly successful Secretary of State for War, and was difficult to succeed. He and Strachey 'fought like cats and avoided each other', Strachey's permanent secretary recalled. Shinwell, mildly, commented that Strachey's appointment 'had not pleased some members of the House of Commons, and there was evidence of opposition to him at the War Office'.[2] Some senior officers were dubious about Strachey's communist past and, although there was never any open problem with any specific officer, Strachey was unable to achieve any real *rapport* with the generals, except with Slim and Brownjohn. At least two generals saw communists everywhere at that time, and one of them referred to Strachey, on one

[1] Later succeeded as Earl of Dundee. He had, in 1922, succeeded Strachey as editor of the *Oxford Fortnightly Review*.
[2] Shinwell, *Conflict without Malice*, p. 214.

occasion, in violent terms, so much so that he was taken to task in consequence by one of his superiors. Furthermore, security was tightened up during Strachey's time as Minister, and precautions had to be taken in respect of one of Strachey's personal friends. Though Strachey, of course, saw the papers of the Chiefs of Staff and the Defence Committee, the papers of the Vice Chiefs of Staff (in effect then a working party of the Chiefs of Staff) were, on occasion, kept from him through the opposition of one Vice Chief. Strachey also seems to have failed to grasp the questions of supply and production which faced the Army during rearmament and, indeed, since these questions had already been decided before he reached the War Office, they did not greatly interest him. He got on well with his civilian staff, among them his permanent secretary Sir George Turner, and private secretary William Geraghty, but his freedom of action in so minutely organized a department as the War Office was much less than it had been at the Ministry of Food.

Strachey wrote to his old colleague, Sir Herbert Broadley, at the Ministry of Food, and now deputy Director of the F.A.O., 'I do not think that anyone would hold that this post at the War Office is especially exciting intellectually. But it is an obvious truth that neglect of military matters, like neglect of lavatories and sewers, can very easily produce a result which will bring an unpleasant end to many forms of intellectual activity.'[1] (This was actually a mild reproof to Broadley who had suggested that he could not understand how Strachey could have an interest in military matters at all.)

But Strachey's first problem of importance at the War Office was personal. At the end of January 1950, Dr Fuchs of the Atomic Energy Research establishment at Harwell was arrested and charged with offences under the Official Secrets Act. On 2 March the *Evening Standard* published a banner headline linking Strachey: 'FUCHS AND STRACHEY: A GREAT NEW CRISIS. War Minister has never disavowed Communism. NOW INVOLVED IN M.I.5 EFFICIENCY PROBE.' The accusation was taken up by the other Beaverbrook papers, apparently on Beaverbrook's personal instructions, despite the

[1] Strachey to Broadley, 26 June 1950.

fact that the news editor of the *Standard*, Ronald Hyde, had advised the editor, Herbert Gunn, not to publish it, on the ground that it was both untrue and was an absurd accusation: Strachey had disavowed communism and he was not concerned in any M.I.5 efficiency probe. The accusation infuriated Strachey. He wished to sue the *Standard*, and not only for libel, but for criminal libel: he wanted the editor of the *Standard*, Herbert Gunn, in gaol. The Attorney General, Sir Hartley Shawcross, advised him against such a course. Shawcross said that no jury would convict for criminal libel. Further, the case would have taken many months to come up, and would have hung over Strachey interminably. Litigation would have been costly, would have given much publicity to Strachey's past views, and would certainly have been counter-productive so far as his political career was concerned. But Strachey and Celia always thought it would have been better to have sued, and that Shawcross's advice was wrong. Certainly the *Standard* staff was alarmed by the rumour that Strachey was proposing litigation, and presumably they would have had to enter a defence in a case which was essentially not defendable. It is, however, rarely wise for a politician to sue, and Attlee never liked ministers so doing.

The incident had one unforeseen consequence of some importance. When it became known that Strachey was not going to sue, Michael Foot wrote a powerful article in *Tribune* in his defence. The title first conceived for this was 'Prostitutes of the Press', but that was thought libellous to Beaverbrook. An alternative title, 'Lower than Kemsley', was introduced. It was, however, Kemsley who sued. *Tribune* fought Kemsley up to the Court of Appeal and to the House of Lords, and eventually won. For many months, however, Michael Foot and Jennie Lee (in whom *Tribune* was, at that time, vested) were on the edge of bankruptcy, as they thought. Strachey, however, never wrote to them, or thanked them for the article that *Tribune* had written in his defence. This oversight was never forgotten by Jennie Lee and the *Tribune* board. It is, doubtless, explicable by the general depression felt by Strachey at the time; it was not only an oversight, but a serious mistake.

Strachey meantime began coping at the War Office with the

innumerable ponderous as well as trivial problems which affected the Secretary of State there; from attendance at the sovereign's parade at Sandhurst, to the problem of housing allocations for civilian employees in Singapore. In the summer of 1950, Strachey made an official visit to Far East Command. In Rangoon, he dined with the Prime Minister, who told him that he was going to retire in six weeks, and then become the fourth incarnation of the Buddha. In Hong Kong, while staying with General Evans, the commander, he was so impressed with the beauty of the scene of the sun rising over China that he wrote a poem, in *vers libre*. On his return he gave it to the *Observer* to publish. But he discovered that, while he had been away, the Prime Minister had issued a new rule that Ministers who wished to publish anything would have to get the Prime Minister's permission. The poem was duly sent to Attlee. Attlee refused permission to publish, and the page in the *Observer* that Sunday had to be reset. A week later, Strachey had to see Attlee on other matters. He asked why the poem had not been published. 'Didn't rhyme,' said Attlee, 'didn't scan either.' The poem ran:

Across a small, muddy stream the worlds meet.
A stone bridge has been broken; over an iron bridge,
With clattering planks, walk pedlars.
They pass through the hands of the officials, too small,
Apparently, to be detected by either authority,
Like the filter passing virus: but they bring no diseases,
Particularly, only some shirts and pieces of dried fish.

The Worlds are enormous; the worlds cannot hear
The patter of the pedlar's feet, or comprehend
Their molecular, random distribution.

My coming to the frontier has caused activity
Amongst the Western police. They search decorously –
Lady searchers for lady pedlars, gentlemen searchers
For gentlemen pedlars: they search the packs.

Oh pedlars who have suffered heavier things
Forgive the incomprehensible visits of Ministers.

Gods, policemen, Commissars or Commissioners
Will give an end to this inconvenience also.
And you will proceed upon bicycles
Through the ricefields and the interstices
Of incommunicable worlds.

A few weeks later, Strachey caused a major row by a speech at
Colchester. This speech contained a passage relating to the
recently proposed Schuman Plan for a European coal and steel
community, as well as various other reflections on the future of
European unity. In essence, he kept close to the attitude expressed
by Attlee and other Ministers, suggesting that it was unacceptable
for Britain to agree without negotiation to a scheme which would
'put real power over Europe's basic industries into the hands of an
irresponsible body free from all democratic control'.[1] This view,
mistaken though it clearly was, was shared by all Strachey's
colleagues and, indeed, by most people in England, except for
Boothby and a few other enthusiasts. But the notes of Strachey's
speech distributed beforehand to the Press, made him refer to
the scheme as a 'plot' on the part of the great capitalist interests
of Europe to avoid nationalization of their industries, 'comparable
to the efforts of Montagu Norman to propose a European central
bank'. He added that he thought that European unity was not
enough – the Commonwealth and the U.S. had to be 'in it',
for the U.S. government was, 'in many ways, a much more
progressive one than many of the Governments of Central
Europe. . . . I would much rather be in a combination which
contained the U.S. than a mere West European federation . . .
[Also] whatever federation will ultimately be joined, [it] must
have a really democratic federal government . . . in the meanwhile,
we are not going to have any bogus federation by which the real
powers of democratically elected parliaments are surrendered in
the name of bogus internationalism to irresponsible, undemocratic
and reactionary super-national bodies.'[2]

Strachey soon withdrew from these harsh remarks. He said, for
instance, that he had not referred to the Schuman plan as a plot,

[1] As expressed by the *Manchester Guardian*, 2 July 1950.
[2] Notes for speech delivered at Colchester, 1 July 1950.

but that that word had been intended to apply to Conservative efforts to overthrow the government in consequence. This explanation is difficult to accept. It is clear that the wording handed out to reporters by Strachey himself or by his private secretary was harsh. He managed, by an adroit statement in a three-and-a-half hour debate devoted specially to his speech at Colchester in the House of Commons on 11 July, to escape from the worst consequences of this affair, but it was clear that he was, at this time, a strong opponent of European unity under the terms then envisaged. Once again the Conservatives devoted much attention to Strachey in a venomous series of exchanges. Churchill intervened in a mean manner in the debate. Attlee, usually tolerant of Strachey's indiscretions, was angry at the sensation caused by the speech; and Boothby, a passionate advocate of European unity, thought him 'mad'.

By then, Strachey had been plunged into the crisis following the outbreak of the Korean War on 20 June 1950. This event had a determining effect on the development of Strachey's general political views. For the attack by North Korea on the South was followed by a heavy U.S. and Western commitment to the South, in the name of the U.N. This military effort, in which Britain was involved from the beginning, was the prelude to prolonged anxiety lest the war in the Far East should herald general war.

The controversy over these matters, and over the priority which defence should have among government costs, dominated the politics of Labour for the next ten years, and became inextricably linked with the clash of the personalities pre-eminently concerned. During the course of the summer of 1950, plans were made by the government for new spending, and by the U.S. government. Strachey, in a speech at Enfield, gave an assurance that 'the work of social and economic reconstruction that has been undertaken' would be safeguarded. He also said that any further defence expenditure would be undertaken 'very differently by the way it has been undertaken in the past. . . . It has often been the case that, when heavier defence expenditure has been necessary, almost the entire burden has fallen on the ordinary people of this country. That is not necessary. It is perfectly possible that that burden should be spread justly among all the classes of this country and that the well-to-do classes should pay their full proportion.' This statement, both provocative and crafty, was meant to imply, as the *Economist* pointed out, that the rich in the past had not paid their fair share.

Strachey also was concerned by the development of the Malayan situation. The communists, entirely Chinese in race, were making a determined effort to capture the peninsula. Strachey, in a note to Attlee in December 1950, made a firm statement of what he believed should be British aims: namely,

(a) a great firmness and vigour on the part of the governing authorities in the military and police side; in fact, ruthlessness where ruthlessness is necessary; but

(b) equal firmness and vigour in pressing on with the economic and political development of the country.[1]

This statement was right; and indeed it laid down the guidelines for the policy successfully pursued by the British in the Malayan emergency. Strachey believed that Malayan civil authorities were too 'squeamish' in their prosecution of the rebels, at the same time as being too conservative in regard to the political and economic development of the country.

In January 1951, Strachey was expressing anxiety lest the U.S. policy should land Britain in a major war. Busy with such matters as the recall of Reservists and endless complaints from Labour party members, or others, about German rearmament, Strachey was worried lest German rearmament should become an end in itself, to be pursued regardless of any offers made by the Russians such as, for example, the disarmament of Eastern Germany or an Austrian Treaty. He also was preoccupied lest any offer by the Russians to accept the West's own plans on Germany of the previous year might be rejected – though no genuine offer was ever made.[2] In April, he was still worried about U.S. policy, in particular Macarthur's. The British Chiefs of Staff had made an estimate of Chinese vulnerability which differed from Macarthur's. Had not the time come, he put it to

---

[1] Personal Note to Attlee, dated December 1950.
[2] Strachey to Attlee, 31 January 1951.

the Minister of Defence, when Britain should tell the U.S. Government that they could not countenance the use of British troops, and sea and air forces, under Macarthur's command, for a policy of which they disapproved? If Macarthur's policies were not repudiated, should Macarthur not be replaced;[1] and, indeed, Macarthur was dismissed within weeks, though it does not seem that British representatives played a major part in assisting this decision.

The question of rearmament, German rearmament, the menaces in the Far East and, finally, the Cabinet's decision to go back, for financial reasons, on one part of the provisions of the welfare state – namely, the imposition, on Gaitskell's recommendations, of charges on false teeth and spectacles – caused a major crisis in the Labour movement. This was the most ambitious rearmament programme ever undertaken in time of peace. But already there had been for months what Crossman described as a 'cold war between Hugh Gaitskell and Nye Bevan', partly on personal grounds. Crossman, in a paper circulated on 20 April, said that, within a few weeks, the issue would have broadened from health charges to include the whole question of the rearmament pro-gramme and the economic programme of the Government. 'Each one of us will be compelled to decide whether he is a Gaitskellian or a Bevanite.' In the interests of the party, Crossman begged for a compromise.[2] The same day, John Freeman, Parliamentary-Under-Secretary at the Ministry of Supply, circulated a similar memorandum which argued that the split in the Labour party was 'not rooted in a dispute over any single act of administration' but was a matter of a difference of approach to the future between 'liberals' in the party and socialists.[3] This was true, in some senses, though there were also personal prob-lems: Morrison's recent promotion to become Foreign Secretary soon after Gaitskell's capture of the Chancellorship played a part, as did the fact that Bevan, as Minister of Labour, was not a member of the Cabinet committee which decided to impose the charges.

[1] Strachey letter to Shinwell, 6 April 1951.
[2] Memorandum from Crossman, sent by him to Strachey, 20 April 1951.
[3] Memorandum from Freeman, sent by him to Strachey, 20 April 1951.

Bevan, accompanied by Harold Wilson and Freeman, resigned on 21 April. Strachey considered resignation, and Jennie Lee recalled him 'crouched by the side of our sitting room fire at 23 Cliveden Place. . . . John hithered and dithered,'[1] but finally decided not to resign. He wrote to Attlee: 'Briefly, I have throughout the crisis considered the imposition of the charges on teeth and spectacles to be a mistake, but have also considered – and still consider – this issue by no means large enough to make me resign. . . . I have made this position clear both to Aneurin and the Chancellor.'[2] Celia was against resignation too, but Strachey's attitude towards Attlee's political leadership, which he now intensely admired, was decisive. Strachey had, anyway, drifted apart from Bevan, for several reasons, some personal, some public. Bevan had never forgiven Strachey for not acknowledging what he considered his help in The Coming Struggle for Power, and Jennie Lee believed that Strachey might have helped her and Michael Foot when they became engaged in their libel case with the Kemsley Press. Strachey, on the other hand, had disapproved of Bevan's long personal association with Beaverbrook, while Bevan had criticized Strachey's hesitation over bread rationing. Strachey was already friendly with Gaitskell, as a glowing letter to him on the occasion of his becoming Chancellor testifies. Gaitskell had written back: 'It seems to me so important that we should be able to give the lie to the famous saying – was it Asquith or Morley? – "There are no friendships at the top". Indeed, with all the agonies one has to endure – and I'm afraid you have had far more than your fair share – I do not think it would be worth while unless one got some fun out of it. And that is only possible if, at least, quite a few of those with whom one works are personal friends.

'I must say we do miss you on the economic side – but at least it is comforting in these times that someone of your intellect and judgement and perception should be looking after the Army, which I hope you do not now find too uncongenial.'[3]

Strachey's first public statement on these matters came in a May

1 Jennie Lee to the Author, 7 January 1972.
2 Strachey to Attlee, 23 April 1951.
3 Gaitskell to Strachey, 29 October 1950.

Day speech at Dundee on 29 April. In this, he pointed out that those who resigned had differed from the Government less on the fact of rearmament than on the question of the speed with which it should be carried out. In a later speech, on 17 June, at a big rally commemorating Keir Hardie, with Bevan on the same platform, he made a general estimate of what he thought should be the next aims of the party, rather than stating expressly what he thought of the current crisis.[1] Much of this time, Strachey was receiving surprised letters of complaint that he had not resigned from old friends and supporters, who had supposed that he was still on the left.

The summer of 1951 was a difficult one for the Secretary of State for War. The Korean War showed no signs of dying down, nor did the controversy over German rearmament. The concept of a European army had also been developed, apparently with Strachey's approval. On 25 August, Strachey, on his way back from a holiday in France, spoke with General Eisenhower at S.H.A.P.E. near Paris, on the subject: Eisenhower plainly thought that the introduction of German units into the European army was far the best, and the only feasible, way of managing the political problem of German rearmament. Strachey echoed this approach in a speech at Dundee on 16 September, in which he went far, from many people's point of view, towards pressing the idea of the European Army, in which continental Europe would contribute to her own defence without British or U.S. troops. On this subject, Strachey made no attempt to avoid an orthodox War Office point of view.

Worn down by the inconveniences of a small majority, Attlee decided on a new election in October 1951. Strachey once again fought in Dundee. A characteristic of this election was the forceful campaign of John Junor, assistant editor of the *Daily Express*, who fought Strachey as a Liberal, with Conservative support. He did so making use of all the arguments which the Beaverbrook Press had employed to pillory the Minister of Food during the past five years. But Strachey won, though with a further reduced

[1] This speech was later published as a Fabian pamphlet, *Towards the Just Society*. For discussion *see* below.

majority of 3,306; he gained 29,020 votes, Junor 25,714, and the communist candidate, D. Bowman, 1,508.

The Government in general lost, as expected, its small majority, the Conservatives getting one almost equally small. Churchill thus returned. Strachey expressed himself 'very satisfied with the Election results and not too dissatisfied politically'.[1] He thought that he could get on with his books. He was happy to abandon the more tedious side of the War Office's work. The parliamentary questions were less numerous, but sometimes no less trivial, than those at the Ministry of Food. His resilience and self-confidence had been severely damaged by his time at the Ministry of Food and by the attacks made on him; the Fuchs headline was the last straw. Beaverbrook and Herbert Gunn were thus successful in their irresponsible attack.

[1] Letter to Colin Clark, 1 November 1951.

Chapter 18 / CONTEMPORARY CAPITALISM AND THE END OF EMPIRE

Strachey, during the long years of Conservative government after 1951, played several parts. First, he was active in a narrow political manner, as a Labour front bench spokesman for military matters, being Chairman of the Labour party 'Defence and Services' group. He spoke frequently in the House of Commons, usually convincingly and often eloquently, and was a regular attender at all the Labour party's defence discussions. He mastered questions of defence to the satisfaction of everyone except George Wigg, his own understudy, whose views on army matters were severely practical, in contrast to Strachey's theoretical approach.

Secondly, in the early 1950s, Strachey, in the 'Keep Calm' group, with Michael Stewart, George Strauss and some others, attempted to achieve a middle position between the Bevanites and the Gaitskellites, thereby incurring the obloquy of both: Dalton, with his customary scorn for those who disagreed with his own approach (he was an ardent promoter of Gaitskell), referred to this trio as the 'Three Sibillant Sisters'.[1] This scorn

---

[1] Strachey was aware how irritating this centre position seemed and stuck to it, defending himself in print, e.g. in the *Dundee Citizen* and *Forward*, 8 November 1952.

was quite misplaced, since unity was desirable, since both Bevanites and Gaitskellites were unreasonable in their factional distrust of each other, and since in the end, after all, Strachey's view was the one which captured the party and led it to victory in 1964 under the leadership of Harold Wilson.

Bevan and his friends resented Strachey's activities more than did the Gaitskellites; first, because Strachey was evidently by now in the centre of the party. (In a Fabian pamphlet, *The Just Society*, published before the election of 1951, Strachey had said that henceforth the 'real struggle . . . is not so much to take the movement further to the left, as to offer an iron resistance to those forces both economical and political which are seeking to take it far to the right'.) In addition, despite his liking for strong leadership, Strachey would never have become a disciple of Bevan's, for he had known Bevan too long, and, indeed, he, Strachey, had once almost been Bevan's mentor. However, an unwillingness to take up a stand on one side or the other is unforgivable in politics, and the consequence was that, even on defence matters, Strachey was not listened to as much as he should have been. Crossman in his diary, for example, noted on 6 March 1953 that Strachey, in the Defence debate, made 'much the best speech of the day', but, 'nobody came in when his name came up. It's puzzling what people count in the House. Somehow, he had made himself not count by sitting on the fence so long.'

Personalities, the recollection of past loyalties or treacheries, and old friendships, play a decisive part in politics. But between Bevan and Strachey there were now differences of principle. Strachey made this clear in a review, in the *Daily Herald* in 1952, of Bevan's book, *In Place of Fear*: 'Bevan is the first to agree that Russia's protestations of peaceful intentions cannot be relied upon. . . . Surely then,' says Strachey, 'it is our duty, precisely for the supreme purpose of preventing war, to undertake a degree of rearmament adequate to put the temptation to acts of aggression out of the way of the Russian Government.' Then, he went on, identifying himself very strongly while doing so with what he called the 'solid' side in the Labour movement rather than the 'militant' one: 'each of us must accept the verdict of the majority. The decisions of the party, democratically arrived at, must be upheld. . . . The party must be, and will be, tolerant, patient, flexible. But it will never let itself degenerate into a mob. . . . Bevan . . . will often succeed in leading us into new and fruitful policies. But the one thing he must not try and do is to *drive* us.'[1]

This caution was the sort of advice which Strachey, and Bevan, had been reluctant to take in 1931. Since then, Strachey had aged; Bevan, partly under the influence of his wife, Jennie Lee, never really did so. How strange to find, among Strachey's papers, a resolution of the Parliamentary Labour party, proposing standing orders to make it obligatory for all members to carry out the decisions of the Parliamentary Labour party ('taking into account the traditional conscience clause'), with a note by Strachey saying, 'Yes, I think so. I will second, or support. . . .'

In the end, Strachey drew close to the Gaitskellites, and began to regard Hugh Gaitskell as the future guide to the party, though Gaitskell, with his iron will, was sometimes critical of Strachey's extreme flexibility. Strachey also retained a romantic attachment towards Bevan, and could never bring himself to attack him. Bevan spoke entertainingly of 'The Coming Struggle for Strachey' as the next battle between left and right. But Strachey never made a reply. The Bevanites never forgave him for not siding with them, and interpreted his actions as opportunistic; and perhaps they were, in the sense that Strachey was determined to obtain political power again; Jennie Lee never forgot the question of the libel action with Kemsley; but, in addition, it was logical that a man as rational as Strachey should be found on the rational, if less romantic, wing of the party rather than on Bevan's. His role as defence spokesman also affected him, though, like many others in the party, he changed his mind over the question of German rearmament: when in power, he had supported it; out of power, he opposed it. Apart from this, his essay in, for example, *New Fabian Essays*, suggested that his experience in the Government had revitalized his belief in Parliament; and he also spoke glowingly of 'Keynesian' methods, as a means whereby the State could manage the economy effectively.[2]

[1] *Daily Herald*, 4 April 1952. Strachey's italics.
[2] 'Tasks and Achievements of British Labour', in *New Fabian Essays*, edited by R. H. S. Crossman (London 1952).

This central position did not make him an exciting candidate, for example, for the Shadow Cabinet, much less the National Executive, for neither of which he ever stood. Nor was he the particular favourite of any trade union; and, in the 1950s, the power of the 'big unions' was never greater in the Labour party, though they gave backing to Gaitskell. Strachey was a frequent lecturer to enthusiastic audiences at the Fabian Society, but the Fabians have never had power, only influence.

The explanation of Strachey's move to the right after 1951 can be found in several things: first, the fact that, as suggested earlier, he found it easier to sympathize with Attlee and then Gaitskell as a leader rather than with Bevan. Second, his revolutionary energy never really recovered from being tested in the fire of actual government. The attacks on him as Minister of Food and Secretary of State for War had shocked him too. Third, the more he learned of communist practice, including communist practice in the 1930s, the more sceptical he became of the idea of revolutionary change. Not that he ever became a militant anti-communist: in a famous review of *Witness* by Whitaker Chambers, he suggested that the ex-communists were becoming as absolutist as the communists themselves; quoting Silone's remark that 'the final conflict will be between communists and ex-communists', he asked 'But will it? . . . Does not the true antithesis lie between absolutists of both kinds and pragmatic, rational, tolerant experimentalists?' This experimentalist outlook, he wrote, is harder to define than its alternative, since 'its very essence will lie in a certain relativism, a cooler temper, a lower claim. This tradition, overwhelmingly dominant in Britain and the U.S., consists in a continuous effort to modify, to adapt, to reform our politics . . . it is that effort at continuous adaptation which amidst so much that is shallow, and even base, in our communities, differentiates them from most others.' These were reflections very far even from the radical ones which had characterized his plan for a 'new association' during the war, for example.

Another impression of the development of the mood of Strachey can be seen in an important argument which he had with Gaitskell over the possible use of controls in a future Labour

Government. Strachey had spoken of the attraction of using this instrument of power, in an article in the *New Statesman*, in February 1954. The Press made much of this. Strachey wrote to Gaitskell:

I'm sincerely sorry the Press has been 'getting at you' as a result of my article.

I may be obsessed about all this. But I did sincerely mean what I said . . . namely, that the future of democratic socialism hangs more on this than on any other single issue. I became a communist supporter in 1931, because I saw no way through the dilemma that the moment a democratic socialist policy began to be implemented, the economy got into crisis – out of control in one way or another – and so democratic socialist governments were bound to be impotent. Keynes and your own group – Douglas [Jay], Evan Durbin and yourself, and the experience of the New Deal, had converted me by 1940 to the view, which I put forward in a book called *Programme for Progress*, that a way through did exist.

In 1945–50, the democratic socialist transformation of our society was wonderfully well begun. But we had that marvellous legacy of Controls – and, even as it was, we lacked some of the skill and, above all, the *will* to insist on their use at the key point of the Control of the balance of payments. *Dare* we shirk the public discussion of this issue – even if it costs us votes . . . ?

Gaitskell replied:

In part, this is really a question of words, of not making unnecessary propaganda for the Tories. But I am also not entirely clear about what you think *precisely* should be done about controls. The plain fact is that there are certain dangers which *no* controls will prevent. We cannot stop Americans thinking that there is going to be a devaluation, and holding up purchases of British goods, as happened in 1949. I should also like to know what additional controls, over and above those now applied, you think should be introduced into the foreign exchange market. I cannot honestly feel that it was a lack of will to apply controls which was reponsible for the three

post-war crises. The first was sheer bad advice and bad judgement, the second we could do very little about anyway, and
in the third case the change in the situation was anticipated,
but not the speed with which it took place. . . . As for people
not taking note of what you say, I am afraid some of the
sentences in the article are certainties for the Tory Handbook.[1]
By themselves they may not count for much, but that some
votes will be lost as a result of them is only too probable.[2]

In 1955, expectations of an early Labour return to power were
damped. Churchill's successor as Prime Minister, Sir Anthony
Eden, put his popularity to the test in May of that year. Strachey
fought this election alongside George Thomson, the ex-editor of
the *Glasgow Forward*. Dundee-born and bred, he had succeeded
Tom Cook as M.P. when the latter had died in a car crash in 1952.
(Strachey became devoted to George Thomson and in consequence became much more settled in his constituency than he had
been.) Strachey was returned for Dundee West by a further
reduced majority of 1,874, polling 26,082 to his Conservative
opponent's 24,208. Once again, the conservative views of
Dundonians whose standard of living had gone up was one
contributory cause. The Conservative candidate, Gordon Pixie,
wrote to Celia, on Strachey's death, how 'he never ceased to
admire the fair way in which Strachey conducted his campaign'.[3]
The communist candidate, Dave Bowman, polled 1,335. In the
country at large, Eden was returned with an increased majority.

Strachey continued on ambiguous terms with his constituency
Labour party in Dundee. Many Dundonian Labour people would
perhaps have preferred a more earthy, if less distinguished,
member. Strachey was not easy for Scottish trade unionists to
get to know or to understand. With outstanding Scottish leaders
such as successive Lords Provost of Dundee, Michael Macmanus
or Ted Hughes (afterwards Lord Hughes), he worked well, but
with less educated men he was not good. Nor did he trouble to
attend often the bi-weekly meetings of Scottish Labour M.P.s in

[1] This prediction was accurate. The Conservative central office's campaign guide
in 1955 made several extracts from the article.
[2] Gaitskell to Strachey, 11 February 1954.
[3] Gordon Pixie to Celia, 17 July 1963.

London. Another problem was the degree to which the communists in Dundee had penetrated some sections of the Labour party, so much so that Strachey and George Thomson could write that the 'City Labour party has chosen to provide the local communist leaders with a means of reaching the public under Labour colours'.[1] (This situation was eventually resolved, but not without much difficulty.)

But, in addition to these political actions, Strachey had a third role: he was the only survivor of the old left in English politics who tried seriously to think out an intellectual position for the 1950s. This really dominated his life between 1951 and 1963 and if, to outward appearances, Strachey, at that time, seemed to be more calm and more complacent than before, in truth there remained in his life the same breathlessness and dedication to continuous work as there had always been.

In 1953, Kingsley Martin asked Strachey to write four articles about modern Marxism for the *New Statesman*, to restate 'the economic bases of the economic and consequential political policy [which] I, and I suppose the lefter portion of the Labour party, support for Britain.'[2] These articles were a 'reconnaissance for a book', as Strachey put it in a letter to Pat Covici, his ex-U.S. publisher, now of Viking Press.[3] By May 1953, the articles were appearing under the title of 'Marxism Revisited', and, by then, Strachey was hoping that the book would be a 'big thing. I shall put everything I know into it. I am only just at the beginning of it, and I cannot hope to have the text in less than two years, so that there is nothing very immediate about it, I am afraid.'[4] Two years later he had indeed a text, but by then he planned it to be the first of three volumes: he wrote to Gollancz about it in September 1955, as being then about 100,000 words, and complete in itself;[5] and, by November, was suggesting that Gollancz could have the typescript in about three or four weeks.[6] He

---

[1] Report on the situation of the Labour party in Dundee, by Strachey and George Thomson, sent to Hugh Gaitskell, Morgan Phillips and Harold Wilson, June 1958.
[2] Strachey to Jo Alsop, 24 March 1953.
[3] Strachey to Pat Covici, 20 May 1953.
[4] Strachey to Donald Klopfer, 20 May 1953.
[5] Strachey to Gollancz, 5 September 1955.
[6] *Ibid.*, 14 November 1955.

showed it to Gollancz before that time, and Gollancz was sending back comments by the end of November. Strachey and Gollancz had a long discussion lasting 'half the night' on 30 November,[1] and Strachey re-wrote certain paragraphs in consequence. Afterwards, Strachey consulted several other intellectuals or economists such as Crossman, Gaitskell (who succeeded Attlee as leader of the Labour party in December 1955), Jay, Paget, Peter Shore, Joan Robinson, Balogh, Colin Clark and Dudley Seers. Most of these advisors were, of course, 'revisionists', even Crossman, who, though a follower of Bevan, was at that time mainly moved by the apparent threat of a 'managerial society'.[2] (Strachey appears frequently in Crossman's wonderful diary of the 1950s – as a dining companion, or a colleague in the Defence group: Crossman, though sometimes tart in his comments on Strachey as on everyone else, generally records him as 'extremely pleasant company and very intelligent', making 'brilliant speeches which were not always politically effective'.)

In the *New Statesman* articles, Strachey summarized his point of view perhaps more sharply than he did in his book by suggesting that Marx's chief error was less one of economic analysis than of political misconception – a fundamental underestimate of the political and trade unionist possibilities open to workers in a democracy. If counter-capitalist pressures became inadequate, Marx's 'economic law of gravity' reasserted itself.[3] Further, the latest stage of capitalism had taken an explicitly democratic form, and, within the system, the counteracting forces of trade unionism and voters had become stronger.

In this book, Strachey writes still as a Marxist; he regarded Marx, not as the prophet that he had seemed to him to be in the 1930s, but as the creator of 'one partial, brilliant rich, prejudiced . . . contribution to our cultural heritage'. Strachey made an attempt to show how economic reality had moved away from Marx, who, nevertheless, was at the centre of the book. Although Strachey may have seemed a Keynesian at the Ministry of Food, and in office in general, and although in his practical political life

1 Gollancz to Donald Klopfer, 15 December 1955.
2 Cf. his essay in *New Fabian Essays*, p. 27.
3 *New Statesman*, 16 May 1953.

he was far from an extremist, in theory he now seemed a Marxist. He reverted to Marx, in fact, in opposition, as a prime pre- occupation, even if he had forgotten him whilst in power, and in *New Fabian Essays*. In the book, Strachey continued to argue that capitalism is unstable and seemed to believe that the existing stage of capitalism was at least as shaky as that preceding it. This was a point where Gaitskell was in disagreement with him.

The best part of this book is Strachey's analysis of Keynes. Strachey's skill at summarizing, dissecting and, finally, absorbing an argument, was exhibited here most effectively – though he could not forgive Keynes for neither knowing, nor caring, what Marx and Lenin had to say about monopoly or imperialism. Keynes, unlike Strachey, was 'only mildly interested in the question of the growing size, and diminishing number, of the units of economic life'. The positive part of Keynes's work was a demand that capitalism should now be regulated by a central authority, since Keynes perceived that capitalism was not self- regulating. But Keynes seemed to Strachey unhistorical, in that he did not think that capitalism was a short phase of human development, to be succeeded by other phases just as it had been preceded by others. Keynes could not imagine that uneducated men and women had any contribution to the solution of con- temporary problems. What he accomplished he did not intend: namely, to help the democratic socialist forces to find a way of continuously modifying the system, despite the opposition of capitalist interests: 'Keynes helped to show the peoples of the West a way forward which did not lead across the dyke of total class war.'

This book was an admirable statement of the economic advantages of democratic socialism, but it was written in a detached style, and dealt mostly with theory. The reviews of *Contemporary Capitalism* were good, and sales reached nearly 5,000. A typical letter came from Boothby:

I have now had the chance to read your book with the care and attention it deserves.
Absolutely first class.

The best since *The Coming Struggle* and, as I naturally think, even better than that. . . .

Now for democracy!

You say . . . that contemporary democracy is the diffusion of power throughout the community. But . . . surely Rathenau was right when he said that the modern state consists of a multiplicity of separate semiautonomous states, enjoying a considerable measure of independence, but individually and collectively stunted because *they lack a foundation in the soil of the people.*

The first thing to do is to separate these interwoven states from one another and then to build them up in a realistic spirit, and give them an independent existence, subordinated though they must be to the supreme political state in certain cardinal respects.

We have not yet begun to build the industrial society of the future. The industrial plant has become a basic social unit, but is not yet a social institution.

I still believe what I wrote in *I fight to live*, that modern democracy can only be founded on the basis of a functionally decentralized state. . . . These are just a few random thoughts inspired by your splendid book. GO ON. You are doing a tremendous work for posterity. . . . Incidentally, I have lost a stone, and look absolutely beautiful.[1]

This book was widely translated. At that time, nobody active in politics had published as thoughtful a reconsideration of Labour thinking – though Anthony Crosland was to do much the same thing, from a different, non-Marxist, standpoint, in his brilliant *The Future of Socialism* (also published in 1956). Crosland, of a younger generation – he had read twice, and been affected by, *A Programme for Progress* as an undergraduate – was looking for a practical guide to the future, but Strachey was looking for a general theory. The difference between Crosland and Strachey (and really between the revisionists and the old left) was that Crosland's arguments seemed moral or ethical, while Strachey's were rooted in economics.

[1] Boothby to Strachey, 30 August 1956.

Meantime, Strachey often travelled, going to France or Italy (later Yugoslavia) for holidays and, in September 1954, he visited the Middle East, both Israel and Egypt, and saw, when there, both Ben Gurion and Nasser. In the 1950s, Strachey's friendships changed somewhat. He remained fond of the Conservative M.P.s, Boothby and Alex Spearman, to both of whom he remained an inspiration, but there also appeared among his friends new figures such as Reggie Paget, another Labour Etonian, elected in 1945, Jim Callaghan, Kenneth Younger, and, later, George Brown and Harold Lever. A bond was Paget's yacht, on which Paget, Strachey, Callaghan and others would make a point of sailing from Hayling Island every Whitsun. Another new friend was Kenneth Galbraith, with whom Strachey travelled in India in 1956. (Celia remained at home, in order to be able to go to Tuscany. She had begun to paint seriously and with Strachey's encouragement henceforth devoted much time to this, being therefore perhaps less concerned in Strachey's political activities.)

This journey to India assumed tremendous importance in Strachey's life. Not only did he begin, as he says, his next book, *The End of Empire*, at Calcutta, 'on the verge of the sparse grass which now separates the low brick wall of Fort William . . . from the river Hooghly,' but the country became a subject of fascination for him. His own subtle mind and conciliatory character had special affinities with the Indians whom he met, and with whom he became friendly. The country also delighted him. His family's connections with India caused him to brood, creatively, on the long history of the imperial experience – hence his next book. The fact that the most prominent member of his family, Sir Henry Strachey, was a member of the rapacious first generation of English conquistadors in India, seems not to have affected his pride in his family achievement.[1] His Indian notebook is full of percipient comments on the new Indian scene – many of these being published in the *New Statesman*. (The best, a long essay on the Black Pagoda of Konarak in Orissa, was later re-published in Strachey's collection of essays, *The Strangled Cry*.) These snippets

[1] Strachey had earlier once begun a historical novel about Sir Henry Strachey. Several chapters of this survive, apparently from the time of the Second World War.

of travel-writing suggest the passionate affection which Strachey afterwards felt for all things Indian. For the next few years, his feelings for India were as strong as they had been in the past for Russia and probably stronger than they had ever been for the U.S.

The visit also created a friendship between Strachey and Galbraith. From the enthusiastic terms in which Strachey later reviewed *The Affluent Society* in *Encounter*, it seems clear that Strachey would have turned to its author as a new prophet if he had himself continued to write on economic subjects.[1] Strachey's review, incidentally, was extremely important in assisting Galbraith to establish his reputation in England.

Also, in 1956, Strachey was in Poland, to lecture, at the time of the Poznan riots. How appropriate that the old revolutionary should be present on the occasion of the first crack in the Soviet system! He was questioned at length by students at the University of Warsaw, and every point of view was heard, from anarchist to conservative. 'We did not succeed in miseducating them,' a member of the Central Committee said afterwards to Strachey, who himself later wrote:

> I was there during those very exciting days in which the Poles called the Eighth Plenum of their Central Committee in order to elect Mr Gomulka as their leader and to displace what they called the 'Natalin Group' (whom they considered to be the agents of the Russians), and, above all, to displace General Rokossovsky, the Russian-appointed General who commanded their army . . . this concerned me personally because I was lecturing that night and one member of the Central Committee had said, 'We are very sorry but we cannot be there tonight, because we have got the Plenum going on from day to day. It's a long Plenum and we have to be there.' But, when I arrived on the platform, I suddenly saw that they were there in the audience after all. I didn't know why. At the end of the lecture, they came to tell me that it was because they had closed the Plenum down, and wouldn't go on with it until the Russians got into their aeroplane, and went back to Moscow. They came to my lecture to fill in the time. . . . I don't think

[1] *Encounter*, September 1958.

anyone could be in Warsaw during that week without seeing the unmistakable reaction of a people which, at any rate, believed it was exploited and dominated by a stronger power and passionately wished for its independence.[1]

Strachey was also taken aside by a member of the Government and asked: 'You, Mr Strachey, are a well-known democratic theorist. . . . We require your advice. We are extremely anxious to conduct absolutely free and democratic elections in our country. But if we do so, how can we ensure that the Government's candidates will be at the top of the poll?'[2]

The book, which became *The End of Empire*, occupied most of Strachey's attention in 1956 and 1957. He did many drafts of it, and his son Charles recalls it as 'at first having not been about empire at all'. At this time, Strachey, as he told Gollancz, really used the House of Commons as a library in which to write, more than as a main preoccupation. He was not very active at the time of the Suez Crisis, though a speech by him in Dundee saying that the British army should not be used to assist French imperialism in Algeria caused furious, if fraternal, complaint from Guy Mollet to Gaitskell.

By this time, his views were moving tranquilly rightwards. Thus, in January 1958, he wrote to Michael Foot *à propos* of Foot's book on Swift: 'In my old age I have reverted to my ancestral tradition of Whiggery – and, after all, there is nothing much in . . . present-day British Socialism which would have shocked the members of the Junta [of 1688].'[3]

The End of Empire was finished in late 1958 and Strachey was busy showing sections of it to friends over that winter. Gaitskell made several useful comments. The book was published by Gollancz in 1959. It was an ambitious, general study of the nature of empires, much revised and changed during the course of composition.

The best part of the book is that which argues convincingly that Britain had made little out of her empire, not merely India, until the acquisition of the Middle East oilfields after 1919.

[1] *The Great Awakening*, p. 17.
[2] Strachey, 'A Politician's view of Democracy', article of July 1958.
[3] Strachey to Michael Foot, 22 January 1958. *See also* p. 243 for more Whiggery.

Certainly the high standard of living in Britain and Europe generally had not depended on the exploitation of the poorer countries. Here Strachey found himself dissenting from both Lenin and Cecil Rhodes.

There were also included in this book a hotch-potch of general ideas: Strachey even gave some suggestions as to what went wrong during his own time at the War Office – an inappropriate addition; while he was specially tolerant to post-imperial Indian and Middle East governments. Strachey, while echoing the Swedish economist Gunnar Myrdal in arguing for the modernization of underdeveloped countries – Myrdal was an important influence in this book – was not sufficiently alive to the problems incurred in over-swift modernization. Nor was Strachey able effectively to counter the argument, put forward by Andrew Shonfield, that the Commonwealth and the Sterling area were both 'expensive luxuries which Britain would be better without'. A sound point was also made by G. L. Arnold (George Lichtheim) in a review: 'the author is rather too inclined to have it both ways where England is concerned. He sees quite clearly that the British Empire has vanished and that the Commonwealth offers no substitute . . . the solution he urges – that Britain should become both a model of socialism and a pioneer of global change – is attractive to ideologists. But why should a socialist Britain provide capital exports for poorer countries?' Strachey finally did not face the fact that all the underdeveloped countries benefited from the cold war; but for the pressure of Soviet 'competition', they would have been much less likely to gain much aid from the West. Strachey seemed to believe that Britain should henceforth give aid for moral reasons alone: a point of view which Crossman, in particular, among his reviewers, vigorously repudiated.

The End of Empire was published on 23 November. This was an exciting experience, since the book was well reviewed almost everywhere. Anthony Crosland called it Strachey's 'best book'.[1] Particularly pleasing to Strachey was the wildly enthusiastic review in *Encounter* by Denis Brogan.[2] Attlee wrote a specially encouraging letter of congratulation.

In October 1959, meantime, Macmillan held his general

[1] *Listener*, 28 November 1959.   [2] *Encounter*, April 1960.

election, like Eden in 1955, primarily on the promise of an, as it turned out, illusory peace. Strachey's campaign was uneventful in West Dundee, but his majority slipped to 714: there was even a recount. The figures were Strachey 25,857, Dr Taylor, the Conservative, 25,143, and Bowman, the persistent communist candidate, 1,087. West Dundee was now a marginal constituency, a fact which undoubtedly had many causes, but Strachey's own personality had something to do with it, since he did not shine in Scotland, and he and Celia always looked forward to the moment when, on their journey south, the signpost proclaimed them to be in England again.

At the end of 1957, Strachey, to his astonishment, suffered a mild heart attack. This incapacitated him for several months. Thereafter he seemed worried about illnesses. This mild hypochondria was not dispelled by three months' rest at the Spanish resort of Estepona. His pattern of life also somewhat changed: he ceased going for walks in the country, and drank whisky to stimulate himself. From 1957 onwards, Strachey, though only fifty-six, began to refer to himself as old, and also to look old. This did not diminish his ambitions or his appetite for variety, but he never, thereafter, seemed in the front rank of practising politicians. He was also somewhat restless and emotionally unpredictable. In this repect, he was much out of sympathy with the complacent world of Macmillan's politics. It was as well that he had an interest, which became an obsession, that took him often out into the wider world. This was the subject of his next book.

Strachey in the 1950s was still a considerable politician, but he seemed in this first (and only) period of his life as a leader of the Opposition less at ease than he had been in the Government in the 1940s, and much less so than he had been as a revolutionary in the 1930s. It was becoming clear to most people, though probably not to himself, that he was primarily a man of ideas, rather than of action. He was too isolated to have followers but too senior to follow anyone else. He lived an easy and agreeable life, more so than most of his colleagues in the Labour leadership. But that did not compensate for him in any way his failure to reach the summits of political leadership which had always been his design and which briefly, in the 1940s, had seemed possible for him.

Chapter 19 / ON THE PREVENTION OF WAR

By the time of the election of 1959, Strachey was busy with an intellectual appreciation of military ideas which led to the last volume in his post-war trilogy, *On the Prevention of War*. This undertaking arose out of his continuing status as spokesman on defence, but he was now entering into close touch with military writers such as Liddell Hart, with whom his association became close. Instinctively, in the late 1950s, Strachey was drawn into the centre of the main controversy in the Labour movement, namely, the role of nuclear weapons. How curious this controversy seems years later! Not simply because both unilateralists and multilateralists seem to have been equally unrealistic; not simply because both sides buried their quarrels quickly at the prospect of power in 1964; but also because even the leading actors in the drama changed their minds very often, and became illogical or contradictory. Even Bevan, the central figure in the unfolding controversy, quarrelled with the party in 1955, because he opposed the British hydrogen bomb, but by 1958 was saying at Brighton that he could not go 'naked into the conference chamber'.

Strachey's position in these matters was expressed by him in many articles and speeches as well as his book. To begin with, he favoured the British independent nuclear deterrent. In 1958, he argued that 'we would become merely pawns of America if we scrapped our nuclear weapons on our own'.[1] In a famous pamphlet urging multilateral, not unilateral, disarmament, he said: 'we must retain the ability to take a different course, even though doing so might deeply alienate America and even drive her towards isolation.'[2] As Stephen Haseler put it in his excellent analysis of the politics of Labour at the time, here was 'an almost Gaullist interpretation of western international relations; a lack of trust in the Americans to defend Europe in a crisis. . . .'[3] In the defence debate of 1958, he became engaged in a furious controversy with his own understudy, George Wigg, who condemned his acceptance of the deterrent theory as an act of murder.

However, by 1959, his view was changing, chiefly in consequence of visits to the U.S. to discuss weapons systems with many of the new U.S. thinkers on this theme. Thus he was in the U.S. both in the spring and in the summer of 1959, on the invitation of the U.S. Government under their so-called 'Foreign Leader Programme', and talked at length with men such as Paul Nitze, Henry Kissinger, Allen Dulles and General Lemnitzer, together with men at the newly-formed Rand Corporation, such as Herman Kahn and William Kauffman: in a thank-you letter to Kauffman Strachey wrote: 'I shall never forget my time at the Rand. I learnt much more there than the rest of my time in the U.S. put together.'[4]

With the new strategic thinkers of the U.S., and later with some practitioners in Kennedy's enterprising government, Strachey was also soon on close terms, and in early 1962, became a member of Herman Kahn's Hudson Institute. He was much impressed by Kahn, who has some claim to be regarded as the latest intellectual leader in Strachey's long experimental life. This was because Kahn and his colleagues were virtually inventing a whole new intellectual discipline, and one where many millions of dollars were at stake – not to speak of many millions of men

---

[1] Reply to question put by *Birmingham Journal*, 24 May 1958.
[2] *Scrap All the H-Bombs*, p. 15.
[3] Stephen Haseler, *The Gaitskellites*, p. 181.
[4] Strachey to William Kauffman, 12 August 1959.

and women. 'I was fascinated by your stuff,' wrote Strachey in March 1960, to Kahn, 'I disagreed passionately with one part of it, and agreed equally passionately with the other.'

'First, the disagreement. . . . You conclude that directly after World War II the United States should have given an ultimatum to Russia to climb down or be bombed. My objection to this sort of stuff is a simple one; whatever merits there might have been of issuing such an ultimatum at that time, the fact is that you did not do it and now you cannot, so why talk about it now? . . .'

Furthermore, after the failure of Blue Streak, the British independent delivery system, Strachey began to believe that the independent deterrent was pointless, and that hope of security, and sanity, depended on the maintenance of a nuclear sanction by the two most powerful countries, the U.S. and the U.S.S.R. His great effort to propogate this view was Strachey's last, and in some ways, his most difficult and demanding task.

In these considerations, Strachey associated himself closely with George Brown, the new Shadow Defence Minister, Reggie Paget, and Brown's aide, Gerry Reynolds – a clever and assiduous group which sought, as Brown put it, 'to educate the Labour Party on defence'. Strachey taught Brown a great deal and thereafter much respected him, as people often do their pupils. But 'education', it seems, was not enough. For, after 1959, the question of defence became the critical problem in the Labour movement as it had never been before.

After the decision about Blue Streak, it at first seemed that Labour policy would be to keep existing nuclear weapons but not go on producing them. But the party obviously could not sort out in mass meeting the problems of first-strike capacity or the differences between 'tactical' and other nuclear weapons. Further problems arose centring more on the relation of Britain, with or without nuclear arms, to the Western alliance. The consequence was a major dispute in the party, leading to the unilateralist victory at the Scarborough conference of 1960 (held three months after the tragic death of Bevan in July 1960). Here Strachey was, with Callaghan, the only major Labour speaker on defence who held firmly to Gaitskell; for even George Brown wavered somewhat, just before the conference, and Healey, in early 1961, committed the party to ending the independent deterrent immediately.

Meanwhile, after his influential 'multilateralist' Fabian pamphlet was published in 1960,[1] Strachey began to put forward his new ideas on the prevention of war by means of an implicit or explicit condominium by the U.S. and Russia. Traditional disarmament matters, such as Strachey himself had supported a few years before, were ignored under this thesis.

Particularly interesting over this topic was Strachey's association with David Astor of the *Observer* and Duncan Sandys, and later George Thomson. The idea which interested this unlikely group – Sandys was still a minister – was the scheme suggested by Strachey in *On the Prevention of War* for some kind of nuclear stabilization on the basis of the retention of nuclear weapons by only the U.S. and the U.S.S.R. Strachey hoped that it might be possible to limit the spread of nuclear weapons by arranging that as many countries as possible should, instead of seeking nuclear arms themselves, try to secure guarantees of protection from one or other of the two super powers. In this, he secured the enthusiastic support of David Astor, and indeed soon after concluded an arrangement guaranteeing a retainer from the *Observer* and £1,000 a year in return for first refusal of all his articles.

These talks at what became a dining club in the House of Commons or at David Astor's house, occupied much of Strachey's attention between 1960 and 1962. Attempts to secure the support of others varied. Thus, Kenneth Younger, who had become a close friend, wrote pessimistically that he could not see any serious possibility of the great powers being able to agree on sanctions against minor powers, such as France (or China), who insisted on going ahead with their nuclear programmes. Strachey wrote back:

'I can see how you feel. It is not so much that you disagree as that you are utterly sceptical about the possibility of the concentration of power, such as would make war inevitable in the long term. No doubt it is entirely a matter of temperament. I do take the horror stories of the nuclear scientists seriously, and, therefore, I cannot see much else to do with one's life than to make people

[1] *The Pursuit of Peace* (Fabian Society 1960).

understand that they really have got to change the nature of the world if they want to survive. In other words, I am still a bit messianic and missionary about this business, thought not about much else nowadays.'[1]

Astor was also active in pressing the views of this group abroad: thus, he put them to Gomulka in Warsaw, and Macnamara in Washington. Strachey himself put his ideas at a meeting at Chatham House to a small group on 7 November 1962 – Sandys, and the historians Michael Howard and Donald Watt, being among those present. Small pressure groups of the intellectual *élite* rather than mass meetings were, of course, the typical political gatherings of the 1960s, and it is typical of Strachey, who began his political life in the latter, to be at home in the former.

Strachey's book on nuclear matters caused a breach, and, as it turned out, a final breach between Strachey and Gollancz, for Gollancz had played a big part in the Campaign for Nuclear Disarmament. The correspondence was prolonged but led nowhere. Strachey was determined not to publish with Gollancz, though Gollancz would have gone ahead as usual.

On the Prevention of War was published by Macmillan in September 1962, with extracts appearing (six months previously) in the *Observer*.[2] Maurice Macmillan was Strachey's editor. Strachey considered that Macmillan's was the publisher most likely to achieve a success with this contribution in strategic thought.

The first section of *On the Prevention of War* is a popularization, in good clear English, of the formidable writings of the new school of U.S. strategists. The second section argued that general disarmament was impossible without world government; and the third suggested that world government was for the moment inconceivable. The best hope, in these 'Hobbesian' circumstances (as the perceptive reviewer in *Punch*, Philip Hengist, put it[3]) of saving the world from nuclear annihilation was to achieve an acceptance of their mutual interests by the superstates. This was as usual a lucid exposition of all the problems, with many interesting

[1] Strachey to Younger, 29 March 1962.
[2] The *Observer*, 24 December, 31 December and 7 January 1962.
[3] *Punch*, 12 December 1962.

reflections on the side. The main criticism of this book must be that Strachey neglected the possibility of smaller states achieving considerable freedom of action: for example, Israel, France or India, Cuba or Chile. It is also possible to doubt whether the disarmament conferences, between 1955 and 1962, were the cynical charades depicted, and whether Strachey's basic premise, that 'war has become intolerable while remaining inevitable', is valid. In general, the book has not stood well the test of time. So much has occurred on the subject of weapons systems that it would be surprising if it did. It bears witness to Strachey's appetite for new and demanding intellectual problems and his realism, but it does not seem very original. Nor was it an accurate prophecy of what would happen.

The book was well-reviewed (save for a paradoxical criticism by A. J. P. Taylor in the *New Statesman*), and Strachey's status as a political writer stood high in 1962. The Cuban missile crisis of October of that year furthermore seemed to prove at least two points which he had been making: namely, that the deterrent did deter, and that a shock was necessary before nations did anything about nuclear weapons.

The Labour party, meanwhile, had become plunged into two new controversies: the first about Clause 4 of its Constitution committing the party to secure the 'common ownership of the means of distribution, production and exchange'. Gaitskell believed this crisis necessary in order to try to convert the party into what Douglas Jay, for a time, hoped would specifically become known as the 'Labour and Radical' party, or 'Labour and Reform'.[1] The Labour movement had moved away from the idea that nationalisation was *ipso facto* a panacea for all social ills, and Gaitskell believed that ambiguity over this was damaging to the picture which Labour presented of itself in the country. Strachey, with John Freeman, called formally on the leader to tell him that they believed that 'seldom had a leader of a party chosen his ground of contest less shrewdly'. Gaitskell, Strachey later reported, was entirely unmoved.[2]

[1] *Forward*, 16 October 1959. Gaitskell drew back at a change of name.
[2] Strachey's obituary on Gaitskell, *Sunday Times*, 20 January 1963.

In this controversy, Strachey remained with Gaitskell, as his recent writings suggested was inevitable. This, together with the increasingly patriotic interpretation of politics which informed his opinion in these years, his preoccupation with military matters and his consequential contacts with the United States military establishment, made him, between 1959 and 1963, a man very much on the right of the Labour party – even becoming popular among, and friendly with, Conservatives who had disliked him greatly in the 1940s.

The second controversy related to the Common Market. Strachey had, to begin with, been suspicious about Britain's possible part in European integration, as his speech at Colchester in 1951 had suggested. He also always had to qualify his growing support for British entry by a recollection of the probable consequences for the jute trade in his own constituency.[1] But, by 1961, Strachey had begun to be favourable to the proposed association of Britain with the new European venture. His son, Charles, of whom he saw a good deal, was one favourable influence, as was the most experienced European of all, Boothby. In the succeeding twelve months, Strachey made several pro-European speeches, and a passage in On the Prevention of War contemplated the idea of considering a united Europe as a 'building block for world government'.[2] When the issue of the Common Market became important from the point of view of the Labour movement, Strachey wrote to Gaitskell (after a holiday in Yugoslavia in mid 1962):

As I told you last week when we met, I would be content, in public at any rate, if the party took the line which you took in your broadcast during the summer, namely that the best thing that could happen would be that we could get satisfactory terms and go into the Market. But that the present terms were unacceptable.

I hear you feel that that is what you did say in your broad-

---

[1] E.g. a speech in Scotland to this effect as late as 19 July 1962. (Hansard, Vol. 668, Col. 680.)

[2] Gaitskell had said that he had been in sympathy with this view, in a speech in Paris in October 1962 to the Conference of the World Parliamentary Association.

cast. Unfortunately I do not think that it came over that way, as the public reponse shows.[1]

Gaitskell replied:

The broadcast I made last week was, of course, made in a new situation created by the Government and the Six between them. This situation is that certain terms have been agreed which, in my opinion which I understand you share, are inconsistent with our pledge and, for that matter, the Government's pledge, to safeguard the Commonwealth. ... But, of course, I spent a great deal of the broadcast not only doing this but showing how I thought a different and far more satisfactory solution could be achieved. ... Had the negotiations in Brussels, as I personally expected three or four months ago, gone the other way and the Six had conceded terms which by and large met our conditions, I should certainly have urged the party not to oppose. In doing so, I should have been confronted with a great deal of opposition from other friends of mine (for this is not a straightforward left/right issue) who would also have been faced with an unavoidable dilemma.[2]

Soon after, at the party conference, Gaitskell came out in complete opposition to the negotiations. With Strachey, therefore, as with other old supporters, Gaitskell was for the first time in dispute during the last half of 1962.

In 1962, Strachey also published several of his 'occasional' articles in book form, beginning with a long *Encounter* article, about anti- or ex-communist literature, which had been entitled *The Strangled Cry* – an allusion to the painting *The Cry* by the Norwegian painter Eduardo Munch.[3] This book of essays did a great deal for Strachey's general literary reputation as it deserved to. The sensitivity and intelligence of these articles made them the most interesting and admired of his minor studies. The other essays included a reprint of one of his wartime air raid warden articles (*Digging for Mrs Miller*), an impression of his nearly

[1] Strachey to Gaitskell, 25 September 1962.
[2] Gaitskell to Strachey, 27 September 1962.
[3] Published November and December 1960. The book was published by The Bodley Head on 14 June 1962.

disastrous journey to North Africa in the troop ship *Scythia* (here described as the *Illyria*), several impressions of contemporaries – the Webbs, Galbraith, Gollancz – and the long essay on the temple of love at Konarak in the State of Orissa. Another essay was a consideration of Rathenau and Schacht in Germany, originally intended for *The End of Empire* but rejected by Strachey for it. This brilliant study boldly stated that the Nazi economy was essentially a Keynesian one, run for Hitler by Schacht.

During these years, Strachey continued to travel a good deal. Thus, at Christmas 1959, he went to Iraq to see his daughter Elizabeth and her family (Elizabeth married the son of an Iraqi judge, Hamid al Qadhi, in 1958); and, in March 1960, he returned to the U.S. to give several lectures. Celia and he went for a holiday in Provence in April 1960, and in Yugoslavia in August, and Strachey was also in the U.S. during January 1961, going from Boston to Washington and California, lecturing on several occasions. A grant from the Rockefeller Foundation assisted him in these undertakings in the U.S., the money being made available through the Institute for Strategic Studies (of which Strachey was a founder member and enthusiastic supporter). In April 1961, he spent a month in Singapore in order to give a series of lectures based on the theme of *The End of Empire*; on the way out he stopped for a further visit to India, passing three days as Nehru's guest. The lectures, later published as an *Encounter* pamphlet entitled *The Great Awakening*, were an immense success, and the distribution of them as a pamphlet was wide. (A modified version was broadcast by Radio Free Europe's Third Programme in Munich.) The visit to India was important since Strachey took great trouble in the course of it to show Celia what he had loved in the country on his previous visit: she, on the other hand, was much more shocked by the poverty and squalor of India than he was. In September 1961, Strachey and Celia were again in Provence and in 1962 they were in Yugoslavia for the summer.

In November 1962, after delivering a Fabian autumn lecture on the theme of his new book on war, he went to a conference in Dakar on African Socialism. He travelled with his sailing companion, Jim Callaghan; in the course of the journey, Strachey said that he was looking forward to playing a big part in the next

Labour Government under Gaitskell. Callaghan recalled also Strachey's melancholy at the news of Esther's death, which came while he was there. After Dakar he went on to Nigeria where he stayed with Antony Head, the High Commissioner, and lectured at Lagos. Afterwards, Lady Head wrote, in a letter which gives a good impression of Strachey's charm as a companion: 'I enjoyed every moment of your visit here – Being with you and talking with you was a pleasure I shall always remember, besides being inspiring you made me feel optimistic (which goodness knows is difficult at times) just through your own wisdom and understanding. I wish you were still here sitting on the terrace watching the sun going down in this magical tropical setting with six parrots and Wa Wa and the crane birds!! . . . Your lecture was so superb. . . .'[1]

Strachey had also prepared a series of new lectures for Radio Free Europe on the theme 'The Challenge of Democracy', still in demand and used as a text on democracy by undergraduates all over the world. He and Celia visited Munich in connection with this series in March 1963.

In January 1963, meantime, Gaitskell died. Strachey's obituary of him, 'The Unreaped Harvest', in the *Sunday Times*,[2] was an eloquent memorial.

This terrible event, following on Bevan's death in 1960, caused yet one more crisis in the Labour party. In this, Strachey worked actively for George Brown, going as far as to call on David Astor in order to beg him to back him. Strachey, having now worked closely with Brown for some years on the defence side of Labour policy, thought him, as Celia recalls, 'intellectually superior to Harold'. But Harold Wilson, nevertheless, maintained Strachey on the front bench, as 'Shadow' Commonwealth Secretary, and he was, therefore, busy in the next few months with the main problems affecting Commonwealth policy, in particular Rhodesia and Chief Enaharo of Nigeria. Strachey also came to recognize, like many others, Wilson's great skill in opposition.

In May 1963 the Indian Government invited him, Douglas Jay,

[1] Lady Head to Strachey, 30 November 1962.
[2] *Sunday Times*, 20 January 1963.

and George Thomson to go to Delhi during the Whitsun recess to talk about Anglo-Indian trade and their economic plans generally. Strachey gave a lecture in Delhi on 'India, Britain and the Commonwealth', ending with the adjuration 'so press on, press on; press on to make India prosperous, strong and great'.

Meantime, in late 1962, Strachey and Celia had sold their old rectory at Lambourne and moved, for a country retreat, to a cottage in Essex near Maldon on the Blackwater estuary, rented from the Wedgwood Benns. They did this with the intention of moving into a house in London which, they thought, would be their permanent home: 12 Wellington Square. Strachey hoped that he would by these arrangements live a more urban political life than was possible in Abridge. The Stracheys moved to Wellington Square in Easter 1963, but did not live there long.

This period of Strachey's life had been characterized by much emotional restlessness and even personal unhappiness. Celia had, for the first time, failed to sympathize with his main intellectual interests: she was primarily a supporter of unilateral disarmament. His obsession with military matters, indeed, had diminished the circle of his friends in Britain. He was furious to find himself getting old, for he regarded himself as still a young man of promise.

EPILOGUE

When in India in 1963, Douglas Jay and George Thomson were anxious to climb a mountain. Strachey desired to be of the party, but others sought to dissuade him on the ground that his health was not up to it. Had he forgotten that he had had a heart attack in 1957? Strachey said that he would come part of the way, and set out with the others, though lagging behind. When Jay and Thomson came down, they found Strachey sitting half-way up the mountain, nursing his back. On returning to their hotel, it became obvious to all that Strachey had a serious back injury. He had had trouble with his back, off and on, all his life, probably as a result of too much fast bowling and other games played all out, to win, when he was young. The pain disappeared when he had had to lie on his back after his heart attack in 1957, but it reappeared after playing tennis with Charles the next year. On his return to England from India in 1963, Strachey experienced acute pain in his leg. Having recently moved, Strachey had, at the time, no regular General Practitioner. He therefore consulted Dr Copeman, a leading doctor who specialised in rheumatism, and whom he had often consulted as a kind of general doctor and in whom he had confidence. Copeman believed that the pain was connected with the trouble in the back, and recommended an operation to fuse the vertebrae. The famous surgeon, Sweetman, concurred. Celia opposed this recommendation, and continued to believe that the diagnosis was wrong. But Strachey was, however, insistent that he make up his own mind about the operation. He refused to allow Celia to see the specialist. He decided to go ahead as advised. In the meantime, he completed a new series of lectures on the theme 'Lenin in April', for Radio Free Europe. These argued that, for the future of Russia and of communism, Lenin made the wrong decision in April 1917 by changing the Bolshevik policy to one of armed revolution.

One event occurred (apart from one speech in the House of Commons, on the Commonwealth Development Corporation, on 19 June) in the month intervening: Strachey went for a sail one weekend with his son, in the Blackwater estuary. It was rough weather and sailing was foolhardy. The boat capsized, and the two of them had to swim for the shore. The swim, only a matter of yards, exhausted Strachey. Weighed down by a corset which he wore against his back troubles, Strachey became convinced that he would drown. He said so to his son. The water was cold and Strachey feared for his heart. Did Strachey remember, perhaps, the death of his own creation, the Abbé, in the novel *The Frontiers*, in the lake of Geneva? By this time, he, Strachey, more resembled the Abbé than the jejune pilot James; but at all events the two reached shore safely. But Strachey was exhausted and shocked.

Perhaps it was a mistake for Strachey to have gone ahead with his plan for an operation so quickly afterwards. But he did so, although it is uncertain whether the surgeon knew of this accident.

The operation took place in July, at King Edward VII's hospital for Officers, 'Sister Agnes's'. It was a difficult one, and Strachey's heart was strained. He lingered afterwards in an unhappy condition, conscious but too weak to talk. Only Celia saw him. She believed that he knew that he was dying. Doubtless in particular he was regretting that he had not finished the social and political study of the River Blackwater, its effect on himself, the memories of the Battle of Maldon which it conjured up and the, to him, evocative view, from the river, of the house of Anthony Wedgwood Benn (then engaged in his fight against his peerage); Strachey's last writing was a correction to the typescript of this study, alluding to his narrow escape from death in that river so short a time before. He was probably furious, on his deathbed, that he was dying perhaps unnecessarily, still at the height of his intellectual powers, when he was a more mature thinker than any other in his party, and when he was expecting to play a major part in a future Labour administration. If he thought of God, or of immortality, there was no anticipation of it before his operation; he had only idly thought that, if he became physically incapable of active politics, he might pass his old age in the House of Lords, speaking occasionally, gossiping and writing. He knew, however, that the operation might be fatal and went ahead with it since he could not stand the idea of living in a wheelchair, with which he was threatened, as an alternative.

Strachey died three days after his operation, early in the morning, on 15 July 1963. Celia, Charles and Elizabeth reached the bedside too late. His will was proved for £50,157 1s. 0d., but he had made dispositions before his death to his children and to Celia so that that sum slightly underestimated his wealth. This was a fairly considerable amount for a Labour politician of his generation.

Strachey was a man of ideas, who 'craved for a system which would embrace every aspect of knowledge', as Michael Foot put it in an obituary.[1] He believed that there must be some universal key, if only it could be found. Hence his dedication to socialism from the early 1920s onwards, to communism and to Marx in the early 1930s and, afterwards, in varying ways – his interest in Toynbee and Teilhard de Chardin being thereby explicable. Except for socialism in a general sense of the word, he never found what he was seeking. Perhaps this derived from the fact that he could not conceive of a system of beliefs which was not a comprehensive one: 'Philosophy,' he wrote, in *The Coming Struggle for Power*, 'seems to have been, on the whole, a kind of grandiose attempt on the part of men for whom what we have called straightforward religious belief had become impossible, to spin out of their own heads, a satisfying substitute for faith.'[2] But he continued himself to make this 'grandiose' effort, though,

[1] *Tribune*, 19 July 1963.
[2] *The Coming Struggle for Power*, p. 173.

at the end of his life, as at its beginning, he was convinced that 'the supreme challenge to the human race . . . is precisely to achieve a higher degree of consciousness in the inevitable process of the continual re-shaping of social life'.[1]

Gollancz thought Strachey's political drive derived from 'a passion for efficiency and a strong feeling, albeit slightly *de haut en bas*, for social justice'.[2] (One can well imagine Prince Mishkin losing the keys of the cabinet boxes, as Strachey did, and refusing to be shocked when as a result all locks had to be changed.) He probably still believed that, as he put it in his review of Whittaker Chambers's *Witness*, the aim of social democracy was 'continuous adaption', and 'defiant reformism';[3] of this view, he was, at the time of his death, an outstanding theoretician; to it he had, in over forty years, between 1923 and 1963, dedicated some hundreds of thousands of words, mostly written in his disjointed long hand. For he was a social democrat far longer than he was either a communist or a member of the New Party.

He influenced the Labour movement on several occasions: towards Marxism in the 1930s; towards Keynes, towards the ideal of the New Deal and away from communism and Marxism generally in the 1940s; and his strategic writing helped towards the formation of a realistic foreign and defence policy in the 1960s. Much of his minor writing was also influential: the patriotic contributions of the war years, the sceptical rapportage of the 1950s, and also the lectures of his last period. The Labour movement which won the election of 1964 owed to him some part of its new, pragmatic, rational, civilized and humane face. But, though he plainly affected the Labour movement, he was also its barometer; and, in some ways, his most original thinking was his earliest – that on monetary policy in *Revolution by Reason*.

Strachey's brain was clear. He was intellectually courageous. He was determined to find a rational explanation for his political conduct. He never stopped working and, indeed, the quantity of his writing has an heroic element about it. He wrote poems, a novel, fragments of others, and innumerable pieces of auto-

[1] Strachey, *The Strangled Cry*, p. 62.
[2] Gollancz, *Reminiscences of Affection*, pp. 131–2.
[3] *Nation*, 4 October 1952, reprinted in *The Strangled Cry*.

biographical journalism. His papers include several incomplete political manuscripts. There were few areas of human intellectual activity which he did not, at one time or another, explore. He had, in some ways, always the attitude towards life of an enthusiastic puppy which impressed his cousin Julia in the 1920s; no idea was too difficult for him to try to seize hold of, and none sufficiently compelling to hold him for long if something new cropped up. But the puppy was often overtaken by a Renaissance man of all crafts. In the 1930s, he was absorbed by Freud as well as by Marx, and attempted to see that the former, as well as the latter, was introduced to a larger public, through the Left Book Club. There was one exception: in a letter to Reinhold Niebuhr, he wrote in 1960, 'I have literally never opened a book on theology in my life'.[1] For Strachey, and this comment was probably as true in 1920 as it was in 1960, sin was a synonym for aggression. In the letter to Niebuhr just quoted, he explained that, for him, even in 1960, 'the word "good" meant that which lay along the evolutionary axis; the word "evil" that which pointed in the reverse direction, down the evolutionary axis on the time scale, or branching off from it at too sharp a tangent. . . . I should prefer,' he said, 'to trust blindly in whatever is visibly propelling creation along that axis: whither it will take us, I would be the first to agree is unknowable . . . [but] the evolutionary perspective is to me infinitely inspiring.'[2] In some respects, this religious emptiness was also a spiritual one; like Maksim Maksimich in Lermontov's novel, he 'did not care, generally, for metaphysical discussions'. Perhaps because of this lacuna, Strachey was a complete intellectual: he would talk seriously about ideas at every opportunity, 'riding, sawing wood, doing anything that didn't occupy his mind. I don't remember comfortable easy silences with him,' his daughter Elizabeth wrote.

Boothby, in a memorial note, recalled Strachey's 'unflinching intellectual integrity . . . he chased ideas wherever they led him and never shrank, as most active politicians would have done, from the practical and ideological consequences'.[3] It may be that

[1] Strachey to R. Niebuhr, 28 June 1960.
[2] *Loc. cit.*
[3] *The Times*, 17 July 1963.

Strachey would have been a more profound thinker if he had concentrated upon the mind and neglected the minor art of practical politics; but he never had any desire to do that and always, perversely, regarded himself as what he was not: first a politician, and secondly a thinker and writer. But such perversity is characteristic of most creative men.

Strachey looked unusual. In Chicago, in the 1930s, he seemed to some to resemble Al Capone in looks, or at least looked a heavy-weight boxer more than an intellectual. Lord Ponsonby said that, in the 1920s, he looked 'most unattractive', despite his charm: but the New Yorker in 1947 found him aristocratic-looking, while Norman Collins, for some years with Gollancz, thought that Strachey 'always looked the most distinguished member of any company in which he found himself'.[1] On the other hand, James MacGibbon, then a young communist, recalls him as seeming 'sinister' as a speaker in the St Pancras Town Hall in 1937. Strachey did not regard himself as being specially Jewish. Thus, in a review of Herman Kahn's book, On Thermonuclear War, in 1961, he wrote that Kahn had one of 'those fantastically effervescent, fertile, ingenious – perhaps over-ingenious minds, which rightly or wrongly, we stolid Anglo-Saxons often associate with the Jewish race'.[2] Strachey was, however, the least stolid of Anglo-Saxons, and looked it.

As to his character, some of Strachey's friends regarded him as 'weak'; Alex Spearman believed him 'contradictory without being untruthful'. In personal or private relations, particularly at the beginning of his life, his tremendous gaiety and love of life masked 'a very sharply defined evasiveness', in Paul Draper's phrase. His evasiveness over his marriage to Esther, so far as Celia was concerned, was a kind of emotional Micawberism. Perhaps he was too sensitive for politics: Strachey was probably writing with a tinge of envy when, in reviewing Roy Jenkins's life of Charles Dilke, he spoke of a man 'coarse-grained and insensitive enough to be able to stand an almost infinite amount of the wear and tear of public life'. Callaghan spoke of Strachey as 'not a political operator', and he certainly did not like political

[1] Norman Collins, letter to the Author.
[2] Washington Post, 16 July 1961.

intrigue or party conferences. Michael Foot described Strachey as appearing, in politics, 'to move timorously, deviously amid inhibiting restraints. He was slow to take sides, wavering and inconclusive.'[1] Indeed, Strachey behaved with Gaitskell and Bevan somewhat as he had between Esther and Celia, hoping for the best, because seeing the points of view of both sides very clearly. On the other hand, Anthony Crosland described him, at his death, as a 'tower of strength in recent years – over Clause 4, defence, Europe: always reliable, shrewd, brave and above all, totally honest.'[2] Similarly, Roy Jenkins wrote that 'his particular combination of great distinction of mind and complete intellectual integrity was quite unique'. He was 'almost the only senior person left in politics for whom one could feel . . . admiration.'[3]

Strachey was an ambitious man, even at the end of his life; 'ambitious, too, for power, and for its own sake, not because he wanted to write about it,' as Peter Shore put it. George Brown spoke of him as 'a backroom character who wanted to be in the front'. In this respect, Strachey was, in Crosland's words, 'a disappointed man'. But then, so are most politicians who fail to become Prime Minister. This mesmeric fascination with the office of premier is one of the weaknesses of our system. Strachey knew his own deficiencies, however, to a greater extent than most do. He spoke often of public office as a mirage. He once compared himself unfavourably to Anthony Wedgwood Benn, his Blackwater neighbour: 'I have never had anything like,' he wrote, 'his instinctive "sense of the House". A lot of my speeches . . . have been open to that deadly barb which Goldsmith stuck into the hide of . . . Burke:

> Too deep for his hearers and always refining;
> He thought of convincing, while they thought of dining.'

In politics, such self-knowledge is unusual; but it was true too that Strachey's great height, wound over the despatch box, and the high drawling Bloomsbury voice which had not changed since Oxford, left the impression that he was instructing the

[1] *Tribune*, 19 July 1963.
[2] A. Crosland to Celia, 17 July 1963.
[3] Roy Jenkins to Celia, 16 July 1963.

Labour party, rather than articulating its thoughts, even though he was, as he put it to a friend, 'the supreme explainer'. Perhaps the most accurate explanation of Strachey is that he was a sensitive man who constantly pressed himself into demanding situations, or into the company of the thick-skinned, in order subconsciously, no doubt, to test himself.

Strachey was influenced by women as much as by men. Women in fact preoccupied him. But Crossman wrote to Celia after Strachey's death: 'You gave John *everything* and *you* made his achievements possible.'[1]

It is difficult to estimate the influence of a wife on a politician. Celia was a strong-minded woman of firm convictions. Though she abandoned communism in 1941 or 1942, she remained to the left of Strachey for some years. She may, however, have influenced him against resignation in 1951, when he was tempted by the Bevanite adventure; and she influenced him when he was undecided as to whether or not to break with Mosley. She dedicated her life to his career, in the importance of which she passionately believed. Family life, too, meant much to Strachey, and, on some matters (such as the Common Market), Strachey was explicitly influenced by his son.

The obituaries of Strachey were generally kind. Most of them pointed out that Strachey, among the last Labour politicians still active who had had senior administrative experience in the government of 1945–51, was certain of high office in a new government. Attlee said that Strachey would have made a good Secretary of Defence: that might have been the case, but Harold Wilson, in a letter to Celia at Strachey's death, said that he would have offered him the Secretaryship of State for Commonwealth Relations.[2] He would thus have been responsible for Rhodesia instead of Arthur Bottomley. Strachey could also have contributed much to the Labour Government in respect of its relations with the East and with the U.S., both of which he probably knew better than any Cabinet Minister of 1964. He might have become Foreign Secretary, in succession to Patrick Gordon Walker. But such things would have depended on how

[1] Crossman to Celia, 16 July 1963.
[2] Harold Wilson to Celia, 17 July 1963.

well he got on with Harold Wilson, and he might even have been relegated to the role of 'elder statesman', with his old friend George Strauss.

Strachey's attitude to money was curious, since he (and Celia) were, as Alex Spearman put it, 'both much concerned with their money, despite their socialism'. Strachey's marriage to Esther Murphy was connected with her being well off. Later in life, he was interested in playing the stock market, being even resentful that he could not devote full attention to it, as could his nephew by marriage, Euan Cooper-Willis, who looked after his financial affairs.

Strachey always attempted to be explicit in private matters. He was sensuous and loved swimming in the nude. He was, however, incapable of any practical work with his hands; he never gardened, though he sawed wood as a relaxation. He could change a gramophone record only with difficulty. He was not at ease with people incapable of understanding ideas and took little trouble to be so. The exceptions were cricketers and boatmen. Otherwise, as Celia put it, he 'had no energy for ordinary people, and no common touch'. His distant manner on first meeting, however, embarrassed everyone and should be attributed to shyness. He was primarily interested in ideas, not people, and, if they had, or seemed to have none, he might not bother to unbend. To his constituents, he often seemed, as the Dundee *People's Journal* put it, 'the man who never smiled'. That journal added: 'his shyness and his remoteness made Dundee folk unaware of his considerable talents, his brilliance as a political writer, and, least obvious of all, his compassion for the world's less favoured human beings.' But Dundee is a hard place and, if Dundee found Strachey austere, the fault lies in the rifts which still divide British society.[1] It was not shyness, but a deep consciousness of the differences between himself and the Scots. Lively and open people, such as Boothby, or Woodrow Wyatt, found him 'generous and warm';[2] doubtless the Dundonians would not have recognized, in their austere M.P., the 'gamesman' friend of Stephen Potter. In some ways a better 'private man'

---

[1] *People's Journal*, 20 July 1963.
[2] Woodrow Wyatt to Celia, 15 July 1963.

than a public one, Strachey had to be either impressed, or amused, to unbend. But he liked doing so, and he liked telling stories. On the other hand, Strachey found it easy to be on good terms with the young, with the friends of his children and their contemporaries. They, in turn, often found this comforting and surprising, without always appreciating that he was, in some ways, an eternal student. When his children were young, Strachey played with them for hours at a time, damming streams, and devising new varieties of old games.

Strachey's methods of writing remained much the same all his life. He would customarily sit on a sofa with his feet up, or on a deck-chair, writing on loose sheets of paper or hard-backed notebooks, oblivious of all around. His concentration was exceptional. He refused to work in a study. He usually sent copies of his books to friends for comments: 'Let me confess,' wrote Crossman, 'that I was often irritated when the manuscript turned up. But long before I had finished the first chapter, I was scoring the margin with the scrawls of the completely engaged reader; and I was always fascinated ... to see how, while refusing all my conclusions, he had woven most of my furious critique into his analysis.' Enmity was difficult to sustain since 'neither of us could resist the temptation of the other's conversation'.[1]

Strachey ended his life still believing in what he called 'the socialist vision of a truly human society', which he believed had been 'degraded' by Stalin.' He also had almost reached the conclusion that the Russian Revolution was a mistake; or, rather, that Lenin had made the wrong decisions in 1917.[2] But he seemed optimistic about Russia in the 1960s – 'a fine country, in many respects' he called it;[3] he could not have known that the age of Khrushchev would be so short. He 'regarded the Labour Movement as the fundamental experience of his life,' recalled Allan Young, despite his frequent heretical actions. To it, he gave many services and made many sacrifices. He could very well have lived a life of ease, or, possibly, as editor of the *Spectator*, of creative ease. On the other hand, the sacrifices of ambitious men are not acts of charity.

[1] *Guardian*, 19 July 1961.
[2] Strachey, *The Strangled Cry*, p. 21.　　[3] *Ibid.*, p. 20.

Despite his scorn for the heredity principle (as expressed in his last unpublished writings about the Stansgate case), he had become concerned, in the end, by his own heredity. He had, also, returned, in all but name, to the Whiggism of his youth, as his letters in 1957 to Foot and Toynbee suggested. His career is so characteristic of his time as to be untypical of other men who lived then: he was the heir to a baronetcy, the comrade of Mosley and also of Burgess, Galbraith and of Bevan, Boothby and Gollancz. The friend of Nancy Cunard he was also the pupil of Palme Dutt, the patient of Ernest Jones and the adjutant to Squadron Leader 'Widge' Gleed. An Etonian cricketer, he became Minister of Food at its most politically difficult time. He moved with the greatest logic from Conservatism to social democracy, Mosleyism (in its New Party stage), communism, patriotism and back to social democracy, ending up on its right flank. Yet he always retained his integrity far more than those who remained more constant. Truly he could say, with Emerson, that consistency is the 'hobgoblin of little minds'. He gave great loyalty to the Labour party, the communist party, and to the R.A.F. He admired Stalin's Five Year Plan and Roosevelt's New Deal, and always sought an orderly world. But he loved India. He planned a Utopia in the 1930s, and tried unsuccessfully to establish one, on a small scale, in Tanganyika in the 1940s. He always made his way to the thick of any controversy, providing excellent arguments for his or for his friends' position, however newly taken up, but was much better equipped to plan a campaign than to fight a battle. Strachey sallied out into the deepest waters of political and intellectual adventure, stopped off on the alluring quays of revolutionary action, psychoanalysis, economic theory and national administration, but, in the end, was returning to the familiar reaches of patriotism, security, family loyalty, tolerance and moderation. When St Loe Strachey died, he had been going leftwards: when John Strachey died, he was heading to the right. Their crafts were ironically almost at the same place, if pointing in different directions, when they each died, only thirty-five years apart, both after many years in the midstream.

Index

73 74 75 76 77 10 9 8 7 6 5 4 3 2 1

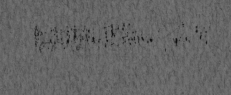